Ru

THE STONES
REVISITED

John Ruskin, *Windows of the Early Gothic Palaces*, photogravure from line engraving, Plate 17 in *The Stones of Venice* II (10:302)

Ruskin's Venice

THE STONES
REVISITED

Sarah Quill

LUND HUMPHRIES

A city of marble, did I say? nay, rather a golden city,
paved with emerald. For truly, every pinnacle and
turret glanced or glowed, overlaid with gold, or
bossed with jasper. Beneath, the unsullied sea drew in
deep breathing, to and fro, its eddies of green wave.
Deep-hearted, majestic, terrible as the sea, the men of
Venice moved in sway of power and war; pure as her
pillars of alabaster stood her mothers and maidens;
from foot to brow, all noble, walked her knights; the
low bronzed gleaming of sea-rusted armour shot
angrily under their blood-red mantle-folds. Fearless,
faithful, patient, impenetrable, implacable – every
word a fate – sate her senate. In hope and honour,
lulled by flowing of wave around their isles of sacred
sand, each with his name written, and the cross
graved at his side, lay her dead. A wonderful piece of
world. Rather, itself a world. It lay along the face of
the waters, no larger, as its captains saw it from their
masts at evening, than a bar of sunset that could not
pass away; but for its power, it must have seemed to
them as if they were sailing in the expanse of heaven,
and this a great planet, whose orient edge widened
through ether, a world from which all ignoble care
and petty thoughts were banished, with all the
common and poor elements of life. No foulness, nor
tumult, in those tremulous streets, that filled or fell
beneath the moon; but rippled music of majestic
change or thrilling silence. No weak walls could rise
above them; no low-roofed cottage, nor straw-built
shed. Only the strength as of rock, and the finished
setting of stones most precious. And around them,
far as the eye could reach, still the soft moving of
stainless waters, proudly pure; as not the flower, so
neither the thorn nor the thistle could grow in the
glancing fields. Ethereal strength of Alps, dream-like,
vanishing in high procession beyond the Torcellan
shore; blue islands of Paduan hills, poised in the
golden west. Above, free winds and fiery clouds
ranging at their will brightness out of the north, and
balm from the south, and the stars of the evening and
morning clear in the limitless light of arched heaven
and circling sea. Such was Giorgione's school – such
Titian's home.

Modern Painters III (5:374–5)

This new edition first published in 2015 by
Lund Humphries
Wey Court East, Union Road
Farnham, Surrey, GU9 7PT, UK
and
Suite 3-1, 110 Cherry Street, Burlington
VT 05401-3818, USA

www.lundhumphries.com

Lund Humphries is part of Ashgate Publishing

PHOTOGRAPHIC ACKNOWLEDGEMENTS:

Ashmolean Museum, Oxford: pp 40, 85, 88, 117; British
Museum, London: p.67; J. N. Bunney and S. E. Bunney:
p.111; Conway Library, Courtauld Institute of Art: p.166;
James S. Dearden: Frontispiece, p.1; Guild of St George
Collection, Ruskin Gallery, Museums Sheffield: pp 61,
63, 225, 227; Ken and Jenny Jacobson: 66, 76, 111, 140;
Museo Correr, Venice: pp 29, 35, 38–9, 112, 177, 209;
National Gallery, London: p.115; Ruskin Foundation,
Ruskin Library and Research Centre, Lancaster: pp 19,
67, 73, 79, 92, 94, 108, 109, 113, 116, 118, 122, 131,
156, 161, 164, 222–3, 231

Compilation, photographs and supplementary texts by
Sarah Quill © Sarah Quill, 2015
Introduction by Alan Windsor © Alan Windsor, 2000
Map copyright © Museo Correr, Venice
British Library Cataloguing-in-Publication Data.
A catalogue record for this book is available from
the British Library.
Library of Congress Cataloging-in-Publication Data
Quill, Sarah.
Ruskin's Venice : the stones revisited / By Sarah Quill.
— [New edition].
pages cm
Includes bibliographical references and index.
ISBN 978-1-84822-145-1 (hardcover : alk. paper)
1. Architecture—Italy—Venice.
2. Architectural photography—Italy—Venice.
3. Venice (Italy)—Buildings, structures, etc.
   —Pictorial works. I. Ruskin, John, 1819-1900.
   Works. Selections. II. Title.
NA1121.V4Q55 2014
720.945'311—dc23
2014029543

ISBN (Hardback) 978-1-84822-145-1
ISBN (Paperback) 978-1-84822-179-6

Edited by Howard Watson

Designed by Oliver Keen

Set in Adobe Garamond Pro

Printed in China

p.1: Photograph of John Ruskin, 1856. The portrait,
almost certainly the first photograph taken of Ruskin,
was made by William Jeffrey, his pupil at the Working
Men's College in London. Photograph courtesy of
James S. Dearden

pp 4–5: View towards Santa Maria della Salute

CONTENTS

PREFACE AND ACKNOWLEDGEMENTS

The Venetians are fond of saying that it takes more than a lifetime to know their own city. By the time John Ruskin's three-volume work *The Stones of Venice* (amounting to almost half a million words, with more than fifty plates reproduced from his own drawings) was published in London in 1851–3, he had visited Venice on six occasions; the first, in 1835, as a boy of sixteen. When he and his wife, Effie, left for London at the end of June 1851, Ruskin had spent, over a period of sixteen years, fewer than eighteen months in Venice, and had already published the first two volumes of *Modern Painters*, and *The Seven Lamps of Architecture*. By any standards *The Stones of Venice* was a massive undertaking; unrivalled in the beauty of its prose, Ruskin's survey of the buildings of Venice laid the foundations for art and architectural historians of the future.

Ruskin possessed an acute eye for colour and detail, and was an accomplished draughtsman. His evocative drawings and watercolours of Venetian architecture now have an added poignancy in view of the city's plight in the first quarter of the twenty-first century, for apart from their value as architectural records, they indicate the extent to which carvings have deteriorated and the colours of incrustation and decoration all but vanished from so many of the buildings he had seen and drawn in his youth. During a long visit to Venice in 1876–7,

Ruskin was struck by the amount of damage that had been caused in a matter of thirty years by the combination of climatic conditions, neglect and (at that time) poor methods of restoration, and sent immediately to England for one of his earlier watercolours to demonstrate the point. He often wrote that he wished life were long enough to illustrate everything that he described in his books, but was frustrated by the limitations and expense of the printing processes of the time.

For the traveller in Venice, Ruskin is still an entertaining, if controversial, guide to the architecture of the city, which has changed remarkably little in its outline since his day. *The Stones of Venice* is, however, too long and discursive a work for anyone but the serious student to attempt to read in its entirety. It seemed appropriate, therefore, in the year 2000, to mark the centenary of Ruskin's death with a compilation of his text and drawings, given with a series of photographs taken towards the end of the twentieth century, to illustrate the degree to which the city's architecture had survived (or, in several cases, changed for the worse) since the middle of the nineteenth century. It was not possible to include and illustrate every building listed alphabetically in the *Venetian Index*, in which several Renaissance buildings were briefly dismissed by Ruskin as being 'of no importance'. The selection of 'stones' became a matter of identifying and photographing those buildings and details about which Ruskin had something definite to say, and rearranging the material into broad chronological sequence to help provide a visual guide to his aesthetic argument. As before, this new edition does not include paintings or interiors but concentrates on the exterior architecture and sculpture described in the *Stones*, all of which may be seen from the street or from the water, without entering a building. A journey along the Grand Canal by *vaporetto* or a crossing by the *traghetto* gondola-ferry must nowadays take the place of the private gondola recommended by Ruskin.

Most of the photographs in the first edition (published in 2000) were taken on film in the last quarter of the twentieth century. There have been changes and developments in the ensuing fifteen years, and many new photographs are included in this new edition. It was necessary to re-photograph as many subjects as possible, so that most of the illustrations would be contemporary with the new book, and would show the significant amount of restoration and cleaning that has taken place in recent years. For instance, the sculptures on the façades of the churches of S. Moisè and S. Stefano (illustrated in the first edition) were so blackened at the time of photography in the 1990s that the details were difficult to distinguish; and the north façade of the Basilica of S. Marco was in a similar state. Certain photographs were taken as long ago as the 1970s, and although digital photography has now replaced film, a few have been used again, where they seemed better to suit the mood of Ruskin's text than a more recent image.

The notebooks, drawings, daguerreotypes and watercolours made by Ruskin during his working visits to Venice tell their own story and are immensely valuable as visual records, for they show us how much has been lost, or how much remains, of the surface decoration of buildings since the mid-nineteenth century. His architectural notebooks and pocket books of drawings,

diagrams, measurements and sketches, made between 1849 and 1850 in preparation for the *Stones*, survive and are held at the Ruskin Library at Lancaster University. Thanks to the work of Ian Bliss, Roger Garside and Ray Haslam, the 1849–50 Venetian notebooks have been transcribed and scanned to produce an electronic edition, now accessible from the website of the Ruskin Library and Research Centre.

From the manuscript list of daguerreotypes held at the Ruskin Library, Lancaster (published by Paolo Costantini and Italo Zannier in *I dagherrotipi della collezione Ruskin*, 1986), it was evident that throughout his working life Ruskin had collected, made or commissioned more than 300 daguerreotype photographs. Of these, it was known that some 131 photographs had survived, the majority of which are held at the Ruskin Library. Then in 2006 Ken and Jenny Jacobson, collectors and historians of photography, acquired at auction in Penrith a box of nineteenth-century photographic plates. The box contained a remarkable discovery: 188 'missing daguerreotypes' from Ruskin's collection, long presumed lost. These are of particular interest and value because many of the Venetian subjects among them had been made as studies for *The Stones of Venice*. The collection includes many further views of architectural details of St. Mark's and the Ducal Palace as well as photographs of lesser-known buildings and their details. (At the time of writing, a book by Ken and Jenny Jacobson describing their discovery and subsequent researches was soon to be published, and they have kindly allowed the reproduction of four of their daguerreotypes in this book.)

Ruskin's mistrust of nineteenth-century restoration was founded on his experience of English methods of the time, and although it is widely believed that he objected in principle to all restoration of ancient buildings, his real concern lay in the manner of its execution. Towards the end of his working life he had the satisfaction of knowing that his 1876–7 collaboration with Count Zorzi, in the campaign to rescue the Basilica of S. Marco from an insensitive restoration, had led to a vigorous British–Italian debate which was soon taken up in other countries. During his last, brief visit in 1888 Ruskin was able to see for himself the benefits that the campaign had conferred on Venice. He might have approved, too, of the situation that developed less than a century later. Following the disastrous floods of 1966, a body of international private committees was formed, under the auspices of UNESCO, and to this day they work closely with the Italian authorities in a continuing programme for the safeguarding of the city. At the forefront of the early campaign to raise funds for the city was the British committee, the Venice in Peril Fund, still in existence after more than forty years. The charity, chaired by John Julius Norwich, was founded in 1971 by Sir Ashley Clarke, whose widow, Frances, continues to work for the benefit of the city.

Invariably prophetic, Ruskin foresaw many of the problems now facing Venice, and his writings in later life reveal deep anxieties about the environment and the effects of industrial pollution in Europe. 'The Storm-Cloud of the Nineteenth Century' was the title of two lectures delivered at the London Institution in February 1884, broadly covering the subject of what we now call 'climate change'. Even Ruskin could not have predicted the extent of the stress that would be imposed on Venice and its lagoon islands by the ever-increasing pressure of mass tourism and the effects of globalisation, together with recent increases in the levels and frequency of *acqua alta* (high water) partly caused by the deep-dredging of canals for the benefit of the traffic of large cruise ships. Venice is a fragile lagoon city and its ecological structure is under continual threat.

I was helped by many people and organisations during the preparation of the first edition, and am grateful once more to the trustees of the Gladys Krieble Delmas Foundation for assistance towards the cost of further research in Venice. Personal thanks are owed to Sarah Bunney, Jeanne Clegg, James S. Dearden, Robert Hewison, Paul Hills, Deborah Howard, Howard Hull, Ken and Jenny Jacobson, John Law, Nigel McGilchrist, John Millerchip, Jenny Newborough, John Julius Norwich, Francis O'Gorman, William Packer, Nicholas Penny, Louise Pullen, Clive Raven, Philip Rylands, Virginia Stevens, Paul Tucker, John Unrau, Michael Wheeler, Stephen Wildman, Clive Wilmer, Tim Williams, Alan Windsor, Wolfgang Wolters and Alvise Zorzi for help and encouragement at various stages. James Dearden kindly read the proofs of the first edition, making many useful suggestions, and the Director of the Ruskin Library Stephen Wildman, together with his staff, has been a continual source of help. The late Ron Parkinson persuaded me to read *The Stones of Venice* before my first working visit to the city in 1971.

For permission to quote extracts from the following published works, thanks are owed to Oxford University Press for *Ruskin in Italy: Letters to His Parents 1845*, ed. H.I. Shapiro; and Yale University Press for *Ruskin's Letters from Venice 1851–52*, ed. J.L. Bradley. Helpful assistance was given by the Abbot Hall Art Gallery, Kendal; the Ashmolean Museum, Oxford; the Biblioteca Marciana, Venice; the British Library, London; the Museo Correr, Venice; the Courtauld Institute, London; the Guild of St George Collection (Museums Sheffield); the National Gallery, London; the Ruskin Library and Research Centre, Lancaster; and the Victoria and Albert Museum, London. I thank Nigel Farrow, Lucy Myers and Sarah Thorowgood at Lund Humphries, and Oliver Keen who designed the new edition, and I am once again grateful to Alan Windsor for his introductory chapter. Howard Watson helped to resolve the intricacies of a new and extended edition.

Sarah Quill

ABBREVIATIONS AND TEXT REFERENCES

Many of the Ruskin passages quoted in this book are taken from *The Works of John Ruskin*, ed. E.T. Cook and A. Wedderburn, Library Edition, London, 1903–12, 39 vols. The references cited from *Works* give the Library Edition volume number followed by the page number. Thus, the reference (10:273) indicates volume 10, page 273. Titles of the relevant volume numbers are given below.

Works 3–7   *Modern Painters* (5 vols)

Works 8   *The Seven Lamps of Architecture*

Works 9–11   *The Stones of Venice* (3 vols)

Works 11   *Examples of the Architecture of Venice* (originally issued in March 1851 as a folio edition of plates engraved from Ruskin's drawings)

Works 20   *Lectures on Art* and *Aratra Pentelici*

Works 24   *Guide to the Academy, Venice* and *St Mark's Rest*

Works 29   *Fors Clavigera*

Works 30   *The Guild of St George*

Works 35   *Praeterita*

Works 36   *Letters (1827–1869)*

Works 37   *Letters (1870–1889)*

References in the text to Ruskin's architectural notebooks and pocket books, held at the Ruskin Library, Lancaster, are given as follows: Notebook followed by 'M', 'M2', 'House Book 1', 'Door Book', 'House Book 2', 'Palace Book', 'Gothic Book', or 'Bit Book'.

Citations to other works are given in a fuller, standard style.

Note: In general, Ruskin's spelling and punctuation have been retained, with some minor amendments made for the sake of consistency and clarity.

CHRONOLOGY OF JOHN RUSKIN'S LIFE

1819
John Ruskin born in London on 8 February, the only child of John James Ruskin and Margaret Cock

1832
For his thirteenth birthday Ruskin is given *Italy* by Samuel Rogers, with vignette illustrations by J.M.W. Turner

1833
Ruskin's first journey abroad, touring France, Switzerland and Italy with his parents

1835
During a six-month tour, the Ruskin family visits Venice in October, staying at the Hotel Danieli

1837
Ruskin enters Christ Church, Oxford, as a Gentleman Commoner

1840
Suffers a breakdown in health and his studies are interrupted, following disappointment in love[1]

1841
The Ruskin family returns to Venice in May
Ruskin completes his Oxford degree

1843
Publication of volume I of *Modern Painters*, Ruskin's response to the critics of the work of J.M.W. Turner[2]

1845
Ruskin makes his first tour abroad without his parents. In Venice, stays at the Hôtel de l'Europe (Ca' Giustinian) for five weeks from early September

1846
The railway bridge, connecting Venice to the mainland, opens in January
Publication of volume II of *Modern Painters*
Ruskin visits Venice in May

1848
Marriage on 10 April to Euphemia ('Effie') Chalmers Gray in Perth, Scotland
Venetian uprising against Austrian rule, led by Daniele Manin

1849
Publication of *The Seven Lamps of Architecture*
Venice, under siege, surrenders to Austrian rule
Ruskin and Effie spend the winter in Venice, staying at the Hotel Danieli from November 1849 until March 1850. They meet Rawdon Brown

1851
Publication of *The Foundations*, volume I of
The Stones of Venice, followed by *Examples of the
Architecture of Venice*, with plates engraved from
Ruskin's drawings
Pamphlet in defence of the work of the Pre-
Raphaelites. Meets John Everett Millais (1829–96),
artist and the founder, with William Holman Hunt
and Dante Gabriel Rossetti, of the Pre-Raphaelite
Brotherhood in 1848
Ruskin and his wife return to Venice on 1
September, staying until June 1852
Death of J.M.W. Turner. Ruskin is named as an
executor

1853
Publication of volumes II and III of *The Stones of
Venice*
Holiday at Glenfinlas (Glen Finglas), Scotland,
with Effie, John Millais and Millais' brother,
William Henry
Ruskin delivers four lectures in Edinburgh,
published in 1854 as *Lectures on Architecture and
Painting*

1854
Effie leaves Ruskin, and their marriage is annulled
Inauguration of the Working Men's College in
London. One of Ruskin's pupils in drawing is John
Wharlton Bunney

1855
Publication of the second edition of *The Seven
Lamps of Architecture*
Effie Ruskin marries John Everett Millais

1856
Publication of volumes III and IV of *Modern
Painters*
Ruskin meets Edward Burne-Jones and Charles
Eliot Norton

1858
Ruskin meets Rose La Touche
Religious 'unconversion' at Turin

1860
Publication of volume V of *Modern Painters* and
Unto This Last

1861
Ruskin presents forty-eight Turner drawings from
his collection to the Ashmolean Museum, Oxford,
and twenty-five drawings to the Fitzwilliam
Museum, Cambridge

1864
Death of Ruskin's father, John James Ruskin

1866
Ruskin proposes marriage to Rose La Touche, and
is asked to wait three years

1869
Ruskin is appointed first Slade Professor of Art at
Oxford
During a summer spent in Switzerland and Italy,
he makes short visits to Venice
Publication of *The Queen of the Air*, a study of the
Greek myths

1870
Visits Venice 25 May – 20 June, staying at the
Hotel Danieli

1871
Publication of the first issue of *Fors Clavigera:
Letters to the Workmen and Labourers of Great
Britain*
Purchase of Brantwood, a house near Coniston in
the Lake District
Death of his mother, Margaret Ruskin
Foundation of the Guild of St George

1872
Ruskin stays at the Hotel Danieli in Venice for
three weeks in the summer

1875
Death of Rose La Touche

1876
Ruskin returns to Venice in September, staying
at the Grand Hotel (Ca' Ferro) on the Grand
Canal, and begins work on *St Mark's Rest*
After meeting Count Alvise Piero Zorzi, he
becomes involved in the campaign to rescue
St Mark's from an insensitive restoration
He commissions J.W. Bunney to paint the west
façade of St Mark's for the Guild of St George

1877
In February, moves to rooms at La Calcina, a small
inn on the Zattere, where he stays until early May
Meets Angelo Alessandri and Giacomo Boni
Publication of *Guide to the Principal Pictures in
the Academy of Fine Art at Venice*
In England, William Morris founds the Society
for the Protection of Ancient Buildings

1877–84
Publication of *St Mark's Rest*

1878
Formal establishment of the Guild of St George at
Walkley in Sheffield
Ruskin suffers a mental breakdown
A court case takes place in London after
a libel suit brought by the painter James
Whistler, following Ruskin's 1877 article
in *Fors Clavigera*

1879
Ruskin resigns his Oxford professorship

1881–3
Periodic breakdowns of health, but work continues

1882
The Ancient Monuments Protection Act is voted
through Parliament in England

1883
Ruskin is reappointed to the Slade professorship

1884
Delivers the lecture 'The Storm-Cloud of the
Nineteenth Century' at the London Institution

1885
Final resignation of his Slade professorship
Publication of the first part of his autobiography,
Praeterita

1888
Ruskin makes his last visit to Venice, cut short
by a severe mental breakdown, which ends his
working life

1890
The collection of the Guild of St George moves to
Meersbrook Park, Sheffield, and opens as the
Ruskin Museum

1900
Ruskin dies at Brantwood on 20 January and is
buried in Coniston churchyard

RUSKIN AND VENICE

Alan Windsor

JOHN RUSKIN WAS, IN HIS LIFETIME, one of the most admired and influential English authors of the nineteenth century, his works known and read by hundreds of thousands of people all over the world.

Ruskin was a poet in his youth, and in maturity a writer, critic and lecturer with a wide range of interests, from geology to political economy, although the visual arts were always the central focus of his attention. Born in London in 1819, he was an exact contemporary of Queen Victoria, and was the only child of elderly, deeply religious Scottish parents who both cosseted and dominated him long after he grew to manhood. His father was a sherry merchant, a self-made man who had built up a considerable fortune from nothing by intensively hard work; he was interested in art and collected good pictures, including those of Turner, with whom he was friendly. Ruskin's mother was an Evangelical Protestant with limited interests outside the household and her religion. Both Ruskin's parents enjoyed travelling widely in England and abroad, particularly in France, Switzerland and Italy, their shared enthusiasm being stimulated by the landscape, the art and the architecture of the places they visited with their son.

Privately tutored for the most part, Ruskin eventually went up to Christ Church, Oxford, where he won the Newdigate Prize for poetry. He was privileged as a young man in having an allowance from his father and he eventually inherited enough money to be able to live as a gentleman; he was never obliged to seek paid employment from anyone. As a result he could publicly express his views on almost any subject in which he was interested with complete independence from any constraints other than those he accepted from his parents. The only formal appointment he held was that of Slade Professor of Art at Oxford from 1869 to 1879 (he was the first) and again, after a period of severe mental breakdown, from 1883 to 1885. His books eventually brought him an income, which replaced the fortune he spent on travel, pictures, illuminated manuscripts and minerals, and on the support of favoured artists and philanthropic schemes, but his writings and his life were driven by his consuming energy in the pursuit of study and teaching: 'learning more, and teaching what truth I knew'.

Ruskin's passionate engagement with Venice began properly with his second visit to the city in 1841, at the age of twenty-two, with his parents. But already, before that, many things had prepared him to respond with the greatest intensity to his mature experience of this unique city: the enthusiasm of his father for the works of Turner; the gift, for his thirteenth birthday, of Samuel Rogers' *Italy*, illustrated with engravings after Turner; his first visit at the age of sixteen, and the development of his interest in architecture and his

John Ruskin, *Archivolt of the north aisle of S. Donato, Murano*,
Plate 5 in *The Stones of Venice* II (10:58)

love of drawing. On that second visit he was able
to draw with an original delicacy and freshness
of vision, endowing his drawings of S. Marco,
the Ducal Palace and other buildings with the
beginnings of an acute sensitivity to their form,
which was to distinguish his architectural studies
from then on.

A third visit in 1845, Ruskin's first journey abroad
without his father and mother, was made with a
clear purpose in mind, but another developed as
a result. Having published the first volume of his
first major book, *Modern Painters* (1843), which
had been an immediate success, he determined to
study Italian artists of the fourteenth and fifteenth
centuries in order to deal with issues deriving from
them in the second volume. He spent five weeks in
Venice towards the end of his tour through Italy, far
longer than he had planned, because this time, his
work on the paintings satisfactorily accomplished,
his awareness of the beauty and tragic decay of the
architecture of the city began to take on a more
urgent and practical dimension than previously.

As a precocious boy he had thrilled with a Byronic
affectation to morbid thoughts of the ghost-haunted
pavements of a doomed city: on his second visit he
had delighted in drawing the great buildings
around St Mark's Square, whilst mourning their
condition; but now he was thoroughly alarmed to
see that hundreds of still-splendid buildings were
being allowed to fall into decrepitude, or were being
altered, insensitively cleaned, gutted, demolished,
drastically restored or simply rebuilt.

Ruskin's approach to drawing changed
dramatically as he no longer strove for pictorial
effect ('taking common loose sketches'). He began
to record details he knew or feared might be gone
forever at any moment, and to convey the beauty of
their colour, their patina and the dynamics of their
patterns. He also bought architectural photographs
from a French artist ('Daguerreotypes taken by this
vivid sunlight are glorious things'), recognising their
precious value as records.

From that time on, Venetian architecture was
never far from his thoughts, and a brief visit of

two weeks in 1846 was devoted almost entirely to drawing details and taking notes.

Ruskin's next major book was immensely successful. *The Seven Lamps of Architecture* was largely the fruit of his work during three months in Normandy studying medieval buildings when on his first trip abroad following his marriage to Euphemia ('Effie') Chalmers Gray, but in it there are many references to the Basilica of St Mark's.

His next visit to Venice was with Effie, and they stayed from November 1849 to March 1850. This time he began to take elaborate, careful measurements and to make an astounding number of detailed analytical drawings of arches, mouldings, capitals, decorative features and sculptures; he made copious notes, climbing to dangerous heights on long ladders and surveying buildings with a care and precision no one had ever done before; he worked exhaustively and single-handedly to build a matchless record of medieval Venetian architecture. Ruskin minutely scrutinised nearly every church and palace of importance in the main group of islands; he wrote to his father in 1852 that he had examined piece by piece buildings covering five square miles, read some forty volumes of the city's archives and made hundreds of architectural drawings. The first volume of *The Stones of Venice* was published in 1851, as well as the three folios of *Examples of the Architecture of Venice, selected and drawn to measurement from the edifices.* Much of the first volume (*The Foundations*) was devoted to the step-by-step elucidation of processes by which practical and constructional methods in architecture lead to characteristic forms of arch masonry, cornice profiles, capitals and so on.

A further long visit, from September 1851 until June 1852, extended and consolidated his surveying and archival work and resulted in the publication, in 1853, of volumes two (*The Sea-Stories*) and three (*The Fall*), the latter including the alphabetical guide to the most important buildings of all periods, the *Venetian Index*.

The Stones of Venice had a didactic and moral theme; *Examples* simply provided plates and commentaries on them. Neither, to begin with, sold especially well, and it is generally accepted that Ruskin's father brought pressure to bear on him to make the second and third volumes of the *Stones* much more poetically rhetorical than the first.

Ruskin made it clear that one of the main aims of *The Stones of Venice* was to deliver an awful warning to contemporary England, the greatest maritime empire of all time. He had begun to look at his own country with a deeply critical eye. He argued that if the lessons to be learned from the downfall of the great powers of Tyre and Venice were fully understood, a less merited pride and a more merited humiliation than theirs might yet be avoided – an idea that was in part derived from Byron and others.

In Ruskin's day, the contemporary Venetians were considered to be a subject people, largely worthless and degenerate when compared to their ancestors. The great achievements in art and architecture of the past were all around, but it was thought that nothing comparable had been created by Venetians for about 200 years. It is worth remembering that Ruskin saw the humiliation of Venice at close hand. Only just over twenty years before he was born, Ludovico Manin, the last Doge of all, had been obliged to leave the Ducal Palace, on the order of Napoleon, and the Venetian Republic, after a thousand years of independence,

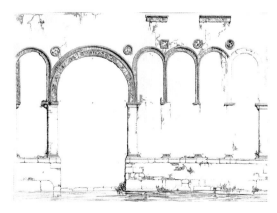

John Ruskin, *Byzantine Ruin in the Rio di Ca' Foscari*, Plate 8 in *Examples of the Architecture of Venice*

had ceased to exist. Since then it had been occupied at will by the French and the Austrians, and all the ancient governing institutions of the Republic had been abolished. The 1848–9 uprising against Austrian rule, heroically led by Daniele Manin, was a tragic failure, and in late 1849, when Ruskin and his young wife Effie arrived, the scars of the Austrian bombardment before the reoccupation were still raw; they were taken together by Austrian officers to see a number of the military installations that ringed the city.

Ruskin believed that the moral integrity of a people could be read in their artefacts, their pictures and in their architecture. These depend, he wrote, 'for their dignity and pleasurableness in the utmost degree, upon the vivid expression of the intellectual life which has been concerned in their production'. In medieval times, 'hand-work' vividly expressed life and imagination; in the nineteenth century, by contrast, machine work or the work of men and women condemned to mindless machine-like activity produced perfectly finished but soulless objects designed by the superior classes for motivations of profit. As Ruskin's love of Gothic and earlier architecture developed, so did his concern with social issues, and with the suffering and misery endured by masses of people throughout Europe. As he was writing *The Seven Lamps*, the two preoccupations began to fuse together as one subject. He now wrote that the most important question to ask, when contemplating stonework, was, 'Was the carver happy while he was about it?'

In the second volume of *The Stones of Venice*, in the famous chapter entitled 'The Nature of Gothic', Ruskin's identification with the working classes and his political theories regarding their role and destiny in society are set out in incandescent prose. Medieval craftsmen might have been primitive, ignorant, clumsy and crude in their character and work, but they had been free, free to express themselves within the ordered fabric of society and building projects alike. Modern workmen were now slaves, more completely so than any such of ancient or modern times. Their enslavement had begun

with the Renaissance, as had the road to the technology of mass-production of goods by a downtrodden humanity shackled to machines and capitalist exploitation, and a pyramidal society dominated by greedy and hypocritical merchants.

Society may make a tool of each individual, or, by freeing him, with all his imperfections, by allowing honest hand craftsmanship, it may make a man of him. Ruskin did explain the odd levels of the windows of the Lagoon side of the Doge's Palace by showing how they owed their positions to the form and functions of the interior rooms, thus emphasising the pleasure he took in organically generated features as opposed to an imposed symmetry on a façade: 'the daring sacrifice of symmetry to convenience which was noticed as one of the chief noblenesses of the Gothic schools.' He otherwise took relatively little interest in the functional aspects of buildings. Apart from St Mark's, he rarely discussed their interiors or their spaces. Exterior mass, form, colour, surface, texture and sculptural decoration meant most to him. He was also deeply moved by the overt or covert symbolism of these elements, often elaborating his own sometimes fanciful, sometimes fascinating interpretation of their meaning. One of the best-known and most amusing of these is his analysis of a series of six cornices of different periods based on floral ornament, in order to show 'the Christian element struggling with the Formalism of the Papacy'; in several examples of those illustrated, 'That officialism of the leaves and their ribs means Apostolic Succession and I don't know how much more, and is already preparing the way for the transition to the old heathenism, and the Renaissance', whilst another cornice, naturalistically carved, reveals 'Protestantism – a slight touch of dissent, hardly amounting to a schism, in those falling leaves, but true life in the whole of it ...'

Ruskin was criticised in his own day for the rather convoluted arguments by which he was able to condemn the Roman Catholic religion of those medieval Venetians he so much admired, whilst praising the health of their Christian morality and

John Ruskin, *Cornice Decoration*, *c.*1851, pencil, brown ink and ink wash, Ruskin Foundation, Ruskin Library, Lancaster

austere, flat and innocent of anatomical correctness or conventional proportion, is to be admired in contrast to some virtuoso mosaic rendering of a composition by a High Renaissance painter ('better than whitewash but that is all'). In the mosaics and sculpture of the Byzantine tradition, he recognised a direct continuity from the art of ancient Greece. The Salomé of the north wall of the baptistery of S. Marco is, he wrote, 'simply the translation of any Greek maid on a Greek vase ... the phantom of some sweet water-carrier from an Arcadian spring'.

Ruskin devoted passages of contemptuous invective to Renaissance architecture in the third volume of *The Stones of Venice*. One of the central interests of *The Stones* lies in the enthusiasm with which he analyses the qualities of Venetian Byzantine and then Gothic architecture, whilst finally denigrating (or, with one or two remarkable exceptions, either damning with qualified praise or pronouncing them to be of no interest) virtually all the most beautiful of the Renaissance buildings, especially those of Palladio.

One of the greatest pleasures of *The Stones of Venice* lies in the poetry of its prose, much of which is still remembered and recited by those who have read it, for its matchless lyricism in the contemplation of Venice, this strangest of cities.

RUSKIN AND THE BYZANTINE STYLE OF ARCHITECTURE IN VENICE

AS AN ARCHITECTURAL CRITIC AND HISTORIAN, Ruskin was early in his admiration for the Byzantine style in Venice. Quite apart from the thousands of fragments of buildings taken from Constantinople and incorporated into the fabric of Venetian ones, Byzantine art was a long-lasting influence on the development of typically Venetian architecture; although he was far from being the first writer to recognise and explain this, Ruskin was and remains one of the most illuminating analysts of its qualities.

Constantinople, today Istanbul, was the capital of the Roman Empire from AD 330, following the adoption of Christianity as the state religion. After

the glories of their art. The explanation, for him, seems to have lain in the independence of the old Venetian state from papal interference and influence; it was pointed out, however, that he appeared by sleight of hand to transform those Venetians into proto-Protestants of some kind. Following his religious 'unconversion' of 1858 in Turin, he adopted a much more relaxed attitude towards Roman Catholicism.

Contemporary architectural enthusiasts were astonished that Ruskin lavished praise on St Mark's, which had hitherto generally been considered to be an uncouth and barbaric building. Ruskin was the first to articulate a peculiarly modern sensibility, in stressing the superior quality of medieval mosaics, in which a Madonna (such as that of the apse of S. Donato at Murano), dramatically elongated and

365 it was a separate empire, which lasted until 1453. Although Roman by administrative practices and by law, it was Greek in its foundation as a city (originally named Byzantium), and a high proportion of its population was of Greek descent and used that language. Byzantine art and architecture derived from those of the ancient Roman Empire, blended with many special characteristics absorbed from the Middle East. Its influence can be seen to have spread to many parts of southern Europe, even as far as Périgueux in France.

Following the disintegration of the Roman Empire, Venice was a connecting link between the East and the West, between the Byzantine and the Frankish Christian empires. Trade and war in the eastern Mediterranean brought an intimate contact with Byzantine art and architecture to the Venetians; and they, lacking an abundance of local stone, looted vast quantities of columns, capitals, panels sculptured in relief and sheets of decorative marble cladding from Constantinople and elsewhere in Asia Minor. Greek artists originating in Constantinople and Athens also no doubt worked in Venice.

Byzantine churches, like those of the West, derived their basic plan from that of the Roman basilica, with a central nave and two or more side aisles, and with a semicircular apsidal end. Their typical buildings were of brick and some mass concrete, with the rugged brickwork making patterns and horizontal bands playing a structural and decorative role.

Often, however, the brickwork was entirely clad inside with thin sheets of marble and other stones for decorative purposes; fresco and mosaics in coloured stones or in glass using tin oxides were also used internally. Mosaics had been used in Roman Italy for flooring, but the Byzantines applied them to the surfaces of walls and domes. Ruskin saw in the style of their imagery a direct continuity from ancient Greek vase-painting: 'a Byzantine *was* nothing else than a Greek, – recognizing Christ for Zeus'. Panels of carved relief were mounted on walls, but three-dimensional sculpture was rare.

Columns were developed from classical types, but new forms of capital were evolved; the typical Byzantine capital was a simple solid forming the transition between the square abacus on top and the cylindrical shaft below, having a gentle concave or, more often, convex profile. Ruskin particularly loved the acute observation of nature in their decorative carving – the plants, animals, birds, fruit, fishes, and representations of human figures

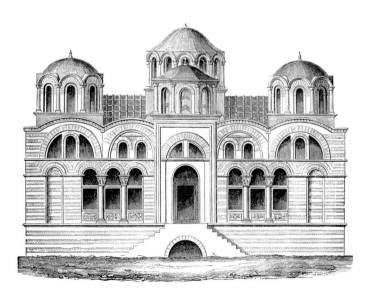

Church of the Theotokos Pammakaristos, Constantinople

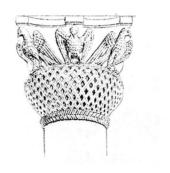

John Ruskin, *Byzantine Capitals* (detail), capitals from Palazzo Donà, Casa Loredan and St Mark's, Plate 8 in *The Stones of Venice* II (10:159)

– which the sculptors brought to their sensitively formalised and endlessly inventive capitals.

Doors, windows and arcades had round-headed arches, the openings often stilted high above the top of the column or pier supporting them. Domes covered square and polygonal spaces, as well as round ones, using pendentives to support the circular base of the dome as it crossed corners. Long rectangular spaces, such as naves, were covered with a row of domes rather than with a timber roof or with vaulting, as in the West. Such domes were commonly exposed externally and made rainproof, rather than being covered with a timber roof, as were the vaults of Western churches. The domes of St Mark's in Venice, however, are surmounted by tall secondary domes constructed on a wooden framework, and their curious forms dominate the external aspect of this unique basilica, 'this multitude of pillars and white domes, clustered into a long low pyramid of coloured light', as Ruskin called it. Elsewhere in the *Stones* he wrote, 'Whatever in St Mark's arrests the eye, or affects the feelings, is either Byzantine, or has been modified by Byzantine influence.' (The Chuch of the Holy Apostles, no longer seen, St Saviour in Chora and the Church of Theotokos Pammakaristos in Contantinople are examples.)

In Venice, a particular type of 'Veneto-Byzantine' palace or large townhouse evolved, usually built back from the edge of the water, and having a waterside façade consisting of a long range of superimposed round-headed, usually stilted, arcades on the ground and first floors, sandwiched between two towers, the whole crowned with a decorative parapet. This basic formula underlay the appearance of Venetian palaces for several hundred years.

RUSKIN AND VENETIAN GOTHIC

GOTHIC IS THE TERM USED FOR the architecture of roughly the twelfth to the fifteenth centuries in northern Europe. It is distinguished by a number of elements that may or may not all be included in a particular building considered Gothic in style. Well aware of the fact that relatively few of such buildings are found in medieval Venetian architecture, Ruskin decided, in writing his chapter in the *Stones* entitled 'The Nature of Gothic', to explain the use of the term to describe the very different elements of Venetian Gothic by trying to evoke the essence of '*Gothicness*', and in so doing he used the subject as a platform for a much wider and deeper argument about the cultural and social morality of modern Europe. He did not at this point make a detailed comparison between Venetian Gothic and that of the north, although one of his most memorable passages is that which introduces the reader for the

John Ruskin, *Fig-tree Angle of the Ducal Palace*, photogravure, Plate H in *The Stones of Venice* II (10:358)

In France, Britain, Germany and elsewhere, pointed arches were used for doors, windows and arcades. Early in the period, windows, filled with pictorial stained glass, became subdivided with tracery; later they were made spectacularly large, while the tracery became audaciously elaborate. Internal spaces were rib vaulted with four or six compartments in each bay, and over time such ribbed vaults were also elaborated into complex stellar patterns with a proliferation of ribs and cells until fan vaulting marked the most elaborate development. The pillars supporting the vaults acquired clusters of shafts around them, until the capital, the earliest of which tended to be modelled along the lines of the Roman Corinthian, became a less and less marked interruption between the slender shafts and the ribs of the vaulting overhead. Extreme heights were achieved, and prominent buttresses and flying buttresses, externally necessary to take the thrust of the vaulting, were crowned with pinnacles. High-pitched steeply sloping roofs were edged with parapets or crenellations. Tall bell towers with very tall spires flanked the west fronts of churches, and the main porches were deep and rich in sculpture, both in relief and wholly in the round. Religious and secular buildings were constructed of stone or brick, according to local traditions, but stone was usually considered to have the greatest prestige.

In Venice, as in other parts of Italy, many of the characteristics listed above are missing, or treated differently. There is nothing in northern Gothic, for example, to compare with the unique composition of the Ducal Palace. Most Venetian medieval buildings were constructed of brick, and few churches were vaulted. The Frari and SS Giovanni e Paolo are notable exceptions, but their vaults are prudently secured from spreading, with wooden tie-beams crossing from between the tops of the tall cylindrical columns supporting them. The relatively soft ground of the islands upon which Venice is built was always a major factor influencing the choice of materials and the constructional methods employed.

Buttresses, where used, are not treated with the prominence they have in northern Europe. Timber

first time to the façade of St Mark's. It is brilliantly orchestrated in terms of a step-by-step evocation of the approach to a typical English cathedral, in contrast to that of the extraordinary Basilica, together with a description of the overall impact of both when fully revealed to the spectator. Elsewhere he illustrated examples of the design and treatment of details as seen in northern as compared with Venetian Gothic, but it is perhaps worth reviewing some broad general differences here.

roofs were usual, and the light barrel vaults and domes of the Byzantine period continued to be built. There were few relatively large windows, and tracery tended to be based on a formula of a quatrefoil in a circle above or between pointed arches. Arches with ogee or double curves were common; strongly cusped, scalloped, horseshoe or undulating variants were derived from Asiatic influences. Plain, single-curved pointed arches were usually used only for main portals or for arcades supporting major burdens. One of Ruskin's most helpful plates in the second volume of *The Stones* (see p.93) demonstrates the evolution of Venetian arch and window types, although he made it clear that a straightforward chronological sequence cannot be assumed from his orders of arches; the use of any one type often overlapped another by a long period. It is worth recalling here that Ruskin did not advocate the literal adoption of the Gothic or of its Venetian variant as a style for the architecture of his own time, although he clearly regarded them as an ideal model. In studying them he sought passionately to determine the basic principles governing the social, artistic and spiritual elements of the periods he admired; he believed that lessons might be drawn from them in order to reform Europe and so incidentally allow an appropriate modern style to evolve. 'All good architecture is the expression of national life and character ...'

Venetian palaces of the Middle Ages were more often built at the water's edge than their Byzantine predecessors, and whilst the façades of the former were not as completely arcaded as those of the latter, they had a very characteristic feature of an open loggia on the first floor with traceried arcading; this feature was often repeated on higher floors. The arcade was also often set in an attractive stone-faced framing panel, as were independent windows.

In plan the ground floor opened with arches directly onto the canal at water level, and a long entrance hall running from the front to the back of the building was flanked by storerooms. On the upper floor another central hall on the same plan ran the depth of the building, flanked by living rooms and bedrooms. An external staircase was at the back, in a small courtyard. The capitals of Venetian Gothic columns were either concave, based on the Corinthian prototype, or convex, like the Byzantine. Projecting balconies (introduced in the fifteenth century) were traceried or balustraded. The campaniles, or bell towers, of churches were usually free-standing in the Italian manner, and finished with tall, plain pyramid-shaped roofs rather than spires. The tops of walls had many varieties of parapet, mostly fanciful variants on Eastern patterns of crenellation. The use of three-dimensional sculpture externally on buildings was rare.

Above all, in all buildings, religious and secular, the Byzantine tradition of clothing the walls (outside, in Venice, as well as inside) with beautiful sheets of veined marble riveted to the brick core was continued, as was, with apparently inexhaustible invention, the deft orchestration of colour and pattern in the overall construction. 'While the burghers and barons of the North were building their dark streets and grisly castles of oak and sandstone,' wrote Ruskin, 'the merchants of Venice were covering their palaces with porphyry and gold ...'

RUSKIN AND VENETIAN RENAISSANCE ARCHITECTURE

RUSKIN WAS HOSTILE TO THE RENAISSANCE in general terms for a number of reasons. He felt that the so-called revival of learning in fifteenth-century Italy marked the beginning, not of a positive new stage of human development, when literary, scientific and historical enquiry, drawing inspiration from the art and the writings of classical antiquity, led to substantial changes for the better in European society (emancipating the individual from the all-pervading control of the Church), but rather of a negative development in which aristocratic and elitist values established themselves throughout art and learning. Of Renaissance architecture he wrote, 'Whatever excellence it has is refined, high-trained, and deeply erudite; a kind which the architect well knows no common mind can taste. He proclaims it to us aloud. "You cannot feel my work unless you study Vitruvius. I will give you no gay colour, no pleasant sculpture, nothing to make you happy; for I am a learned man. All the pleasure you can have in anything I do is in its proud breeding, its rigid formalism, its perfect finish, its cold tranquillity. I do not work for the vulgar, only for the men of the academy and the court ...'"

Nevertheless, Ruskin appreciated much of the early Renaissance architecture in Venice, particularly where any colourful or decorative influence from the Byzantine era could be discerned on the façades of these later buildings. Although his description of the interior of the church of Sta Maria dei Miracoli is mainly a list of faults, he admired this gem of the late fifteenth century, and described the Palazzo Manzoni, of the same period, as a 'perfect and very rich example of the Byzantine Renaissance'. Disliking much of what he called Central or Roman Renaissance, principally that of the sixteenth century, he did not include Sansovino's exquisite Loggetta at the base of the Campanile of S. Marco in the *Venetian Index*, and dismissed his fine Palazzo Dolfin (later Manin) with a characteristic 'Of no importance'. He believed Palladio – accepted universally today as one of the greatest of all architects – to be completely lacking in architectural imagination and, what is more, an architect who had 'given up all colour'. He despised almost all of the 'Grotesque' Renaissance buildings, his term for the Baroque of the seventeenth century and later; the churches of S. Moisè and Sta Maria Zobenigo (del Giglio) were the subjects of his most withering scorn.

Ruskin's views were based partly on the political opinions touched on in the passage quoted at the beginning of this section, and partly on his purely visual response to such features as walls and their decoration with pattern, colour and sculpture. As always, he interpreted what he saw as being symptomatic of the virtues and vices of the architects and their craftsmen, qualified by the moral fibre of the period in which they were working.

Ruskin had little interest in the sort of ideal proportions applied to whole buildings or to their component parts, so much explored by classicists ancient and modern. Indeed, his exhaustive measurements of St Mark's led him to note with immense satisfaction that shafts of the columns of the façade 'by no means match each other, and their differences are accommodated with the help of the good-natured capitals and bases – which stretch or shorten themselves as need may be'. He also cared nothing for precise symmetry; he strongly appreciated the irregularity of St Mark's precisely because 'the builder has varied every magnitude in this *generally* symmetrical composition'. The studied symmetry and the exquisitely calculated proportions of Palladio's buildings consequently meant nothing to him, nor did their wall surfaces or their carved decoration.

Ruskin liked walls to be suggestive of natural geological structures, of cliffs and mountain faces. In a stone wall, if some horizontal bands of stone expressed the strength and robustness of their material, other parts of the surface, supported by them, could be delicate and obviously non-loadbearing. This was analogous in his view to the variety of material to be seen in some great natural structure like a mountain: 'Do not think that nature rusticates her foundations. Smooth sheets of rock, glistening like sea waves, and that ring under the hammer like a brazen bell – that is her preparation for the first stories.' Classical treatments such as the rustication or vermiculation of the surface of the stones of the base or of ground-floor parts of a building, for example, struck him as being weak and rotten-looking, 'like wet slime honeycombed by sand-eels'. The plainer, smooth-surfaced ashlar kind of rustication, with square-sectioned channels emphasising the division between each stone, also repelled him – he wondered ironically if those on Soane's Bank of England in London were not intended to symbolise account books. And yet he thought that the fifteenth- and sixteenth-century side of the Ducal Palace, facing the narrow Rio del Palazzo, 'though very sparing in colour, is yet, as an example of finished masonry in a vast building ... one of the finest things, not only in Venice, but in the world'. The variety of its surface treatment, and the massive positive-and-negative truncated pyramid-pattern rustication of its base, aroused the greatest enthusiasm in him.

But colour was of major importance to Ruskin in walls. Colour was a delight when it came about as the result of different materials being used, polychromy deriving from structure, or, as in the façade of St Mark's, from the nonfunctional ranges of columns. It could also, he pointed out, be deliberately introduced as encrustation, as seen in the thin sheets of precious marble and other stones attached to the surface of brick walls in order to decorate them, independent of any structural purpose.

Ruskin also appreciated smooth stuccoed surfaces intended for painted decoration. In these respects, much Renaissance architecture failed to provide any interest for his eye or his mind and spirit. 'The exteriors of all the latter palaces were built of barren stone.'

The quality of sculptural decoration on Renaissance buildings was another major element that disappointed and angered him. 'Feebleness and want of soul' are to be observed. He found it always either crudely imitative (as he relentlessly spelled out in his description of those capitals of the arcade of the Ducal Palace, which date from the fifteenth century, on the Piazzetta side), or dull, empty and theatrical; or, as in the grotesque head on Sta Maria Formosa, blasphemous and obscene. Despite his condemnation of just about all architectural and sepulchral monumental sculpture of the periods in question, he nevertheless was unrestrained in his admiration for Verrocchio's equestrian statue of Bartolomeo Colleoni, 'certainly one of the noblest works in Italy'.

There are many surprises in Ruskin's descriptions of Renaissance buildings in Venice. The Palazzo Grimani, for example, comes in for high praise, for example (although it has been pointed out that, whilst sincere, the glowing

generosity of his description is in part designed to contrast with his vitriolic denunciation of the Renaissance as a whole, which follows later). He was appreciative of Sta Maria della Salute. Whilst it is true that he found many appalling faults in it and, in order to justify his qualified praise of the building as a whole, argues (reasonably enough) that 'An architect trained in the worst schools ... may yet have a natural gift of massing and grouping', he cannot nevertheless quite conceal his liking for it. On the other hand, he might have been expected to like the bizarre external spiral staircase (*bòvolo* ['snail-shell' in Venetian dialect]) of the Palazzo Contarini (Palazzo Minelli as he knew it), which he dismisses as being 'very picturesque, but of the fifteenth century, and without merit'. He also ignored, as noted above, Sansovino's Loggetta, even though it is so rich and satisfying in colour, but was civil about the same architect's 'graceful' Libreria Vecchia in the Piazzetta, even if pointing out many faults. The Procuratie Vecchie, whilst of 'no particular interest', are considered to be a graceful series of buildings, and the sixteenth-century Procuratie Nuove form 'a more majestic, though less graceful side for the great square'. The whole ensemble of these buildings, in his famous description of the approach to St Mark's, is characterised as being 'struck back into lovely order', their arches 'charged with goodly sculpture, and fluted shafts of delicate stone'. Here again, however, these favourable adjectives are used only in a rhetorical context where the poetic drama of the façade of St Mark's is to be evoked in contrast; they seem to be inconsistent with his more considered evaluation of them as architecture.

It is not difficult to see how, following Ruskin's preferences, the dazzlingly white and fastidiously symmetrical façades of Palladio's churches, executed in smooth Istrian stone, failed to please him. It remains, however, something of a mystery that he should have felt so much contempt for both the interiors and the exteriors of such beautiful works.

M. Moro dis dal vero

BEFORE 'THE STONES'

The greatest thing a human soul ever does in this world is to *see* something, and tell what it *saw* in a plain way. Hundreds of people can talk for one who can think, but thousands can think for one who can see. To see clearly is poetry, prophecy, and religion – all in one.

Modern Painters III (5:333)

On my thirteenth birthday, 8th February 1832, my father's partner, Mr. Henry Telford,[1] gave me Rogers' *Italy*[2] and determined the main tenor of my life. At that time I had never heard of Turner ... But I had no sooner cast eyes on the Rogers vignettes than I took them for my only masters and set myself to imitate them as far as I possibly could by fine pen shading.

Praeterita (35:79)

In March 1845, aged twenty-six, Ruskin embarked on a long continental tour – the first visit abroad without his parents – accompanied by his valet and general amanuensis, John ('George') Hobbs.[3] The main purpose of the tour was to make further drawings of landscapes for the second volume of Modern Painters *and to begin a serious study of Italian painting. After travelling through France and Switzerland, they were joined in Geneva by Joseph Couttet, a guide from Chamonix known to the Ruskin family. The party travelled widely in Italy, and arrived in Venice in September, having been joined in Baveno by the painter J.D. Harding, Ruskin's drawing teacher since 1841. Ruskin had planned to spend two weeks in Venice, but postponed his departure twice, and eventually stayed for five weeks. After years of neglect, the city, under the Austrian administration, was undergoing a programme of drastic modernisation, and Ruskin resolved to record whatever he could and to 'get a few of the more precious details before they are lost for ever'. He wrote almost daily to his parents, his letters taking the place of the diary he had no time to keep.*

Letters from John Ruskin to his father:

> Venice, 10th September [1845]
> Hôtel de l'Europe[4]

My Dearest Father,

I went to Mestre in order to recall to mind as far as I could our first passing to Venice [in 1835]. The afternoon was cloudless, the sun intensely bright, the gliding down the canal of the Brenta exquisite. We turned the corner of the bastion, where Venice *once*

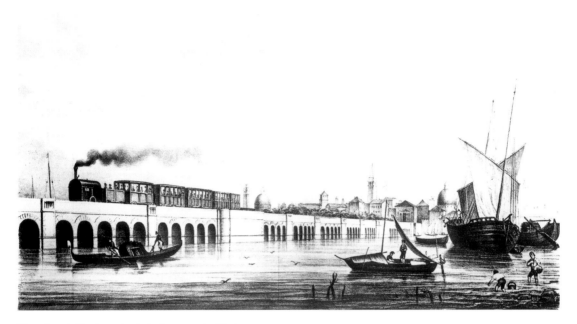

The railway bridge (completed 1846), connecting Venice to the mainland at Mestre, *c.*1846, anon. engraving, Museo Correr, Venice

appeared, & behold – the Greenwich railway, only with less arches and more dead wall, entirely cutting off the whole open sea & half the city, which now looks as nearly as possible like Liverpool at the end of the dockyard wall. The railway covered with busy workmen, scaffolding & heaps of stones, an iron station where the Madonna dell'Acqua used to be, and a group of omnibus gondolas.[5]

When we entered the Grand Canal, I was yet more struck, if possible, by the fearful dilapidation which it has suffered in these last five years. Not only are two thirds of the palaces under *repair* – we know what that means – but they could not stand without it – they are mouldering down as if they were all leaves & autumn had come suddenly. Few boats about – all deathlike & quiet, save for the scaffolding & plastering ... it began to look a little better as we got up to the Rialto, but, it being just solemn twilight as we turned under the arch, behold, all up to the Foscari palace – *gas lamps!* on each side, in grand new iron posts of the last Birmingham fashion, and sure enough, they have them all up

the narrow canals, and there is a grand one, with more flourishes than usual, just under the Bridge of Sighs. Imagine the new style of serenades – by gas light. Add to this, that they are repairing the front of St. Mark's, and appear to be destroying its mosaics ... What makes me sadder is, that the divine beauty of the yet uninjured passage about the Salute and Piazzetta has struck me more intensely than ever. I have been standing (but the moment before I began this letter) on the steps at the door – the water is not even plashing in the moonlight, there is not even a star twinkling, it is as still as if Venice were beneath the sea, but beautiful beyond all thought.[6]

14th September – how painful it is to be in Venice now I cannot tell you. There is no single spot, east or west, up or down, where her spirit remains – the modern work has set its plague spot everywhere – the moment you begin to feel, some gas pipe business forces itself on the eye, and you are thrust into the 19th century ... I am but barely in time to see the last of dear old St. Mark's. They have ordered him to be '*pulito*' and after whitewashing the Doge's palace, and daubing it with the Austrian national distillation of coffins and jaundice,[7] they are *scraping* St. Mark's clean. Off go all the glorious old weather stains, the rich hues of the marble which nature, mighty as she is, has taken ten centuries to bestow – and already the noble corner farthest from the sea, that on which the sixth part of the age of the generations of man was dyed in gold, is reduced to the colour of magnesia, the old marbles displaced & torn down – what is coming in their stead I know not ... One only consolation I have – the finding, among the wrecks of Venice, authority for all that Turner has done of her ... All his skies are here too, or would be, if man would let them alone, but yesterday as I was trying to note some morning clouds, a volume of smoke from a manufactory on the Rialto blotted everything as black as the Thames.[8]

14th September [2nd letter] – As our regular time for starting to work is ½ past 5, I cannot write much at night. I can only tell you the delight I have had, as well as the sorrow, in examining tonight the architecture of St. Mark's, which is going to be destroyed. Every capital of its thousand columns is different, and their grace inimitable – and these are in the *renewed* parts, either scraped down, or cleaned with an acid which has so destroyed the carving that it is not even legible – as I said before, I am just in time & no more.[9]

20th September – I have been hunting up the churches a little, and find them in the most awful condition – stonemasons everywhere, monuments torn down & pavements up, the cloisters everywhere turned into barracks and the carvings defaced or repainted ... There are some wonderful & beautiful churches on the islands too, far better preserved than any at Venice except St Mark's.[10]

1st October – What would I not give to have back again ten years, & to be set, with my present powers and feelings, in St. Mark's place, as it was when I sketched the little clock dial vignette in my white paper and pencil book of 1835.[11]

7th October – I have been lucky enough to get from a poor Frenchman here, said to be in distress, some most beautiful, though small, Daguerreotypes of the palaces I have been trying to draw – and certainly Daguerreotypes taken by this vivid sunlight are glorious things. It is very nearly the same thing as carrying off the palace itself – every chip of stone & stain is there – and of course, there is no mistake about *proportions*.[12]

Ruskin was quick to recognise the potential importance of photography in providing an accurate historical record of the state of endangered buildings, and he began to collect daguerreotypes of architecture and sculpture.[13] By 1846 he considered the daguerreotype photograph to be 'certainly the most marvellous invention in the century; given us, I think, just in time to save some evidence from the great public of wreckers' (3:210), and to Samuel Prout he wrote, 'They are of course more valuable than any sketch can be in the way of information.' (38:341) In the third volume of The Stones of Venice *(1853) he concluded, 'Of one thing ... I have little doubt: that an infinite service will soon be done to a large body of our engravers; namely, the making them draughtsmen (in black and white) on paper instead of steel.' (11:199)*

From Praeterita, *Ruskin's autobiography, written between 1885 and 1889:[14]*

It must have been during my last days at Oxford that Mr. Liddell,[15] the present Dean of Christ Church, told me of the original experiments of

Daguerre.[16] My Parisian friends obtained for me the best examples of his results; and the plates sent to me in Oxford were certainly the first examples of the sun's drawings that were ever seen in Oxford, and, I believe, the first sent to England.[17]

Wholly careless at that time of finished detail, I saw nothing in the Daguerreotype to help or alarm me; and inquired no more concerning it, until now at Venice I found a French artist producing exquisitely bright small plates (about four inches square) which contained, under a lens, the Grand Canal or St. Mark's Place as if a magician had reduced the reality to be carried away into an enchanted land. The little gems of picture cost a napoleon each; but with two hundred francs I bought the Grand Canal from the Salute to the Rialto; and packed it away in thoughtless triumph.

I had no time then to think of the new power, or its meaning; my days were overweighted already. Every morning, at six by the Piazza clock, we were moored, Harding and I, among the boats in the fruit-market; then, after eight o'clock breakfast, he went on his own quest of full subjects, and I to the Scuola di San Rocco, or wherever else in Venice there were Tintorets.[18] In the afternoon we lashed our gondola to the stern of a fishing-boat, sailing, as the wind served, within or outside the Lido, and sketching the boat and her sails in their varied action – or Venice, as she shone far away beyond her islands. (35:373)

The second volume of Modern Painters *was published in April 1846, followed in September by the third revised edition of volume I. During the summer of the same year Ruskin made a brief visit to Venice with his parents. In April 1848 he married Euphemia ('Effie') Chalmers Gray (1828–97), the daughter of George Gray, a friend of John James Ruskin. The marriage took place at Bowerswell, her parents' house in Perth, Scotland, on 10 April 1848. The couple had hoped to visit Venice, but the unsettled political situation in Europe made this impossible, and they spent time in northern France instead. In the summer of 1849 Venice was under siege, following the 1848–9 uprising against*

Austrian rule, led by the Venetian patriot Daniele Manin. The Austrian bombardment of the city lasted for three months, leading to famine, outbreaks of typhus and cholera, and eventual capitulation. The new railway bridge connecting Venice to the mainland was destroyed, and when Ruskin and Effie arrived in November 1849 for an extended visit, they crossed the lagoon by gondola. They took rooms at the Hotel Danieli, staying until March 1850.

During this four-month visit, Ruskin began his detailed and laborious researches for The Stones of Venice, *which he later described as the giving of three years of 'close and incessant labour to the examination of the chronology of the architecture of Venice'. (16: 126–7). In his preface to the first edition of volume I of* The Stones of Venice *(1851), he recalled:*

I went to Venice finally in the autumn of 1849, not doubting but that the dates of the principal edifices of the ancient city were either ascertained, or ascertainable without extraordinary research. To my consternation, I found that the Venetian antiquaries were not agreed within a century as to the date of the building of the façade of the Ducal Palace ... and it became necessary for me to examine not only every one of the older palaces stone by stone, but every fragment throughout the city which afforded any clue to the formation of its styles. This I did as well as I could ... (9:3–4)

By now Ruskin possessed his own daguerreotype equipment, which he took to Venice on the 1849–50 visit. John Hobbs was pressed into service as photographer, and soon became proficient at taking and developing the daguerreotype plates. Occasionally Ruskin would operate the equipment himself, as a letter from Effie to her mother in February 1850 suggests: 'Nothing interrupts him, and whether the Square is crowded or empty he is either seen with a black cloth over his head taking Daguerreotypes or climbing about the capitals covered with dust'.[19]

Ruskin had begun to make extensive use of photographs, both as studies for drawings and for recording architectural details, writing in his preface

to Examples of the Architecture of Venice (1851):
'I have used the help of the Daguerreotype without scruple in completing many of the mezzotinted subjects for the present series, and I much regret that artists in general do not think it worth their while to perpetuate some of the beautiful effects which the Daguerreotype alone can seize.' (11:312)[20]

From The Stones of Venice I:

Stroke by stroke we count the plunges of the oar, each heaving up the side of the boat slightly as her silver beak shoots forward ... In front, nothing to be seen but long canal and level bank; to the west, the tower of Mestre is lowering fast, and behind it there have risen purple shapes, of the colour of dead rose-leaves, all round the horizon, feebly defined against the afternoon sky – the Alps of Bassano. Forward still: the endless canal bends at last, and then breaks into intricate angles about some low bastions, now torn to pieces and staggering its ugly rents towards the water – the bastions of the fort of Malghera. Another turn and another perspective of canal, but not interminable. The silver beak cleaves it fast – it widens; the rank grass of the banks sinks lower and lower, and at last dies in tawny knots along an expanse of weedy shore. Over on the right, but a few years back, we might have seen the lagoon stretching to the horizon, and the warm southern sky bending over Malamocco to the sea. Now we can see nothing but what seems a low and monotonous dock-yard wall, with flat arches to let the tide through it – this is the railroad bridge, conspicuous above all things. But at the end of those dismal arches there rises, out of the wide water, a straggling line of low and confused brick buildings, which, but for the many towers which are mingled among them, might be the suburbs of an English manufacturing town. Four or five domes, pale, and apparently at a greater distance, rise over the centre of the line; but the object which first catches the eye is a sullen cloud of black smoke brooding over the northern half of it, and which issues from the belfry of a church.

  It is Venice. (9:415)

Giovanni Pividor, The deconsecrated church of S. Girolamo in Cannaregio, mid 19th-century drawing. Suppressed by the Napoleonic administration in 1806, the church was converted in 1842 into a steam flour mill by the architect G.B. Meduna (1800–80), who was also responsible for controversial restorations at the Ca' d'Oro and the Basilica of San Marco

During the winter of 1850–51 Ruskin worked intensively in London on the first volume of The Stones of Venice *(entitled* The Foundations *and published on 3 March 1851 by Smith, Elder & Co.). On 1 May he began work on the second volume, writing in his diary from Denmark Hill, 'All London is astir, and some part of all the world. I am sitting in my quiet room, hearing the birds sing, and about to enter on the true beginning of the second part of my Venetian work. May God help me to finish it – to his glory, and man's good.' (10:xxiii)*

  He found, though, that there were too many gaps in his notes, and that it would be necessary to spend more time in Venice. He and Effie returned to the city on 1 September 1851 for an extended visit, staying for a week with Rawdon Brown at Casa Businello before moving into rooms at the Casa Wetzlar (now the Gritti Palace Hotel) for eight months. Venice was still occupied by the Austrian army, and troops and fortifications were to be seen everywhere. Although visitors were beginning to return to the city, many Venetians continued to suffer extreme hardship and poverty, and there were recurring outbreaks of cholera. In May 1852 the lease on the Casa Wetzlar expired, and the Ruskins found alternative lodgings in Piazza San Marco, where they stayed until June.

The major part of the research for volumes II and III of The Stones of Venice *was undertaken during this visit. It was another intense period of work for Ruskin, whose letters, notebooks, drawings and daguerreotypes testify to the long cold hours spent out of doors each day, examining and measuring the buildings and recording their details.*

Letters from John Ruskin to his father:

Venice, 2nd September [1851] – We got here yesterday evening, true to our day, and found Mr. Brown[21] waiting for us, but no letters; however I suppose you have not calculated on our keeping our time so exactly – but I am certainly now getting a little anxious – though also I hear that letters are very often lost in this post office – not very consolatory information for in general I had rather wait for a letter than lose one.

Venice is more beautiful than ever, and I am most thankful to be able to finish or retouch my descriptions on the spot.[22]

4th September – … We have got very good lodgings at last and I hope shall be quietly settled on the Grand Canal out of reach of all noise and trouble – by the beginning of the week.[23]

12th October – I never saw such tides – up and down to all manner of heights at all manner of times – The sea cannot be said to ebb and flow. It shakes up and down. However I shall have an interesting paragraph about the tides in the first chapter of next volume. For it is curious, rather, that the place where Venice

was built was the only place in the world where it *could* have been built. Had the tide been the *least* less than it is – had it been 2½ feet instead of three, the run of water through the streets would not have been enough for their healthy drainage – they would have become slow sewers – and the people would have been compelled to roof them in – and the town would have become pestiferous … Had the tide been a foot more than it is – had it been *four* feet instead of three – no access could have been had to the gondolas at low water except down slimy steps.[24]

From London, Ruskin's father was sending him reviews of the first volume of The Stones of Venice. *Some were unfavourable, criticising its theoretical discourse on the elements of architecture and the technical nature of the text and drawings. Ruskin replied on 15th October 1851, 'The reviews do not annoy me by their malice … I am often much more worried in a small way by people's not understanding me than by their differing with me.'*[25]

Letters from John Ruskin to his father:

16th October [1851] – This second volume [of *The Stones of Venice*] is to be called 'The Sea Stories' – for what on land we call a ground floor, I always call in speaking of Venetian buildings the *Sea* Story: and this will give the same kind of double meaning to the title of the second volume that there is in the first.[26]

2nd November – We have had a superb high tide this morning – in all over our courtyard – and over the greater part of St. Mark's place – and nothing could be more exquisite than the appearance of the church from the other end, with the reflection of its innumerable pillars white and dark green and purple, thrown down far over the square in bright bars, fading away in confused arrows of colour – with here and there a touch of blue and gold from the mosaics. Had there been sunshine it would have been like a scene from the Arabian nights.[27]

8th November – I am obliged to send you this shabby sheet of paper, being to my surprise out of writing paper – and at a very inconvenient moment – the water being just now half a foot deep in the stationers' shops – and all access cut off to St. Mark's place except in the lightest boats – and to the shops except on people's backs ... Last Sunday when the water was in the streets Effie and I went out before breakfast to St. Mark's place in the gondola.[28]

10th November – A sunny morning at last – very beautiful to behold. It is high time, the distress in the country being very great, but I am glad to have seen the stormy weather – there were pieces of scenery thoroughly noble – and among them the way the top of the tower of St. Mark's entangled itself among the rainclouds, not the least interesting ... I have never staid in a day for the weather – took my row, rain or fair – and changed my things when I came in – last Tuesday or Wednesday was a tremendous day for Wind as well [as] rain, and I rowed over to Lido to look at the sea. As I came back I saw Mr. Brown's boat at the public garden's steps: his boat is too small for rough weather, and he could not get across to the Lido – and was taking his walk in the gardens. I went in search of him and we had a pleasant walk together in the beating rain and North wind: the Venetians have certainly some reason to think the English odd people. Lord Dufferin[29] was paddling about in the lagoons, all the while he was here, in one of those indian-rubber boats which you may see landing up at the door of a shop in Bond St. He took it over to Lido, and rowed some way in the sea with it: when he landed, an Austrian coastguard came to investigate him,

and wanted to rip up his boat to see what was inside! (10:xxxiii and xxxvi)[30]

16th November – I get very angry every time I pass the guns in St. Mark's place, or the pontoons opposite it; and very much provoked – and indeed it is sufficiently tiresome – that there is now no 'lonely isle' in all the lagoons of Venice. Wherever you go, where once there were quiet little gardens among ruins of island churches, there is now a Sentinel and a powder magazine, and there is no piece of unbroken character to be found anywhere. There is not a single shore, far or near, which has not in some part of it the look of fortification, or violent dismantling or renewing, for military purposes of some kind or another; and there is hardly an old convent window out of which you will not see a Croat's face peeping – or his pipeclayed swordbelt hanging. (10:422n)

23rd November – I have begun to study the tides carefully, as I found it was hopeless to arrive at any result by mere watching – I have got a tide book – and am putting down the hours of turning very carefully, the first curious result being that we have had high water at the same hour for three days running in the morning – and low water twenty minutes later in the afternoon of the second day – what it will be today remains to be seen. (10:16n)[31]

30th November – Crossing to Lido in a *storm* in a gondola, sounds very grand: and indeed there is some sublimity in it – but not the sublimity of danger. The lagoon – as you know – is only covered two foot deep with water at high tide – therefore to have a wave four feet high – the sand must be laid dry between each surge, which is impossible – therefore the waves never can rise – in the wildest gale more than a couple of feet –

The deconsecrated church of S. Giorgio in Alga[32] with its campanile converted into an observatory, drawing by A. Tosini, *c.* 1850, Museo Correr, Venice

and this is of course mere trifle when your boat is thirty feet long. In the deep canals the waves are something larger and stronger, but constantly broken at their turns, so that unless one could get out of the port (which the Austrians do not allow – even if one wanted) it would be a matter of great difficulty and ingenuity to get upset. But the great green foaming waste of water is thoroughly magnificent – though it cannot rise like the sea. I enclose you today, four pages of *nearly* the beginning of the chapter on St. Mark's – if you keep the pages in order – I will send you them in a regular sequence as they are finished – or as George can write them, for you may suppose he has a good deal to do – the house depending on his stewardship.[33]

From The Stones of Venice II

The average rise and fall of the tide is about three feet (varying considerably with the seasons) but this fall, on so flat a shore, is enough to cause continual movement in the waters and in the main canals to produce a reflux which frequently runs like a mill stream. At high water no land is visible for many miles to the north or south of Venice, except in the form of small islands crowned with towers or gleaming with villages: there is a channel, some three miles wide, between the city and the mainland, and some mile and a half wide between it and the sandy breakwater called the Lido, which divides the lagoon from the Adriatic, but which is so low as hardly to disturb the impression of the city's having been built in the midst of the ocean, although the secret of its true position is partly, yet not painfully, betrayed by the clusters of piles set to mark the deep-water channels, which undulate far away in spotty chains like the studded backs of huge sea-snakes, and by the quick glittering of the crisped and crowded waves that flicker and dance before the strong winds upon the uplifted level of the shallow sea. But the scene is widely different at low tide. A fall of eighteen or twenty inches is enough to show ground over the greater part of the lagoon; and at the complete ebb the city is seen standing in the midst of a dark plain of sea-weed of gloomy green, except only where the larger branches of the Brenta and its associated streams converge towards the port of the Lido.

Through this salt and sombre plain the gondola and the fishing boat advance by tortuous channels, seldom more than four or five feet deep, and often so choked with slime that the heavier keels furrow the bottom till their crossing tracks are seen through the clear sea water like the ruts upon a wintry road, and the oar leaves blue gashes upon the ground at every stroke, or is entangled among the thick weed that fringes the banks with the weight of its sullen waves, leaning to and fro upon the uncertain sway of the exhausted tide. The scene is often profoundly oppressive, even at this day, when every plot of higher ground bears some fragment of fair building: but in order to know what it was once, let the traveller follow in his boat at evening the windings of some unfrequented channel far into the midst of the melancholy plain; let him remove, in his imagination, the brightness of the great city that still extends itself in the distance, and the walls and towers from the islands that are near; and so wait, until the bright investiture and sweet warmth of the sunset are withdrawn from the waters, and the black desert of their shore lies in its nakedness beneath the

John Ruskin, *St George of the Seaweed*, 1849, etching by T.S. Boys, engraving by T.G. Lupton, Plate 15 in *Modern Painters* III

night, pathless, comfortless, infirm, lost in dark languor and fearful silence, except where the salt runlets plash into the tideless pools, or the sea-birds flit from their margins with a questioning cry; and he will be enabled to enter in some sort into the horror of heart with which this solitude was anciently chosen by man for his habitation.

They little thought, who first drove the stakes into the sand, and strewed the ocean reeds for their rest, that their children were to be the princes of that ocean, and their palaces its pride; and yet, in the great natural laws that rule that sorrowful wilderness, let it be remembered what strange preparation had been made for the things which no human imagination could have foretold, and how the whole existence and fortune of the Venetian nation were anticipated or compelled, by the setting of those bars and doors to the rivers and the sea. Had deeper currents divided their islands, hostile navies would again and again have reduced the rising city into servitude; had stronger surges beaten their shores, all the richness and refinement of the

Venetian architecture must have been exchanged for the walls and bulwarks of an ordinary sea-port. Had there been no tide, as in other parts of the Mediterranean, the narrow canals of the city would have become noisome, and the marsh in which it was built pestiferous. Had the tide been only a foot or eighteen inches higher in its rise, the water-access to the doors of the palaces would have been impossible: even as it is, there is sometimes a little difficulty, at the ebb, in landing without setting foot upon the lower and slippery steps: and the highest tides sometimes enter the courtyards, and overflow the entrance halls. Eighteen inches more of difference between the level of the flood and ebb would have rendered the doorsteps of every palace, at low water, a treacherous mass of weeds and limpets, and the entire system of water-carriage for the higher classes, in their easy and daily intercourse, must have been done away with. The streets of the city would have been widened, its network of canals filled up, and all the peculiar character of the place and the people destroyed. (10:12–14)

8th January [Venice 1852] – I don't think the Ducal Palace will stand 50 years more, its capitals are so rent and worn. I am having some of its sculpture cast – there is a poor sculptor here whom it is a charity to employ – and for a few shillings I can get the most accurate facsimiles of pieces of sculpture, which will soon be lost forever – and their freight home will be very little. (10:466)

16th January – I am really very sorry ... at the continual drain I am making upon your purse, giving you no return ... but I am taken quite by surprise at the sums which go in candles and fuel and house expences. I have spent also about £25 in casts – of which I am packing up to-day 21 pieces of Ducal Palace capitals &c., which are both invaluable in themselves – if I can get them sent safe home – and have saved me for the present some laborious drawing; as I can work out what refinements I want better from these than from the original pieces, which are so high as to be out of convenient sight.[34]

January 18, 1852 – This six months in Venice has been little enough for what I desired to do. Take all the time that I have had here, about twelve months in all, in which I have had to examine piece by piece buildings covering five square miles of ground – to read, or glance at, some forty volumes of history and chronicles – to make elaborate drawings – as many as most artists would have made in the time, and to compose my book, what of it is done (for I do not count the first volume anything), and you will not, I think, wonder that I grudge the losing of a single day. (10:xxxvii)

John James Ruskin's reaction to the arrival in London of a consignment of plaster casts of details of Venetian sculpture was unenthusiastic. He queried their necessity, the cost of commissioning them and the additional expense of their transport to England. Neither the first volume of The Stones of Venice *nor its accompanying folio work* Examples of the Architecture of Venice (*published in three parts with plates engraved from Ruskin's drawings) were selling particularly well, and Ruskin's father believed the works to be too dry and technical for the taste of the general reader, who had come to expect from his son the style of lyrical writing embodied in the first two volumes of* Modern Painters.

Letters from John Ruskin to his father:

30th April 1852 – You say that you suppose they [the casts] are necessary. They are not *necessary*, only great helps and great possessions ... I have also spared myself a great deal of labour for the present, in making drawings, for which my eyes are all the better. A cast of a piece of detail is better than the best sketch for information, though the sketch is usually more delightful. (10:466–7)

Venice, Feb. 18, 1852 – I am sorry you are not at all interested in my antiquarianism, but I believe you will like the book better when you see it finished; at all events it would be foolish to abandon the labour of two whole years, now that it is just approaching completion ... I never have written except under the conviction of a thing's being important, wholly irrespective of the public's thinking it so; and all my power, such as it is, would be lost, the moment I tried to catch people by fine writing. You know I promised them no Romance: I promised them stones ... I believe that what I have done will be found useful at last. (9:xxxviii)

The second volume of The Stones of Venice (The Sea-Stories) *was published in July 1853, and the third volume* (The Fall), *which included the* Venetian Index, *in October of the same year.*

VENEZIA

PUBBLICATA
LLA CONGREGAZIONE MUNICIPALE
all'Occasione del IX Congresso
degli Scienziati Italiani
nell'Anno 1847

ZI PRINCIPALI DEL CANAL GRANDE
ro, dalla Stazione della Strada Ferrata.

ISOLA
DI S. CHIARA

Area
della Stazione
a costruirsi

Campo
di Marte

Spiaggia di S. Marta

STABILIMENTI CIVILI

Canale per Fusina

Punta
di S. Biagio

Canale della Giu...

ISOLA DELLA GIUDECCA

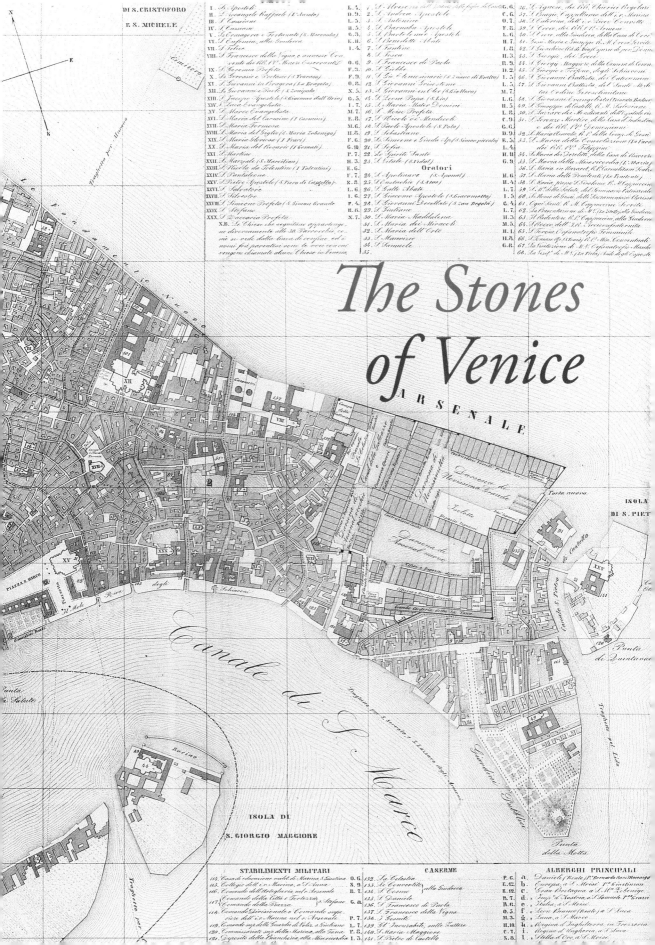

The Stones of Venice

Since first the dominion of men was asserted over the ocean, three thrones, of mark beyond all others, have been set upon its sands: the thrones of Tyre, Venice, and England. Of the First of these great powers only the memory remains; of the Second, the ruin; the Third, which inherits their greatness, if it forget their example, may be led through prouder eminence to less pitied destruction.

The exaltation, the sin, and the punishment of Tyre have been recorded for us, in perhaps the most touching words ever uttered by the Prophets of Israel against the cities of the stranger. But we read them as a lovely song; and close our ears to the sternness of their warning: for the very depth of the Fall of Tyre has blinded us to its reality, and we forget, as we watch the bleaching of the rocks between the sunshine and the sea, that they were once 'as in Eden, the garden of God'.

Her successor, like her in perfection of beauty, though less in endurance of dominion, is still left for our beholding in the final period of her decline: a ghost upon the sands of the sea, so weak – so quiet, – so bereft of all but her loveliness, that we might well doubt, as we watched her faint reflection in the mirage of the lagoon, which was the City, and which the Shadow.

I would endeavour to trace the lines of this image before it be for ever lost, and to record, as far as I may, the warning which seems to me to be uttered by every one of the fast-gaining waves, that beat like passing bells, against The Stones of Venice.

The Stones of Venice I (9:17)

The island of Torcello: view from the lagoon, with the Basilica of
Santa Maria Assunta and Church of Santa Fosca (Photograph 2007)

BYZANTINE

TORCELLO

SEVEN MILES TO THE NORTH OF VENICE, the banks of sand, which nearer the city rise little above low-water mark, attain by degrees a higher level, and knit themselves at last into fields of salt morass, raised here and there into shapeless mounds, and intercepted by narrow creeks of sea. One of the feeblest of these inlets, after winding for some time among buried fragments of masonry, and knots of sunburnt weeds whitened with webs of fucus, stays itself in an utterly stagnant pool beside a plot of greener grass covered with ground ivy and violets. On this mound is built a rude brick campanile, of the commonest Lombardic type, which, if we ascend towards evening (and there are none to hinder us, the door of its ruinous staircase swinging idly on its hinges) we may command from it one of the most notable scenes in this wide world of ours. Far as the eye can reach, a waste of wild sea moor, of a lurid ashen grey; not like our northern moors with their jet-black pools and purple heath, but lifeless, the colour of sackcloth, with the corrupted sea-water soaking through the roots of its acrid weeds, and gleaming hither and thither through its snaky channels. No gathering of fantastic mists, nor coursing of clouds across it; but melancholy clearness of space in the warm sunset, oppressive, reaching to the horizon of its level gloom. To the very horizon on the north-east; but, to the north and west, there is a blue line of higher land along the border of it, and above this, but farther back, a misty band of mountains, touched with snow. To the east, the paleness and roar of the Adriatic, louder at momentary intervals as the surf breaks on the bars of sand; to the south, the widening branches of the calm lagoon, alternately purple and pale green, as they reflect the evening clouds or twilight sky; and almost beneath our feet, on the same field which sustains the tower we gaze from, a group of four buildings, two of them little larger than cottages (though built of stone, and one adorned by a quaint belfry), the third an octagonal chapel, of which we can see but little more than the flat red roof with its rayed tiling, the fourth, a considerable church with nave and aisles, but of which, in like manner, we can see little but the long central ridge and lateral slopes of roof, which the sunlight separates in one glowing mass from the green field beneath and grey moor beyond. There are no living creatures near the buildings, nor any vestige of village or city round about them. They lie like a little company of ships becalmed on a far-away sea.

View from the lagoon towards the north shore of Venice
(Photograph 2014)

Then look farther to the south. Beyond the widening branches of the lagoon, and rising out of the bright lake into which they gather, there are a multitude of towers, dark, and scattered among square-set shapes of clustered palaces, a long and irregular line fretting the southern sky.

Mother and daughter, you behold them both in their widowhood – Torcello and Venice.

The inlet which runs nearest to the base of the campanile is not that by which Torcello is commonly approached. Another, somewhat broader, and overhung by alder copse, winds out of the main channel of the lagoon up to the very

The approach to Torcello and the Ponte del Diavolo (Photograph 1978)

edge of the little meadow which was once the Piazza of the city, and there, stayed by a few grey stones which present some semblance of a quay, forms its boundary at one extremity. Hardly larger than an ordinary English farmyard, and roughly enclosed on each side by broken palings and hedges of honeysuckle and briar, the narrow field retires from the water's edge, traversed by a scarcely traceable footpath, for some forty or fifty paces, and then expanding into the form of a small square, with buildings on three sides of it, the fourth being that which opens to the water. Two of these, that on our left and that in front of us as we approach from the canal, are so small that they might well be taken for the outhouses of the farm, though the first is a conventual building, and the other aspires to the title of the 'Palazzo Pubblico', both dating as far back as the beginning of the fourteenth century; the third, the octagonal church of Santa Fosca, is far more ancient than either, yet hardly on a larger scale. Though the pillars of the portico which surrounds it are of pure Greek marble, and their capitals are enriched with delicate sculpture, they, and the arches they sustain, together only raise the roof to the height of a cattle-shed; and the first strong impression which the spectator receives from the whole scene is, that whatever sin it may have been which has on this spot been visited with so utter a desolation, it could not at least have been ambition. Nor will this impression be diminished as we approach, or enter, the larger church, to which the whole group of buildings is subordinate. It has evidently been built by men in flight and distress, who sought in the hurried erection of their island church such a shelter for their earnest and sorrowful worship as, on the one hand, could not attract the eyes of their enemies by its splendour, and yet, on the other, might not awaken too bitter feelings by its contrast with the churches which they had seen destroyed. There is visible everywhere a simple and tender effort to recover some of the form of the temples which they had loved, and to do honour to God by that which they were erecting, while distress and humiliation prevented the desire, and prudence precluded the admission, either of luxury of ornament or magnificence of plan. The exterior is absolutely devoid of decoration, with the exception only of the western entrance and the lateral door, of which the former has carved side posts and architrave, and the latter, crosses of rich sculpture; while the massy stone shutters of the windows, turning on huge rings of stone, which answer the double purpose of stanchions and brackets, cause the whole building rather to resemble a refuge from Alpine storm than the cathedral of a populous city. (10:17–21)

Torcello: View of the Piazza, anon. 19th-century engraving; the Basilica of Santa Maria Assunta and the octagonal church of Santa Fosca are to the right of the scene in the engraving

The first flight to the lagoons for shelter was caused by the invasion of Attila in the fifth century, so that in endeavouring to throw back the thought of the reader to the former solitude of the islands, I spoke of them as they must have appeared '1300 years ago'. Altinum, however, was not finally destroyed till the Lombard invasion in 641, when the episcopal seat was removed to Torcello, and the inhabitants of the mainland city, giving up all hope of returning to their former homes, built their Duomo there. (10:444–5)

View of Torcello, looking towards Santa Fosca (Photograph 2013)

Basilica of Santa Maria Assunta and the church of Santa Fosca, Torcello (Photograph 1997)

MURANO

CHURCH OF SAN DONATO
(SS MARIA E DONATO)

OUR BOAT SHOOTS SWIFTLY FROM BENEATH the last bridge of Venice, and brings us out into the open sea and sky ...

To the north, there is first the great cemetery wall, then the long stray buildings of Murano and the island villages beyond, glittering in intense crystalline vermilion, like so much jewellery scattered on a mirror, their towers poised apparently in the air a little above the horizon, and their reflections, as sharp and vivid and substantial as themselves, thrown on the vacancy between them and the sea. And thus the villages seem standing on the air; and, to the east, there is a cluster of ships that seem sailing on the land; for the sandy line of the Lido stretches itself between us and them, and we can see the tall white sails moving beyond it, but not the sea, only there is a sense of the great sea being indeed there, and a solemn strength of gleaming light in sky above.

The most discordant feature in the whole scene is the cloud which hovers above the glass furnaces of Murano; but this we may not regret, as it is one of the last signs left of human exertion among the ruinous villages which surround us. The silent gliding of the gondola brings it nearer to us every moment; we pass the cemetery, and a deep sea-channel which separates it from Murano, and finally enter a narrow water-street, with a paved footpath on each side, raised three or four feet above the canal, and forming a kind of quay between the water and the doors of the houses. These latter are for the most part low, but built with massy doors and windows of marble or Istrian stone, square-set and barred with iron; buildings evidently once of no mean order, though now inhabited only by the poor. Here and there an

Lion at Ponte de Mezo, Murano (Photograph 2013)

ogee window of the fourteenth century, or a doorway deeply enriched with cable mouldings, shows itself in the midst of more ordinary features; and several houses, consisting of one story only carried on square pillars, forming a short arcade along the quay, have windows sustained on shafts of red Verona marble, of singular grace and delicacy ...

We push our way on between large barges laden with fresh water from Fusina, in round white tubs seven feet across, and complicated boats full of all manner of nets that look as if they could never be disentangled, hanging from their masts and over their sides; and presently pass under a bridge with the lion of St. Mark on its archivolt, and another on a pillar at the end of the parapet, a small red lion with much of the puppy in his face, looking vacantly up into the air (in passing we may note that, instead of feathers, his wings are covered with hair, and in several other points the manner of his sculpture is not uninteresting).

Presently the canal turns a little to the left, and thereupon becomes more quiet, the main bustle of the water-street being usually confined to the first straight reach of it, some quarter of a mile long, the Cheapside of Murano. We pass a considerable church on the left, S. Pietro, and a little square opposite to it with a few acacia trees, and then find our boat suddenly seized by a strong green eddy, and whirled into the tide-way of one of the main

Church of SS Maria e Donato, Murano, 19th-century engraving by Marco Moro

Palazzo Corner on the rio dei Vetrai, Murano
(Photograph 2013)

channels of the lagoon, which divides the town of Murano into two parts by a deep stream some fifty yards over, crossed only by one wooden bridge. We let ourselves drift some way down the current, looking at the low line of cottages on the other side of it, hardly knowing if there be more cheerfulness or melancholy in the way the sunshine glows on their ruinous but whitewashed walls, and sparkles on the rushing of the green water by the grass-grown quay. It needs a strong stroke of the oar to bring us into the mouth of another quiet canal on the farther side of the tide-way, and we are still somewhat giddy when we run the head of the gondola into the sand on the left-hand side of this more sluggish stream, and land under the east end of the church of San Donato, the 'Matrice' or 'Mother' church of Murano.

It stands, it and the heavy campanile detached from it a few yards, in a small triangular field of

Church of SS Maria e Donato, Murano
(Photograph 2013)

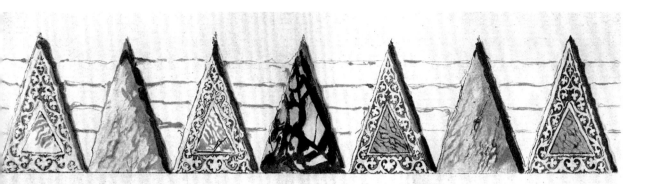

John Ruskin: *Inlaid Bands of Murano*, chromolithograph,
Plate 3 in *The Stones of Venice* II (10:51)

somewhat fresher grass than is usual near Venice,
traversed by a paved walk with green mosaic of
short grass between the rude squares of its stones,
bounded on one side by ruinous garden walls, on
another by a line of low cottages; on the third, the
base of the triangle, by the shallow canal from
which we have just landed ...

The cathedral itself occupies the northern angle
of the field, encumbered with modern buildings,
small outhouse-like chapels, and wastes of white
wall with blank square windows, and itself utterly
defaced in the whole body of it, nothing but the
apse having been spared; the original plan is only
discoverable by careful examination, and even then
but partially. The whole impression and effect of
the building are irretrievably lost, but the fragments
of it are still most precious.

The ground plan is composed, like that of
Torcello, of nave and aisles only, but the clerestory
has transepts extending as far as the outer wall of
the aisles. The semi-circular apse, thrown out in the
centre of the east end, is now the chief feature of
interest in the church, though the nave shafts and
the eastern extremities of the aisle, outside, are also
portions of the original building; the latter having
been modernized in the interior.

The feature which is most to be noted in this
apse is a band of ornament, which runs round it
like a silver girdle, composed of sharp wedges of
marble, preciously inlaid, and set like jewels into
the brickwork; above it there is another band of
triangular recesses in the bricks, of nearly similar
shape, and it seems equally strange that all the
marble should have fallen from it, or that it should
have been originally destitute of them.

The reader may choose his hypothesis; but there
is quite enough left to interest us in the lower band,
which is fortunately left in its original state, as is
sufficiently proved by the curious niceties in the
arrangement of its colours, which are assuredly to
be attributed to the care of the first builder.

The building [is] for the most part, composed
of yellow brick. This yellow is very nearly pure,
much more positive and somewhat darker than
that of our English light brick, and the material
of the brick is very good and hard, looking in
places almost vitrified, and so compact as to
resemble stone. Together with this brick occurs
another of a deep full red, and more porous
substance, which is used for decoration chiefly,
while all the parts requiring strength are
composed of the yellow brick. Both these
materials are *cast into any shape and size* the
builder required, either into curved pieces for
the arches, or flat tiles for filling the triangles;
and, what is still more curious, the thickness
of the yellow bricks used for the walls varies
considerably, from two inches to four; and their

Church of SS Maria e Donato: detail of the
apse (Photograph 2013)

apse is the uppermost in Plate III, and that used for
the centre of the apse, and of the whole series, is the
lowermost in the same plate; *the piece of black and
white marble being used to emphasize the centre of the
chain*, exactly as a painter would use a dark touch
for a similar purpose. (10:51–2)

We come now to the most interesting portion of
the whole east end, the archivolt at the end of the
northern aisle.

It was above stated that the band of triangles was
broken by two higher arches at the ends of the aisles.
That, however, on the northern side of the apse does
not entirely interrupt, but lifts it, and thus forms a
beautiful and curious archivolt, drawn in the Plate.
The upper band of triangles cannot rise together with
the lower, as it would otherwise break the cornice
prepared to receive the second story; and the curious
zigzag with which its triangles die away against the
sides of the arch, exactly as waves break upon the sand,
is one of the most curious features in the structure.

It will be also seen that there is a new feature
in the treatment of the band itself when it turns
the arch. Instead of leaving the bricks projecting
between the sculptured or coloured stones, reversed
triangles of marble are used, inlaid to an equal
depth with the others in the brickwork, but
projecting beyond them so as to produce a sharp
dark line of zigzag at their junctions.

The keystone, if it may be so called, is of white
marble, the lateral voussoirs of purple; and these are

length also, some of the larger pieces used in
important positions being a foot and a half long.

With these two kinds of brick, the builder
employed five or six kinds of marble: pure white,
and white veined with purple; a brecciated marble
of white and black; a brecciated marble of white
and deep green; another, deep red, or nearly of the
color of Egyptian porphyry; and a grey and black
marble, in fine layers. (10:38–50)

The band, composed of these triangles, set close to
each other in varied but not irregular relations, is
thrown, like a necklace of precious stones, round
the apse and along the ends of the aisles; each side
of the apse taking, of course, as many triangles as its
width permits ... Of these groups of seven triangles
each, that used for the third and fifth sides of the

Church of SS Maria e Donato, Murano:
inlaid bands on the apse (Photograph 2013)

John Ruskin, *Archivolt of the Duomo of Murano*,
chromolithograph, Plate 5 in *The Stones of Venice* II (10:58)

the only coloured stones in the whole building which are sculptured; but they are sculptured in a way which more satisfactorily proves that the principle above stated was understood by the builders, than if they had been left blank. The object, observe, was to make the archivolt as rich as possible; eight of the white sculptured marbles were used upon it in juxtaposition. Had the purple marbles been left altogether plain, they would have been out of harmony with the elaboration of the rest. It became necessary to touch them with sculpture as a mere sign of carefulness and finish, but at the same time destroying their coloured surface as little as possible. *The ornament is merely outlined upon them with a fine incision*, as if it had been etched out on their surface preparatory to being carved.

ST MARK'S

Whatever in St. Mark's arrests the eye, or affects the feelings, is either Byzantine, or has been modified by Byzantine influence; and our inquiry into its architectural merits need not therefore be disturbed by the anxieties of antiquarianism, or arrested by the obscurities of chronology.

The Stones of Venice II (10:78)

All European architecture, bad and good, old and new, is derived from Greece through Rome, and coloured and perfected from the East. The history of architecture is nothing but the tracing of the various modes and directions of this derivation. Understand this, once for all: if you hold fast this great connecting clue, you may string all the types of successive architectural invention upon it like so many beads. The Doric and the Corinthian orders are the roots: the one of all Romanesque, massy-capitaled buildings – Norman, Lombard, Byzantine, and what else you can name of the kind; and the Corinthian of all Gothic, Early English, French, German, and Tuscan.

The Stones of Venice I (9:34)

[WE] EMERGE ON THE BRIDGE and Campo San Moisè, whence the entrance into St. Mark's Place, called the Bocca di Piazza (mouth of the square), the Venetian character is nearly destroyed, first by the frightful façade of San Moisè, which we will pause at another time to examine, and then by the modernizing of the shops as they near the piazza, and the mingling with the lower Venetian populace of lounging groups of English and Austrians. We will push fast through them into the shadow of the pillars at the end of the 'Bocca di Piazza', and then we forget them all; for between those pillars opens a great light, and, in the midst of it, as we advance slowly, the vast tower of St. Mark seems to lift itself visibly forth from the level field of chequered stones; and, on each side, the countless arches prolong themselves into ranged symmetry, as if the rugged and irregular houses that pressed together above us in the dark alley had been struck back into sudden obedience and lovely order, and all their rude casements and broken walls had been transformed into arches charged with goodly sculpture, and fluted shafts of delicate stone.

And well may they fall back, for beyond those troops of ordered arches there rises a vision out of the earth, and all the great square seems to have opened from it in a kind of awe, that we may see it far away – a multitude of pillars and white domes,

St Mark's: detail of the west façade (Photograph 1998)

Capitals of the Porta di San Pietro (Photograph 2012)

clustered into a long low pyramid of coloured light; a treasure-heap, it seems, partly of gold, and partly of opal and mother-of-pearl, hollowed beneath into five great vaulted porches, ceiled with fair mosaic, and beset with sculpture of alabaster, clear as amber and delicate as ivory – sculpture fantastic and involved, of palm leaves and lilies, and grapes and pomegranates, and birds clinging and fluttering among the branches, all twined together into an endless network of buds and plumes; and in the midst of it, the solemn forms of angels, sceptred, and robed to the feet, and leaning to each other across the gates, their figures indistinct among the gleaming of the golden ground through the leaves beside them, interrupted and dim, like the morning light as it faded back among the branches of Eden, when first its gates were angel-guarded long ago.

And round the walls of the porches there are set pillars of variegated stones, jasper and porphyry, and deep-green serpentine spotted with flakes of snow, and marbles ... their capitals rich with interwoven tracery, rooted knots of herbage, and drifting leaves of acanthus and vine, and mystical

Far right: St Mark the Evangelist above the upper central arch, St Mark's (Photograph 1997)

Right: Gilded angel on the upper central arch of the Basilica (Photograph 1997)

Marble revetment on west
wall of the Treasury, St Mark's
(Photograph 2013)

signs, all beginning and ending in the Cross; and
above them, in the broad archivolts, a continuous
chain of language and of life – angels, and the
signs of heaven, and the labours of men, each in
its appointed season upon the earth; and above
these, another range of glittering pinnacles, mixed
with white arches edged with scarlet flowers – a
confusion of delight, amidst which the breasts of
the Greek horses are seen blazing in their breadth
of golden strength, and the St. Mark's Lion, lifted
on a blue field covered with stars, until at last, as
if in ecstasy, the crests of the arches break into a
marble foam, and toss themselves far into the blue

sky in flashes and wreaths of sculptured spray, as
if the breakers on the Lido shore had been frost-
bound before they fell, and the sea-nymphs had
inlaid them with coral and amethyst. (10:82–3)

Now the first broad characteristic of the building,
and the root nearly of every other important
peculiarity in it, is its confessed *incrustation*. It
is the purest example in Italy of the great school
of architecture in which the ruling principle is the
incrustation of brick with more precious materials.

Suppose a nation of builders, placed far from
any quarries of available stone, and having

Carved panels on south exterior wall of the Treasury of St Mark's (Photograph 2003)

Four porphyry tetrarchs on the exterior wall of the Treasury (Photograph 2003). In 1965 the tetrarchs' Byzantine origins were confirmed when the 'missing foot' was identified during excavations at the monastery of the Myrelaion, Istanbul, near the site of the Philadelphion.[1]

Columns of the central porch, St Mark's (Photograph 1997)

precarious access to the mainland where they exist; compelled therefore either to build entirely with brick, or to import whatever stone they use from great distances, in ships of small tonnage, and, for the most part, dependent for speed on the oar rather than the sail. The labour and cost of carriage are just as great, whether they import common or precious stone, and therefore the natural tendency would always be to make each shipload as valuable as possible. But in proportion to the preciousness of the stone, is the limitation of its possible supply; limitation not determined merely by cost, but by the physical conditions of the material, for of many marbles, pieces above a certain size are not to be had for money. There would also be a tendency in such circumstances to import as much stone as possible ready sculptured, in order to save weight; and therefore, if the traffic of their merchants led

Detail of the west-facing wall of the Treasury, St Mark's
(Photograph 2008)

them to places where there were ruins of ancient edifices, to ship the available fragments of them home. Out of this supply of marble, partly composed of pieces of so precious a quality that only a few tons of them could be on any terms obtained, and partly of shafts, capitals, and other portions of foreign buildings, the island architect has to fashion, as best he may, the anatomy of his edifice. It is at his choice either to lodge his few blocks of precious marble here and there among his masses of brick, and to cut out of the sculptured fragments such new forms as may be necessary for the observance of fixed proportions in the new building; or else to cut the coloured stones into thin pieces, of extent sufficient to face the whole surface of the walls, and to adopt a method of construction irregular enough to admit the insertion of fragmentary sculptures; rather with a view of displaying their intrinsic beauty, than of setting them to any regular service in the support of the building. (10:93–6)

[The Venetians] were exiles from ancient and beautiful cities, and had been accustomed to build with their ruins, not less in affection than in admiration; they had thus not only grown familiar with the practice of inserting older fragments in modern buildings, but they owed to that practice a great part of the splendour of their city, and whatever charm of association might aid its change from a Refuge into a Home. The practice which began in the affections of a fugitive nation was prolonged in the pride of a conquering one; and beside the memorials of departed happiness were elevated the trophies of returning victory. The ship of war brought home more marble in triumph than the merchant vessel in speculation; and the front of St. Mark's became rather a shrine at which to dedicate the splendour of miscellaneous spoil, than the organized expression of any fixed architectural law or religious emotion. (10:96–7)

In the fifth chapter of the 'Seven Lamps' the reader will find the opinion of a modern architect of some reputation, Mr. Woods,[2] that the chief thing remarkable in this church 'is its extreme ugliness'; and he will find this opinion associated with another, namely that the works of the Carracci are far preferable to those of the Venetian painters. This second statement of feeling reveals to us one of the principal causes of the first; namely that Mr. Woods had not any perception of colour, or delight in it. The perception of colour is a gift just as definitely

John Ruskin, *The Vine. Free and in Service*, photogravure from line engraving, Plate 6 in *The Stones of Venice* II (10:115)

trained in the composition of form only, to discern the beauty of St. Mark's. It possesses the charm of colour in common with the greater part of the architecture, as well as of the manufactures, of the East; but the Venetians deserve especial note as the only European people who appear to have sympathized to the full with the great instinct of the Eastern races. They indeed were compelled to bring artists from Constantinople to design the mosaics of the vaults of St. Mark's, and to group the colours of its porches; but they rapidly took up and developed, under more masculine conditions, the system of which the Greeks had shown them the example: while the burghers and barons of the North were building their dark streets and grisly castles of oak and sandstone the merchants of Venice were covering their palaces with porphyry and gold; and at last, when her mighty painters had created for her a colour more priceless than gold or porphyry, even this, the richest of her treasures, she lavished upon walls whose foundations were beaten by the sea; and the strong tide, as it runs beneath the Rialto, is reddened to this day by the reflection of the frescoes of Giorgione.[3]

If, therefore, the reader does not care for colour, I must protest against his endeavour to form any judgment whatever of this church of St. Mark's. But if he both cares for and loves it, let him remember that the school of incrusted architecture is *the only one in which perfect and permanent chromatic decoration is possible*; and let him look upon every piece of jasper and alabaster given to the architect as a cake of very hard colour, of which a certain portion is to be ground down or cut off, to paint the walls with. (10:97–8)

Nothing is so rare in art, as far as my own experience goes, as a fair illustration of architecture; *perfect* illustration of it does not exist. For all good architecture depends upon the adaptation of its chiselling to the effect at a certain distance from the eye ...

It would be easier to illustrate a crest of Scottish mountain, with its purple heather and pale harebells

granted to one person, and denied to another, as an ear for music; and the very first requisite for true judgment of St. Mark's, is the perfection of that colour-faculty which few people ever set themselves seriously to find out whether they possess or not. For it is on its value as a piece of perfect and unchangeable colouring, that the claims of this edifice to our respect are finally rested; and a deaf man might as well pretend to pronounce judgment on the merits of a full orchestra, as an architect

Archivolt of the Porta di S. Pietro of the Basilica and detail of the spandrel (Photographs 2013)

at their fullest and fairest, or glade of Jura forest, with its floor of anemone and moss, than s single portico of St Mark's. The fragment of one of its archivolts, given at the bottom of the Plate [*The Vine. Free and in Service*], is not to illustrate the thing itself, but to illustrate the impossibility of illustration.

It is left a fragment, in order to get it on a larger scale; and yet even on this scale it is too small to show the sharp folds and points of the marble vine-leaves with sufficient clearness. The ground of it is gold, the sculpture in the spandrils is not more than an inch and a half deep, rarely so much. It is in fact nothing more than an exquisite sketching of outlines in marble, to about the same depth as in the Elgin frieze; the draperies, however, being filled with close folds, in the manner of the Byzantine pictures, folds especially necessary here, as large masses could not be expressed in the shallow sculpture without becoming insipid; but the disposition of these folds is always most beautiful, and often opposed by broad and simple spaces, like that obtained by the scroll in the hand of the prophet.

The balls in the archivolt project considerably, and the interstices between their interwoven bands of marble are filled with colours like the illuminations of a manuscript; violet, crimson, blue, gold, and green, alternately: but no green is ever used without an intermixture of blue pieces in the mosaic, nor any blue without a little centre of pale green; sometimes only a single piece of glass a quarter of an inch square, so subtle was the feeling for colour which was thus to be satisfied.

No two tesserae of the glass are exactly of the same tint, the greens being all varied with blues, the blues of different depths, the reds of different clearness, so that the effect of each mass of colour is full of variety, like the stippled colour of a fruit piece.

The intermediate circles have golden stars set on an azure ground, varied in the same manner; and the small crosses seen in the intervals are alternately blue and subdued scarlet, with two small circles of white set in the golden ground above and beneath them, each only about half an inch across (this work, remember, being on the outside of the building, and twenty feet above the eye), while the blue crosses have each a pale green centre. Of all this exquisitely mingled hue, no plate, however large or expensive, could give any adequate conception; but, if the reader will supply in

THE CENTRAL PORCH

There are four successive archivolts, one within the other, forming the great central entrance of St. Mark's. The first is a magnificent external arch, formed of obscure figures mingled among masses of leafage, as in ordinary Byzantine work; within this there is a hemispherical dome, covered with modern mosaic; and at the back of this recess the other three archivolts follow consecutively, two sculptured, one plain; the one with which we are concerned is the outermost. (10:316)

Its ornaments, to the front, are of leafage closing out of spirals into balls interposed between the figures of eight Prophets (or Patriarchs?) – Christ in their midst on the keystone. No one would believe at first it was thirteenth-century work, so delicate and rich as it looks; nor is there anything else like it that I know, in Europe, of the date: but pure thirteenth-century work it is, of rarest chiselling. I have cast two of its balls with their surrounding leafage, for

John Ruskin, *The North-west Porch of St Mark's*, Ruskin's 1879 copy of part of his 1877 drawing, photogravure, Plate D in *The Stones of Venice* II (10:116)

imagination to the engraving what he supplies to a common woodcut of a group of flowers, the decision of the respective merits of modern and of Byzantine architecture may be allowed to rest on this fragment of St. Mark's alone. (10:116–17)

The doors actually employed for entrance in the western façade are as usual five, but the Byzantine builder could not be satisfied with so simple a group, and he therefore introduced two minor arches at the extremities, by adding two small porticos which are *of no use whatever* except to consummate the proportions of the façade, and themselves to exhibit the most exquisite proportions in arrangements of shaft and archivolt with which I am acquainted in the entire range of European architecture. (10:152–3)

Carvings on the outer arch (left side) of the central porch of St Mark's (Photograph 2014)

The third (central) porch of St Mark's (Photograph 1998)

John Ruskin, *Carved Acanthus Boss from the Face of the Outer Central Arch of St Mark's*, 1877, pencil and bodycolour, Guild of St George Collection, Museums Sheffield

St. George's Museum; the most instructive pieces of sculpture of all I can ever show there.[4]

You see, in the first place, that the outer foliage is all of one kind – pure Greek acanthus – not in the least transforming itself into ivy, or kale, or rose: trusting wholly for its beauty to the varied play of its own narrow and pointed lobes.

Narrow and pointed – but not jagged; for the jagged form of acanthus, look at the two Jean d'Acre columns [see 'Pillars of the Piazzetta', pp 65–7], and return to this – you will then feel why I call it *pure*; it is as nearly as possible the acanthus of early Corinth, only more flexible, and with more incipient blending of the character of the vine which is used for the central bosses. You see that each leaf of these last touches with its point a stellar knot of inwoven braid; (compare the ornament round the low archivolt of the porch on your right below), the outer acanthus folding all in spiral whorls. (24:286–7).

Carvings on archivolts of the central porch (Photograph 2014)

Female figures of the Virtues and Beatitudes on the second
decorated arch, central porch (Photograph 2006)

Detail of the outer central arch, lower left side
(Photograph 2013)

[The outermost arch] is carved both on its front and under-surface or soffit; on the front are seventeen female figures bearing scrolls, from which the legends are unfortunately effaced. These figures were once gilded on a dark blue ground, as may still be seen in Gentile Bellini's picture of St. Mark's in the Accademia delle Belle Arti.[5]

The sculptures of the months are on the under-surface, beginning at the bottom on the left hand of the spectator as he enters, and following in succession round the archivolt; separated, however, into two groups at its centre, by a beautiful figure of the youthful Christ, sitting in the midst of a slightly hollowed sphere covered with stars to represent the firmament, and with the attendant sun and moon, set one on each side, to rule over the day and over the night. (10:316–17)

The Translation of the Body of St Mark to the Basilica, 13th-century mosaic on the Porta S. Alipio, west façade (Photograph 1999)

A cast commissioned by Ruskin (1880s) from the western façade of the Basilica, Collection of the Guild of St George, Museums Sheffield

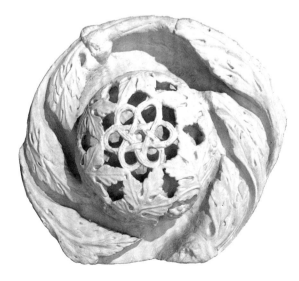

Sculptures of the months (January, February, March, reading upwards) on the second decorated arch of the third porch (Photograph 2008)

The *naïveté* of barbaric Christianity could only be forcibly appealed to by the help of coloured pictures: so that, both externally and internally, the architectural construction became partly merged in pictorial effect; and the whole edifice is to be regarded less as a temple wherein to pray, than as itself a Book of Common Prayer, a vast illuminated missal, bound with alabaster instead of parchment, studded with porphyry pillars instead of jewels, and written within and without in letters of enamel and gold. (10:112)

THE NORTH SIDE OF ST MARK'S (PIAZZETTA DEI LEONCINI)

Go round to the side farthest from the sea, where, in the first broad arch, you will see a panel, set horizontally, the sculpture of which represents twelve sheep – six on one side, six on the other – of a throne: on which throne is set a cross; and on the top of the cross a circle, and in the circle a little caprioling creature.

And outside of all are two palm trees, one on each side; and under each palm tree two baskets of dates; and over the twelve sheep is written in delicate Greek letters 'The Holy Apostles'; and over the little caprioling creature 'The Lamb'. (24:241–2)

Hetoimasia (the empty throne), Byzantine low-relief sculpture on north façade of St Mark's (Photograph 2012). Ruskin commissioned a cast of this relief in 1852, writing on 1 March to his father: 'Among the pieces sent home I should think you would be interested by the very ancient symbolical Greek sculpture of six sheep under a palm tree – part of a tablet of which I have cast the centre also, which will come in next box.' (10:466)

PILLARS OF THE PIAZZETTA

The two magnificent blocks of marble, brought from St Jean d'Acre, which form one of the principal ornaments of the Piazzetta, are Greek sculpture of the sixth century, and will be described in my folio Work. (11:398)[6]

These pillars are known to be not later than the sixth century, yet wherever external violence has spared their decoration it is as sharp as a fresh-growing thistle. (24:418)

Of the 325 or so photographic plates known to survive from Ruskin's collection of daguerreotypes, 136 are Venetian subjects, of which some twenty images include one or both of the freestanding carved pillars or piers in the Piazzetta. The pillars held lasting interest for Ruskin, and were the subject of many of his photographs and drawings. These two blocks of marble, which had been placed outside the entrance to the Baptistery on the south side of St Mark's in the thirteenth century, are carved on all four sides with cantharus vases, grapes, vine-leaves, pomegranates, acanthus leaves, egg-friezes, six-pointed stars and Greek monograms.[7] For hundreds of years they have been known by the Venetians as the 'Pilastri Acritani' (Pillars of Acre) because it was believed that they had been brought back as war trophies from the church of St Saba at Ptolemais (St Jean d'Acre) in Palestine, where the Venetians defeated the Genoese in 1258. One of them is no longer in its original position: at one time both pillars had flanked the great arch of the Porta da Mar, the sea-facing door to the church, now blocked up by a Renaissance addition dating from c.1501. One of the pillars was badly scarred by a fire in 1482.[8]

Then, in 1960 in Istanbul (formerly Constantinople), various architectural fragments, blocks of marble and brick vaults were uncovered by municipal workers bulldozing in the Saraçhane area of Istanbul in preparation for the building of a road underpass, and it was quickly realised that the remains of an important Byzantine church of late antiquity had been discovered. Work on the

The Pilastri Acritani or 'Pillars of Acre' in the Piazzetta
(Photograph 1997)

underpass was diverted, and what must have been one of the most exciting archaeological excavations of the twentieth century began in 1964. It was carried out by Dumbarton Oaks (Harvard's centre for Byzantine research) and the Istanbul Archaeological Museum, with other members of the team from the universities of Oxford and Newcastle upon Tyne. The works lasted six years, with the findings published in the Dumbarton Oaks papers[9] and in a number of illuminating publications by R.M. Harrison,

N. Firatli, and M. Vickers.[10] *Following the discovery of pieces of marble bearing parts of a carved inscription from verses[11] in praise of the Princess Anicia Juliana, the descendant of Roman and Byzantine emperors, the remains were identified as being from the long-lost sixth-century Byzantine church of St Polyeuktos. Dedicated to the Christian martyr, the church was completed in 527.*

The Istanbul excavations revealed that St Polyeuktos had been modelled in its details on biblical

John Ruskin and John Hobbs, 'The Vine Pillar', daguerreotype, *c.*1850–52 (reversed image), courtesy of K. and J. Jacobson

The easternmost pillar, showing the south- and west-facing sides (Photograph 2013)

descriptions of the Temple of Solomon with its 'nets of chequer work, and wreaths of chainwork for the chapiters [capitals] that were on top of the pillars … and the top of the pillars were of lily work in the porch, four cubits'.[12] This extended to the use of the Solomonic or royal cubit of measurement, of which Michael Vickers has written extensively.[13] The placing of the pillars in Venice at the principal sea-facing entrance to St Mark's, close to the sculptures of the Judgment of Solomon on the Ducal Palace, indicates that the Venetians were conscious of the connection. After some capitals and other fragments identical to those of the Pilastri Acritani were uncovered, it became clear that the two pillars of the Piazzetta had once belonged to this sixth-century church, from whose ruins they were taken in 1204 after the Fourth Crusade.[14]

The association between the pillars and the Temple of Solomon re-emerged in Ruskin's thoughts in later life. In c.1877 he made a drawing on purple paper[15] from an earlier daguerreotype, and in 1879 exhibited the photograph and the watercolour side by side at the Fine Art Society in an attempt to draw

Detail of the west side of the easternmost pillar (Photograph 1994)

John Ruskin, *The St Jean d'Acre Pillars, Venice* (reversed image), 1879, copied by Ruskin from his daguerreotype of c.1849–52, pencil and watercolour, heightened with white on purple paper, British Museum. The drawing is reproduced as Plate XXI in *Academy Notes* (14:426); the daguerreotype is held at the Ruskin Library, Lancaster

public attention to the fate of the west façade of St Mark's, which was threatened with a drastic reconstruction.

Habit and tradition die hard in Venice; and although fifty years have elapsed since the Istanbul excavations uncovered the remains of St Polyeuktos, the pillars are still known as the 'Pilastri Acritani' (Pillars of Acre), and doubtless will remain so.

A restoration of the pilastri was completed in 1993 by Save Venice, the American Committee for Venice.

LION OF ST MARK

The next figure is the most important capital of the whole transitional period: that employed on the two columns of the Piazzetta.

These two pillars are said to have been *raised* in the close of the twelfth century, but I cannot find even the most meagre account of their bases, capitals, or, which seems to me most wonderful, of that noble winged lion, one of the grandest things produced by mediaeval art, which all men admire, and none can draw. I have never yet seen a faithful representation of his firm, fierce, and fiery strength. I believe that both he and the capital which bears him are late thirteenth-century work. I have not been up to the lion, and cannot answer for it; but if it be not thirteenth century work, it is as good; and, respecting the capitals, there can be small question. They are of exactly the date of the oldest tombs, bearing crosses, outside of St. John and Paul; and are associated with all the other work of the transitional period, from 1250 to 1300 (the bases of these pillars, representing the trades of Venice, ought, by the by, to have been mentioned as among the best early efforts of Venetian grotesque); and, besides, their abaci are formed by

The bronze Lion of St Mark in the Piazzetta (Photograph 2005)

four reduplications of the dentilled mouldings of St. Mark's, which never occur after the year 1300. (11:275)

In St. Mark's Rest *(1877) Ruskin added:* 'In the first place, the Lion of St. Mark is a splendid piece of eleventh or twelfth-century bronze. I know that by the style of him; but have never found out where he came from. I may now chance on it, however, at any moment in other quests. Eleventh- or twelfth-century, the Lion – fifteenth, or later, his wings; very delicate in feather-workmanship, but with little lift or strike in them: decorative mainly. Without doubt his first wings were thin sheets of beaten bronze, shred into plumage; far wider in their sweep than these.' (24:225)

In 1985 the lion was removed from its column for analysis and cleaning, and was exhibited in the summer of 1989 at the Archaeological Museum, Piazza San Marco. In October 1990 it travelled to London for a three-month exhibition at the British Museum, and was returned to its column in 1991.

John Ruskin, *Gothic Capitals*, Plate 2, Fig. 8 in *The Stones of Venice* III (11.12)

Columns of the Lion of St Mark and St Theodore in the
Piazzetta (Photograph 1997)

ST THEODORE

Whether St. Mark was first bishop of Aquileia or not, St. Theodore was the first patron of the city; nor can he yet be considered as having entirely abdicated his early right, as his statue, standing on a crocodile, still companions the winged lion on the opposing pillar of the Piazzetta. A church erected to this saint is said to have occupied, before the ninth century, the site of St. Mark's; and the traveller, dazzled by the brilliancy of the great square, ought not to leave it without endeavouring to imagine its aspect in that early time when it was a green field, cloister-like and quiet, divided by a

13th-century sculpted figures depicting the Trades at the base of the St Theodore column (Photograph 2009)

St Theodore and crocodile in the Piazzetta: 20th-century copy of the original sculpture (Photograph 2013)

small canal, with a line of trees on each side; and extending between the two churches of St. Theodore and St. Geminian, as the little piazza of Torcello lies between its palazzo and cathedral. (10:71)

In St. Mark's Rest (1877) Ruskin noted: 'The statue of St. Theodore, whatever its age, is wholly without merit. I can't make it out myself, nor find record of it: in a stonemason's yard I should have passed it as modern.' (24:225) *The sculptures of St Theodore and the crocodile seen by Ruskin were taken down during the Second World War, and replaced by the identical copy seen in the Piazzetta today. The original sculptures are preserved inside the Ducal Palace.*

ORDERS OF CAPITALS

There are two great orders of capitals in the world: one of these is convex in its contour, the other concave; richness of ornament, with all freedom of fancy, is for the most part found in the one, and severity of ornament, with stern discipline of the fancy, in the other.

Of these two families of capitals both occur in the Byzantine period, but the concave group

John Ruskin, *The Four Venetian Flower Orders* (detail), Plate 10 in *The Stones of Venice* II (10:164)

John Ruskin, *The Four Venetian Flower Orders* (detail), Plate 10 in *The Stones of Venice* II (10:164)

is the longest-lived, and extends itself into the Gothic times. We must now investigate their characters more in detail; and these may be best generally represented by considering both families as formed upon the types of flowers; the one upon that of the water-lily, the other upon that of the convolvulus. There was no intention in the Byzantine architects to imitate either one or other of these flowers; but all beautiful works of art must either intentionally imitate or accidentally resemble natural forms; and the direct comparison with the natural forms which these capitals most resemble, is the likeliest mode of fixing their distinctions in the reader's mind.

The convex family is modelled according to the commonest shapes of that great group of flowers which form rounded cups, like that of the water-lily, the leaves springing horizontally from the stalk, and closing together upwards. The rose is of this family, but her cup is filled with the luxuriance of her leaves; the crocus, campanula, ranunculus, anemone, and almost all the loveliest children of the field, are formed upon the same type.

The other [concave] family resembles the convolvulus, trumpet-flower, and such others, in which the lower part of the bell is slender, and the lip curves outwards at the top. There are fewer flowers constructed on this than on the convex model; but in the organization of trees and of clusters of herbage it is seen continually. Of course, both of these conditions are modified, when applied to capitals, by the enormously greater thickness of the stalk or shaft, but in other respects the parallelism is close and accurate; and the reader had better at once fix the flower outlines in his mind, and remember them as representing the only two orders of capitals that the world has ever seen, or can see.

The examples of the concave family in the Byzantine times are found principally either in large capitals founded on the Greek Corinthian, used chiefly for the nave pillars of churches, or in

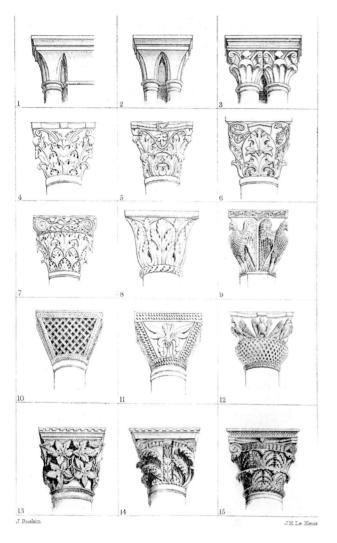

John Ruskin, *Byzantine Capitals: Concave Group*, photogravure from line engraving, Plate 8 in *The Stones of Venice* II (10:159)

Capital on the Porta di S. Pietro, west façade of the Basilica (Photograph 2014)

the small lateral shafts of the palaces. It appears somewhat singular that the pure Corinthian form should have been reserved almost exclusively for nave pillars, as at Torcello, Murano and St. Mark's; it occurs indeed, together with almost every other form, on the exterior of St. Mark's also, but never so definitely as in the nave and transept shafts. The other characteristic examples of the concave group in the Byzantine times are as simple as those resulting from the Corinthian are rich. They occur on the small shafts at the flanks of the Fondaco de' Turchi, the Casa Farsetti, Casa Loredan, Terraced House [Palazzo Barzizza on the Grand Canal], and upper story of the Madonnetta House [Palazzo Donà della Madonnetta on the Grand Canal]. (10:156–7)

The concave group, however, was not naturally pleasing to the Byzantine mind. Its own favourite capital was of the bold convex or cushion

Impost capitals on the exterior of the Cappella Zen, with undercutting and openwork (Photograph 2008)

Capitals on the north façade of the Basilica (Photograph 2009)

John Ruskin, *Capitals: Convex Group*, c.1851, pencil, ink, watercolour and bodycolour, engraved by George Allen, aquatint by T.S. Boys, for Plate 18 in *The Stones of Venice* I. Ruskin Library, Lancaster

shape, so conspicuous in all the buildings of the period. (10:158)

The reader must always remember that the examples given are single instances, and those not the most beautiful but the most intelligible, chosen out of thousands: the designs of the capitals of St. Mark's alone would form a volume. (10:165)

LILY CAPITALS

[These] are representations of a group with which many interesting associations are connected. It was noticed ... that the method of covering the exterior of buildings with thin pieces of marble was likely to lead to a system of lighting the interior by minute perforation. In order to obtain both light and air without admitting any unbroken body of sunshine, in warm countries it became a constant habit of the Arabian architects to pierce minute and star-like openings in slabs of stone, and to employ the stones so pierced where the Gothic architects employ traceries. Internally, the form of stars assumed by the light as it entered was in itself an exquisite decoration, but externally it was felt necessary to add some slight ornament upon the surface of the perforated stone; and it was soon found that, as the small perforations had a

Byzantine impost capital with openwork (*lavorato a giorno*), exterior of the Cappella Zen, San Marco (Photograph 2005)

tendency to look scattered and spotty, the most effective treatment of the intermediate surfaces would be one which bound them together and gave unity and repose to the pierced and disturbed stone. Universally, therefore, those intermediate spaces were carved into the semblance of interwoven fillets, which alternately sank beneath and rose above each other as they met.

This system of braided or woven ornament was not confined to the Arabs; it is universally pleasing to the instinct of mankind. I believe that nearly all early ornamentation is full of it – more especially, perhaps, Scandinavian and Anglo-Saxon; and illuminated manuscripts depend upon it for their loveliest effects of intricate colour, up to the close of the thirteenth century. (10:162–3)

Byzantine ornamentation, like that of almost all nations in a state of progress, is full of this kind of work; but it occurs most conspicuously, though

John Ruskin, *Lily Capital of the North-west Angle of St Mark's*, photogravure from line engraving, Plate 9 in *The Stones of Venice* II

most simply, in the minute traceries which surround their most solid capitals; sometimes merely in a reticulated veil, sometimes resembling a basket, on the edges of which are perched birds and other animals. The capitals which show it most definitely are those so often spoken of as the lily capitals of St. Mark's, of which the northern one is carefully drawn. (10:164)

These capitals, called barbarous by our architects, are without exception the most subtle pieces of composition in broad contour which I have ever met with in architecture.

Upon these profoundly studied outlines, as remarkable for their grace and complexity as the general mass of the capital is for solid strength and proportion to its necessary service, the braided work is wrought with more than usual care; perhaps, as suggested by the Marchese Selvatico, with some idea of imitating those 'nets of chequerwork and

Capitals and columns of the south-west portico of St Mark's (Photograph 2012)

Split-palmette 'lily' basket capital on the north-west porch of St Mark's (Photograph 2013)

wreaths of chainwork' on the chapiters [capitals] of Solomon's temple, which are, I suppose, the first instances on record of an ornamentation of this kind thus applied. The braided work encloses on each of the four sides of the capital a flower whose form [is] derived from that of the lily. It is never without the two square or oblong objects at the extremity of the tendrils issuing from its root, set like vessels to catch the dew from the points of its leaves; but I do not understand their meaning. No amount of illustration or eulogium would be enough to make the reader understand the perfect beauty of the thing itself, as the sun steals from interstice to interstice of its marble veil, and touches with the white lustre of its rays at midday the pointed leaves of its thirsty lilies. (10:164–5)

VENETO-BYZANTINE BUILDINGS

IF WE PASS THROUGH THE CITY looking for buildings which resemble St. Mark's – first, in the most important feature of incrustation; secondly, in the matter of the mouldings, we shall find a considerable number, not indeed very attractive in their first address to the eye, but agreeing perfectly, both with each other, and with the earliest portions of St. Mark's in every important detail; and to be regarded, therefore, with profound interest, as indeed the remains of an ancient city of Venice, altogether different in aspect from that which now exists. From these remains we may with safety deduce general conclusions touching the forms of Byzantine architecture, as practised in Eastern Italy, during the eleventh, twelfth and thirteenth centuries.

They agree in another respect, as well as in style. All are either ruins, or fragments disguised by restoration. Not one of them is uninjured or unaltered; and the impossibility of finding so much as an angle or a single story in perfect condition is a proof, hardly less convincing than the method of their architecture, that they were indeed raised during the earliest phases of the Venetian power. The mere fragments, dispersed in narrow streets,

and recognizable by a single capital, or the segment of an arch, I shall not enumerate; but of important remains, there are six in the immediate neighbourhood of the Rialto, one in the Rio di Ca' Foscari, and one conspicuously placed opposite the great Renaissance palace known as the Vendramin Calerghi ... (10:143–4)

FONDACO DEI TURCHI

It is a ghastly ruin; whatever is venerable or sad in its wreck being disguised by attempts to put it to present uses of the basest kind. It has been composed of arcades borne by marble shafts, and walls of brick faced with marble; but the covering stones have been torn away from it like the shroud from a corpse; and its walls, rent into a thousand chasms, are filled and refilled with fresh brickwork, and the seams and hollows are choked with clay and whitewash, oozing and trickling over the marble – itself blanched into dusty decay by the frosts of centuries.

Of its history little is recorded, and that little futile. That it once belonged to the dukes of Ferrara, and was bought from them in the sixteenth

The Fondaco dei Turchi,
*c.*1845, daguerreotype
(unknown photographer),
courtesy of K. and J. Jacobson

John Ruskin, *The Fondaco dei Turchi*, c.1850,
frontispiece to *The Stones of Venice* II (*Works* 10)

The Fondaco dei Turchi on the Grand Canal (Photograph 2009)

century to be made a general receptacle for the goods of the Turkish merchants, whence it is now generally known as the Fondaco, or Fontico, de' Turchi, are facts just as important to the antiquary as that in the year 1852 the municipality of Venice allowed its lower story to be used for a 'deposito di Tabacchi'. Neither of this, nor of any other remains of the period, can we know anything but what their own stones will tell us. (10:145)

Rented by the Venetian Republic to Turkish merchants from 1621, the Fondaco dei Turchi eventually fell into disrepair. The abandoned building was purchased in 1858 by the Municipality, and in 1869 a complete reconstruction by the architect Federico Berchet was undertaken, with unfortunate results, including the addition of two towers that had not featured in the original Veneto-Byzantine structure. From 1887 to 1922 the building was used for the storage and display of the sculpture collection of Teodoro Correr, before it was moved to its present location at the Museo Correr in Piazza San Marco. The Fondaco dei Turchi now houses the collection of the Natural History Museum.

RIO FOSCARI HOUSE

We must now descend the Grand Canal as far as the Palazzo Foscari, and enter the narrower canal called the Rio di Ca' Foscari, at the side of that palace. Almost immediately after passing the great gateway of the Foscari courtyard, we shall see on our left, in the ruinous and time-stricken walls which totter over the water, the white curve of a circular arch covered with sculpture, and fragments of the bases of small pillars entangled among festoons of the Erba della Madonna [ivy-leaved toadflax]. I have already, in the folio plates (*Examples of the Architecture of Venice*) which accompanied the first volume, partly illustrated this building. In what references I have to make to it here, I shall speak of it as the Rio Foscari House. (10:454)

Fortunately, enough of the ruins remained in the year 1849 to enable me to reconstruct the ground or, as I shall always call it in Venice, the water-story, with very slight chance of error ... I have drawn the central arch on a larger scale in this Plate [*Stilted Archivolts from a Byzantine Ruin in the Rio di Ca' Foscari, Venice*] exactly as it appeared in 1849. It was a beautifully picturesque fragment; the archivolt sculptures being executed in marble, which seemed, in some parts, rather to have gained than lost in whiteness by its age, and set off by the dark and delicate leaves of the Erba della Madonna, the only pure piece of modern addition to the old design, all else being foul plaster and withering wood. There is a curious instance, however, in this drawing, of the difficulty of being absolutely faithful, however earnestly we desire it. There was no way of drawing this arch but out of a gondola immediately underneath, in a position from which it was quite impossible to see the upper portion of the archivolt distinctly. I made the sketch before I fully appreciated the importance of the building, chiefly for the sake of its picturesqueness; and coming to the piece of archivolt which I could not clearly discern, drew it carelessly, with what appeared to me to be an upright leaf in its centre. Afterwards, discovering the great importance of these remains,

Rio Ca' Foscari: archivolt on the canal façade of a house in Corte de l'Aseo, Dorsoduro (Photograph 2006)

I went up to examine every piece of them, and found the supposed upright leaf to be the Byzantine symbol – a hand, between the Sun and Moon, in the attitude of benediction. This sign is almost always used in the centres of Byzantine arches and crosses.[16] (11:336–7)

John Ruskin, *Stilted Archivolts from a Byzantine Ruin in the Rio di Ca' Foscari, Venice*, 1849, pencil, water and bodycolour. Ruskin Library, Lancaster

CASA LOREDAN

Though not conspicuous, and often passed with neglect [this palace] will, I believe, be felt at last by all who examine it carefully, to be the most beautiful palace in the whole extent of the Grand Canal. It has been restored often, once in the Gothic, once in the Renaissance times – some writers say even rebuilt; but if so, rebuilt in its old form. The Gothic additions harmonize exquisitely with its Byzantine work, and it is easy, as we examine its lovely central arcade, to forget the Renaissance additions which encumber it above. It is known as the Casa Loredan. (10:454–5)

The capitals resemble those of St. Mark's more than any we have hitherto met with, and the reader will notice, in the double shaft, the lily pattern with which he is so familiar ... all these Loredan capitals are excessively rude in cutting, blunt and imperfect ... Yet the effect of the capitals from beneath is altogether admirable ... I am inclined

Palazzo Loredan on the Grand Canal (Photograph 2012)

Detail of window arch and capitals, Palazzo Loredan (Photograph 2013)

to consider the whole series as of true ancient workmanship, contemporary with St. Mark's, but more cheaply and hastily executed, and retained with the shafts in the rebuilding of the palace. (10:149)

And as for these Byzantine buildings, we only do not feel them, because we do not *watch* them; otherwise we should as much enjoy the variety of proportion in their arches as we do at present that of the natural architecture of flowers and leaves. (10:154)

VENETO-BYZANTINE SCULPTURE

IN THE PRIVATE PALACES, THE RANGES of archivolt are for the most part very simple, with dentilled mouldings; and all the ornamental effect is entrusted to pieces of sculpture set in the wall above or between the arches. These pieces of sculpture are either crosses, upright oblongs, or circles. The cross was apparently an invariable ornament, placed either in the centre of the archivolt of the doorway, or in the centre of the first story above the windows; on each side of it the circular and oblong ornaments were used in various alternation. In too many instances the wall marbles have been torn away from the earliest Byzantine palaces, so that the crosses are left on their archivolts only. The best examples of the cross set above the windows are found in houses of the transitional period: one in the Campo S. Maria Formosa [Palazzo Vitturi]; another, in which a cross is placed between every window, is still well preserved in the Campo S. Maria Mater Domini [Casa degli Zane]; another, on the Grand Canal, in the parish of the Apostoli [Ca' da Mosto] has two crosses, one on each side of the first story, and a bas-relief of Christ enthroned in the centre; and finally, that from which the larger cross in the Plate [*Byzantine Sculpture*] was taken is the house once belonging to Marco Polo at San Giovanni Grisostomo [in the Corte Seconda del Milion]. (10:166)

13th-century patera of two peacocks drinking from the Fountain of Life, on the porch of the Carmini church (Photograph 2013)

John Ruskin, *Byzantine Sculpture*, photogravure from line engraving by J.H. Le Keux, Plate 11, *The Stones of Venice* II (10:166). The motif of peacocks and eagles from the façade of St Mark's was used to illustrate the covers of the three volumes of *The Stones of Venice*, first edition (1851–3)

The Corte Seconda del Milion in Cannaregio (Photograph 2007)

PALAZZO POLO AT SAN GIOVANNI GRISOSTOMO (IN THE CORTE SECONDA DEL MILION)

Its interior court is full of interest, showing fragments of the old building in every direction; cornices, windows, and doors of almost every period, mingled among modern rebuilding and restoration of all degrees of dignity. (10:399)

This cross, though graceful and rich, and given because it happens to be one of the best preserved, is uncharacteristic in one respect; for, instead of the

Patera and cross above a Byzantine arch in the Corte Seconda del Milion (Photograph 2009)

central rose at the meeting of the arms, we usually find a hand raised in the attitude of blessing, between the sun and the moon, as in the two smaller crosses seen in the Plate [*Byzantine Sculpture*]. In nearly all representations of the Crucifixion, over the whole of Europe, at the period in question, the sun and the moon are introduced, one on each side of the cross – the sun generally, in paintings, as a red star. (10:166)

The Byzantine cross [at S. Sebastiano church], with the doves at its feet, is a beautiful example of quaint and early architectural sculpture. (10:466)

Crosses and paterae on the façade of the Casa degli Zane, Campo S. Maria Mater Domini (Photograph 2013)

BIRDS AND BEASTS

This habit of placing the symbol of the Christian faith in the centres of their palaces was universal in early Venice; it does not cease till about the middle of the fourteenth century. The other sculptures, which were set above or between the arches, consist almost invariably of groups of birds or beasts; either standing opposite to each other with a small pillar or spray of leafage between them, or else tearing and devouring each other.

The multitude of these sculptures, especially of the small ones enclosed in circles, which are now scattered through the city of Venice, is enormous, but they are seldom to be seen in their original positions. When the Byzantine palaces were destroyed, these fragments were generally preserved, and inserted again in the walls of the new buildings,

Griffon with its prey, marble patera on north façade of St Mark's (Photograph 2014)

Greek marble cross (11th to 12th century) and patera of birds (12th to 13th century) on the campanile of the church of S. Sebastiano (Photograph 2014)

with more or less attempt at symmetry; fragments of friezes and mouldings being often used in the same manner; so that the mode of their original employment can only be seen in St. Mark's, the Fondaco de' Turchi, Braided House [Palazzo Donà on the Grand Canal], and one or two others. (10:167–8)

The groups of contending and devouring animals are always much ruder in cutting, and take somewhat the place in Byzantine sculpture which the lower grotesques do in the Gothic; true, though clumsy, grotesques being sometimes mingled among them, as four bodies joined to one head in the centre; but never showing any attempt at variety of invention, except only in the effective disposition of the light and shade, and in the vigour and thoughtfulness of the touches which indicate the plumes of the birds or foldings of the leaves. Care, however, is always taken to secure variety enough to keep the eye entertained, no two sides of these Byzantine ornaments being in all respects the same: for instance, in the chain-work round the first figure in Plate 11 [peacocks, St Mark's] there are two circles enclosing squares on the left-hand side of the arch at the top, but two smaller circles and

A 13th-century marble relief sculpture of peacocks and eagles, west façade of St Mark's (Photograph 2006)

Veneto-Byzantine low-relief carving of peacocks on the south wall of the Treasury, St Mark's (Photograph 2013)

a diamond on the other, enclosing one square, and two small circular spots or bosses; and in the line of chain at the bottom there is a circle on the right, and a diamond on the left, and so down to the working of the smallest details. (10:168–9)

The peacock, used in preference to every other bird, is the well-known symbol of the Resurrection; and when drinking from a fountain or from a font is, I doubt not, also a type of the new life received in faithful baptism. The vine, used in preference to all other trees, was equally recognized as, in all cases, a type either of Christ Himself, or of those who were in a state of visible or professed union with Him. The dove, at its foot, represents the coming of the Comforter; and even the groups of contending animals had, probably, a distinct and universally apprehended reference to the power of evil. But I lay no stress on these more occult meanings. The principal circumstance which marks the seriousness of the early Venetian mind is perhaps the last in which the reader would suppose it was traceable: that love of bright and pure color which, in a modified form, was afterwards the root of all the triumph of the Venetian schools of painting, but which, in its utmost simplicity, was characteristic of the Byzantine period only. (10:171–2)

☙ ☙ ☙

How far the system of grounding with gold and colour, universal in St. Mark's, was carried out in the sculptures of the private palaces, it is now impossible to say. The wrecks of them which remain, as above noticed, show few of their ornamental sculptures in their original position; and from those marbles which were employed in succeeding buildings during the Gothic period, the fragments of their mosaic grounds would naturally rather have been removed than restored. Mosaic, while the most secure of all decorations if carefully watched and refastened when it loosens, may, if neglected and exposed to weather, in process of time disappear so as to leave no vestige of its existence. However this may have been, the assured facts are that both the

John Ruskin, *Study of Marble Inlaying on the Front of the Casa Loredan, Venice*, 1845, pencil, ink, watercolour and bodycolour, Ashmolean Museum, Oxford

shafts of the pillars and the facing of the whole building were of veined or variously coloured marble: the capitals and sculptures were either, as they now appear, of pure white marble, relieved upon the veined ground; or, which is infinitely the more probable, grounded in the richer palaces with mosaic of gold, in the inferior ones with blue colour, and only the leaves and edges of the sculpture gilded. These brighter hues were opposed by bands of deeper colour, generally alternate russet and green in the archivolts – bands which still remain in the Casa Loredan and Fondaco de' Turchi, and in a house in the Corte del Remer, near the Rialto, as well as in St. Mark's; and by circular disks of green serpentine and porphyry, which, together with the circular sculptures, appear to have been an ornament peculiarly grateful to the Eastern mind, derived probably in the first instance from the suspension of shields upon the wall, as in the majesty of ancient Tyre. The sweet and solemn harmony of purple with various green remained a favourite chord of colour with the Venetians, and was constantly used even in the later palaces; but never could have been seen in so great perfection as when opposed to the pale and delicate sculpture of the Byzantine time. (10:169–71)

The builders of our great cathedrals veiled their casements and wrapped their pillars with one robe of purple splendour. The builders of the luxurious Renaissance left their palaces filled only with cold white light, and in the paleness of their native stones. (10:174)

previous pages: The south-west portico of St Mark's
looking towards the Ducal Palace (Photograph 2014)

John Ruskin, *The Exterior of the Ducal Palace, Venice,* 1852,
pen, wash and pencil, Ashmolean Museum, Oxford

GOTHIC

It requires a strong effort of common sense to shake ourselves quit of all that we have been taught for the last two centuries, and wake to the perception of a truth just as simple and certain as it is new: that great art, whether expressing itself in words, colours, or stones, does not say the same thing over and over again; that the merit of architectural, as of every other art, consists in its saying new and different things; that to repeat itself is no more a characteristic of genius in marble than it is of genius in print; and that we may, without offending any laws of good taste, require of an architect, as we do of a novelist, that he should be not only correct, but entertaining.

The Nature of Gothic (10:206–7)

Let us then understand at once that change or variety is as much a necessity to the human heart and brain in buildings as in books; that there is no merit, though there is some occasional use, in monotony; and that we must no more expect to derive either pleasure or profit from architecture whose ornaments are of one pattern, and whose pillars are of one proportion, than we should out of a universe in which the clouds were all of one shape, and the trees all of one size.

The Nature of Gothic (10:207)

THE CHARM WHICH VENICE still possesses, and which for the last fifty years has rendered it the favourite haunt of all the painters of picturesque subject, is owing to the effect of the palaces belonging to the period we have now to examine, mingled with those of the Renaissance.

This effect is produced in two different ways. The Renaissance palaces are not more picturesque in themselves than the club-houses of Pall Mall; but they become delightful by the contrast of their severity and refinement with the rich and rude confusion of the sea-life beneath them, and of their white and solid masonry with the green waves. Remove from beneath them the orange sails of the fishing-boats, the black gliding of the gondolas, the cumbered decks and rough crews of the barges of traffic, and the fretfulness of the green water along their foundations, and the Renaissance palaces possess no more interest than those of London or Paris. But the Gothic palaces are picturesque in themselves, and wield over us an independent power. Sea and sky, and every other accessory might be taken away from them, and still they would be beautiful and strange. They are not less striking in the loneliest streets of Padua and Vicenza (where many were built during the period of the Venetian authority in those cities) than in the most crowded thoroughfares of Venice itself; and if they could be transported into the midst of London, they would still not altogether lose their power over the feelings.

The best proof of this is in the perpetual attractiveness of all pictures, however poor in skill, which have taken for their subject the principal of these Gothic buildings, the Ducal Palace. In spite of all architectural theories and teachings, the paintings of this building are always felt to be delightful; we cannot be wearied by them, though often sorely tried; but we are not put to the same trial in the case of the palaces of the Renaissance. They are never drawn singly, or as the principal subject, nor can they be. The building which faces the Ducal Palace on the opposite side of the Piazzetta is celebrated among architects, but it is not familiar to our eyes; it is painted only incidentally, for the completion, not the subject, of a Venetian scene; and even the Renaissance arcades of St. Mark's Place, though frequently painted, are always treated as a mere avenue to its Byzantine church and colossal tower. And the Ducal Palace itself owes the peculiar charm which we have hitherto felt, not so much to its greater size as compared with other Gothic buildings, or nobler design (for it never yet has been rightly drawn), as to its comparative isolation. The other Gothic structures are as much injured by the continual juxtaposition of the Renaissance palaces, as the latter are aided by it; they exhaust their own life by breathing it into the Renaissance coldness: but the Ducal Palace stands comparatively alone, and fully expresses the Gothic power.

And it is just that it should be so seen, for it is the original of nearly all the rest. It is not the elaborate and more studied development of a national style, but the great and sudden invention of one man, instantly forming a national style, and

Apse windows of the Frari church (Photograph 2009)

becoming the model for the imitation of every architect in Venice for upwards of a century. It was the determination of this one fact which occupied me the greater part of the time I spent in Venice. It had always appeared to me most strange that there should be in no part of the city any incipient or imperfect types of the form of the Ducal Palace; it was difficult to believe that so mighty a building had been the conception of one man, not only in disposition and detail, but in style; and yet impossible, had it been otherwise, but that some early examples of approximate Gothic form must exist. There is not one. The palaces built between the final cessation of the Byzantine style, about 1300, and the date of the Ducal Palace (1320–1350), are all completely distinct in character ... and there is literally no transitional form between them and the perfection of the Ducal Palace. Every Gothic building in Venice which resembles the latter is a copy of it. I do not mean that there was no Gothic in Venice before the Ducal Palace, but that the mode of its application to domestic architecture had not been determined. The real root of the Ducal Palace is the apse of the church of the Frari. The traceries of that apse, though earlier and ruder in workmanship, are nearly the same in mouldings, and precisely the same in treatment (especially in the placing of the lions' heads), as those of the great Ducal Arcade; and the originality of thought in the architect of the Ducal Palace consists in his having adapted those traceries, in a more highly developed and finished form, to civil uses. In the apse of the church they form narrow and tall window lights, somewhat more massive than those of Northern Gothic, but similar in application: the thing to be done was to adapt these traceries to the forms of domestic building necessitated by national usage. The early palaces consisted, as we have seen, of arcades sustaining walls faced with marble, rather broad and long than elevated. This form was kept for the Ducal Palace; but instead of round arches from shaft to shaft, the Frari traceries were substituted, with two essential modifications. Besides being enormously increased in scale and thickness, that they might better bear the superincumbent weight, the quatrefoil, which in the Frari windows is above the arch, was, in the Ducal Palace, put between the arches; the main reason for this alteration being that the bearing power of the arches, which was now to be trusted with the weight of a wall forty foot high, was thus thrown between the quatrefoils, instead of under them, and thereby applied at far better advantage. (10:270–73)

Church of the Frari: detail of windows of the apse (Photograph 2013)

CHURCH OF THE FRARI

Founded in 1250, and continued at various subsequent periods. The apse and adjoining chapels are the earliest portions, and their traceries have been above noticed as the origin of those of the Ducal Palace. The best view of the apse, which is a very noble example of Italian Gothic, is from the door of the Scuola di S. Rocco. The doors of the church are all later than any portion of it, very elaborate Renaissance Gothic. (11:379)

Madonna and Child with angels: 15th-century Tuscan relief sculpture above the portal of the Cappella Corner (Photograph 2013)

SCHOOLS OF VENETIAN GOTHIC
AND ORDERS OF VENETIAN ARCHES

From Ruskin's Notebook 'M', 23 November 1849:

I obtained to-day for the first time a clue to the whole system of pure Venetian Gothic.

School No 1. There is first *a* vide opposite: pure Byzantine with double line of dentils, first school to seek for examples of.

School No 2. *b* opposite. A saracenic – q. 12th or 11th century innovation. Line of dentils pointed above, round below.

School No 3. *c* opposite, both lines pointed: I find this arch at the ponte dei Caleghieri with the simple section *c* on next page, the shaded part being the dentil. And now comes a great step. At this point the Saracenic arches in St Mark's must have been built and from them, by merely sharpening the bend of the arch, we have directly – School no.4 – the arch *d*. This I find in the same house with *c*, ponte dei Caleghieri; executed with the moulding *d*. This change in the moulding is a great step, and must be examined thoroughly. Now

I find in the same house, the window *e*, worked with the simpler section *e* opposite, the shaded part on the right being the cusp: and without any finial – the dentils meeting in sharp point. (Diary 1849–50, Notebook 'M', p.47)

During the winter of 1849–50 Ruskin was developing a typology to illustrate the evolution of the successive phases of Venetian Gothic, as seen in its window arches and doors. His system of the 'Orders of Venetian Arches' is still considered a valid guide. On 23 November he recorded his discovery of a house near Ponte (Storto) dei Calegheri in which his window arch types (c), (d) and (e) from Schools 3 and 4 were all incorporated into one building. This is undoubtedly the early Gothic fourteenth-century Palazzo Moroni on the rio della Fenice. Unremarked in modern guide books, its austere façade tends to be passed without a second glance, although it is noted in a number of Italian publications for the purity and coherence of its Gothic windows and mouldings.[1]

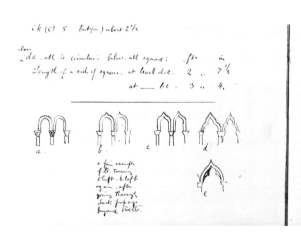

John Ruskin, *Schools of Venetian Gothic*, 1849, ink drawing from Notebook 'M'. p.47. Ruskin Library, Lancaster

The 14th-century Palazzo Moroni on the rio della Fenice (Photograph 2013)

Palazzo Moroni: view from Campiello dei Calegheri (Photograph 2009)

Fifth-order Gothic windows of the canal façade of Palazzo Moroni (Photograph 2008)

On the approach from Campiello dei Calegheri, Ruskin's arch type (e) is seen in the five-light 'fifth-order' window on the canal façade; with (d) visible in the fourth-order trefoiled arch of the upper second-floor windows on the extreme left and right of the façade. Continuing along the Fondamenta della Fenice and looking back to the side of the building facing Calle del Piovan o Gritti, one sees another example of type (d) on the upper floor, with a fifth-order (e) below it, echoing the façade windows of the piano nobile.

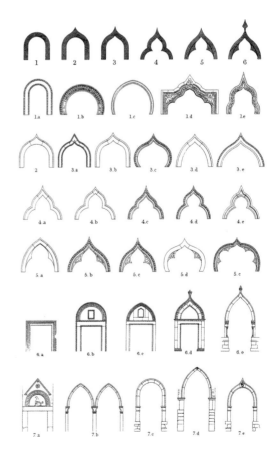

Those features of the Gothic palaces in which the transitions of their architecture are most distinctly traceable [are] namely, the arches of the windows and doors ... The Gothic style had formed itself completely on the mainland, while the Byzantines still retained their influence at Venice; and the history of early Venetian Gothic is therefore not that of a school taking new forms independently of external influence, but the history of the struggle of the Byzantine manner with a

John Ruskin, *The Orders of Venetian Arches*, photogravure from line engraving, Plate 14 in *The Stones of Venice* II (10:290)

contemporary style quite as perfectly organized as itself, and far more energetic.

The uppermost shaded series of six forms of windows represents, at a glance, the modifications of this feature in Venetian palaces, from the eleventh to the fifteenth century. Fig. 1 [see *The Orders of Venetian Arches*] is Byzantine, of the eleventh and twelfth centuries; figs. 2 and 3 transitional, of the thirteenth and early fourteenth centuries; figs. 4 and 5 pure Gothic of the thirteenth, fourteenth and early fifteenth; and fig. 6 late Gothic, of the fifteenth century, distinguished by its added finial. Fig. 4 is the

longest-lived of all these forms: it occurs first in the thirteenth century; and, sustaining modifications only in its mouldings, is found also in the middle of the fifteenth.

I shall call these the six orders of Venetian windows, and when I speak of a window of the fourth, second, or sixth order, the reader will only have to refer to the numerals at the top of the Plate. Then the series [bottom page 93] shows the principal forms found in each period, belonging to each several order; except 1*b* to *c* and the two lower series, numbered 6*a* to 7*e*, which are types of Venetian doors. (10:290–91)

DOOR IN SALIZZADA DEL FONDACO DE' TURCHI

In the angle: it is of stone and very graceful ... the roses mere captain's biscuits[2] with holes in them. (Notebook 'Gothic Book', p.51)

Remains of a Veneto-Byzantine archivolt with low-relief carvings (10th to 11th century) in Salizzada del Fondaco dei Turchi (S. Croce); within the arch is a 15th-century gothic shield (Photograph 2013)

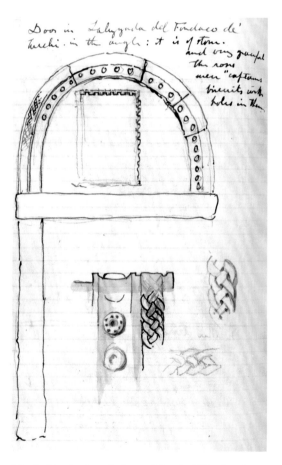

John Ruskin, drawing of a door in Salizzada del Fondaco dei Turchi from Notebook 'Gothic Book', p.51. Ruskin Library, Lancaster

CORTE DEL REMER (CA' LION-MOROSINI)

The woodcut represents the door and two of the lateral windows of a house in the Corte del Remer, facing the Grand Canal, in the parish of the Apostoli. It is remarkable as having its great entrance on the first floor, attained by a bold flight of steps sustained on pure pointed arches wrought in brick. I cannot tell if these arches are contemporary with the building, though it must always have had an access of the kind. The rest of its aspect is Byzantine, except only that the rich sculptures of its archivolt show in combats of animals, beneath the soffit, a beginning of the Gothic fire and energy. The moulding of its plinth is of a Gothic profile, and the windows are pointed, not with a reversed curve, but in a pure straight gable, very curiously contrasted with the delicate bending of the pieces of marble armour cut for the shoulders of each arch. There is a two-lighted window, such as that seen in the vignette,

Ca' Lion-Morosini in the Campiello
del Remer, Cannaregio (Photograph 2013)

John Ruskin, *Door and Two Lateral Windows from a House in the Corte del Remer*, woodcut, Fig.26 in *The Stones of Venice* II (10:293)

on each side of the door, sustained in the centre by a basket-worked Byzantine capital: the mode of covering the brick archivolt with marble, both in the windows and doorway, is precisely like that of the true Byzantine palaces. (10:292–3)

Campiello del Remer: Romanesque horseshoe arch and third-order windows of the Ca' Lion-Morosini (Photograph 2013)

WINDOW IN CALLE DEL PISTOR

The endeavour to reconcile the grace of the reversed arch with the strength of the round one, and still to build in brick, ended at first in conditions such as that represented at *a*, which is a window in the Calle del Pistor, close to the church of the Apostoli, a very interesting and perfect example.

Window in the Calle del Pistor (Photograph 2006)

John Ruskin, window in Calle del Pistor, woodcut, Fig. 28(a) in *The Stones of Venice* II (10:294)

HOUSE IN SALIZZADA SAN LIO

At *b* is given one of the earliest and simplest occurrences of the second-order window from a most important fragment of a defaced house in the Salizzada San Lio, close to the Merceria. It is associated with a fine pointed brick arch, indisputably of contemporary work, towards the close of the thirteenth century. (10:294)

Arch and windows of a 13th-century house in the Salizzada S. Lio (Photograph 2013)

John Ruskin, *Second-order Windows from a House in the Salizzada S. Lio*, woodcut, Fig. 28(b) in *The Stones of Venice* II (10:294)

CA' DA MOSTO: PALACE AT APOSTOLI ON THE GRAND CANAL, NEAR THE RIALTO, OPPOSITE THE FRUIT MARKET

The second-order window soon attained nobler development. At once simple, graceful and strong, it was received into all the architecture of the period, and there is hardly a street in Venice which does not exhibit some important remains of palaces built with this form of window in many stories, and in numerous groups. The most extensive and perfect is one upon the Grand Canal in the parish of the Apostoli, near the Rialto, covered with rich decoration, in the Byzantine manner, between the windows of its first story; but not completely characteristic of the transitional period, because still retaining the dentil in the arch mouldings, while the transitional houses all have the simple roll. (10:295)

A most important transitional palace. Its sculpture in the first story is peculiarly rich and curious; I think Venetian, in imitation of Byzantine. The sea story and first floor are of the first half of the thirteenth century, the rest modern. Observe that only one wing of the sea story is left, the other half having been modernized.[3] (11:362)

Façade of the Ca' da Mosto at Santi Apostoli (Photograph 2006)

Ca' da Mosto: detail of the façade, with second-order windows and paterae (Photograph 2014)

Newly restored section; part of the façade of Ca' da Mosto (Photograph 2014)

Second-order windows, paterae and *formelle* of Palazzo Falier at Santi Apostoli (Photograph 2014)

Formella of an eagle with rabbits and peacocks, façade of Palazzo Falier (Photograph 2009)

John Ruskin, *Windows of the Second Order: Casa Falier, St. Apostoli*, Plate 15 in *The Stones of Venice* II (10:295)

CASA FALIER

But for this range of windows, the little piazza SS Apostoli would be one of the least picturesque in Venice; to those, however, who seek it on foot, it becomes geographically interesting from the extraordinary involution of the alleys leading to it from the Rialto. In Venice, the straight road is usually by water, and the long road by land; but the difference of distance appears, in this case, altogether inexplicable. Twenty or thirty strokes of the oar will bring a gondola from the foot of the Rialto to that of Ponte SS Apostoli.

Looking back, on the other side of this canal, [the reader] will see the windows which, with the arcade of pointed arches beneath them, are the

Palazzo Falier at Santi Apostoli (Photograph 1998)

remains of the palace once belonging to the unhappy Doge Marino Faliero.[4] The balcony is, of course, modern, and the series of windows has been of greater extent, once terminated by a pilaster on the left hand, as well as on the right; but the terminal arches have been walled up. What remains, however, is enough, with its sculptured birds and dragons, to give the reader a very distinct idea of the second-order window in its perfect form. (10:295–7)

PALAZZO PRIULI BON AT SAN STAE

The advance of the Gothic spirit was, for a few years, checked by this compromise between the round and pointed arch. The truce, however, was at last broken, in consequence of the discovery that the keystone would do duty quite well in the form *a*, and the substitution of *b* at the head of the arch gives us the window of the third order, 3*b*, 3*d* and 3*e* in the Plate [*The Orders of Venetian Arches*]. The forms 3*a* and 3*c* are exceptional; the first occurring as we have seen, in the Corte del Remer, and in one other palace on the Grand Canal close to the church of St. Eustachio [Palazzo Priuli Bon]. (10:297)

Third-order windows of Palazzo Priuli Bon on the Grand Canal at S. Stae (Photograph 2013)

PONTE DEL PARADISO

At side of this house, above the pretty gabled
Madonna is a window of 3rd order ...
(Notebook 'House Book 1', p.5)

:
Arco del Paradiso on rio di S. Maria Formosa, with late
15th-century relief of the Madonna and donor, and
arms of the Foscari and Mocenigo families; behind the
Arco is a third-order window (Photograph 2013)

Third-order windows of Palazzo Querini, Campo delle Beccarie, Rialto (Photograph 2006). The Ca' Mazor, the house of Marco and Pietro Querini, was demolished after the plot of Bajamonte Tiepolo in 1310

PALAZZO QUERINI
(CAMPO DELLE BECCARIE, RIALTO)

The most perfect examples of the third order in Venice are the windows of the ruined palace of Marco Querini, the father-in-law of Bajamonte Tiepolo, in consequence of whose conspiracy against the government this palace was ordered to be razed in 1310; but it was only partially ruined, and was afterwards used as the common shambles. The Venetians have now made a poultry market of the lower story (the shambles being removed to a suburb), and a prison of the upper, though it is one of the most important and interesting monuments in the city, and especially valuable as giving us a secure date for the central form of these very rare transitional windows. (10:298)

Third-order windows of Palazzo Moro in Campo S. Bartolomeo (Photograph 2006)

PALAZZO MORO

Another example [of third order windows], less refined in workmanship, but, if possible, still more interesting, owing to the variety of its capitals, remains in the little piazza opening to the Rialto, on the St. Mark's side of the Grand Canal [in Campo S. Bartolomeo]. The house faces the bridge, and its second story has been built in the thirteenth century, above a still earlier Byzantine cornice remaining, or perhaps introduced, from some other ruined edifice, in the walls of the first floor. The windows of the second story are of pure third order, with their flanking pilaster and capitals varying constantly in the form of the flower or leaf introduced between their volutes. (10:299)

PALAZZO SAGREDO ON
THE GRAND CANAL

Another most important example [of the third-order window] exists in the lower story of the Casa Sagredo, on the Grand Canal, remarkable as having the early upright form (3b) with a somewhat later moulding. Many others occur in the fragmentary ruins in the streets; but the two boldest conditions which I found in Venice are those of the Chapter-house of the Frari, in which the Doge Francesco Dandolo was buried circa 1339; and those of the flank of the Ducal Palace itself, absolutely corresponding with those of the Frari, and therefore of inestimable value in determining the date of the palace. (10:299)

John Ruskin, *Windows of the Third and Fourth Orders: The Casa Sagredo*, photogravure, Plate F in *The Stones of Venice* II (10:299)

Palazzo Sagredo on the Grand Canal at S. Sofia (Photograph 1994)

Windows of Palazzo Sagredo on the Grand Canal at S. Sofia (Photograph 1994)

[The Palazzo Sagredo is] much defaced, but full of interest. Its sea story is restored; its first floor has a most interesting arcade of the early thirteenth-century third-order windows; its upper windows are the finest fourth and fifth orders of early fourteenth century; the group of fourth orders in the centre being brought into some resemblance to the late Gothic traceries by the subsequent introduction of the quatrefoils above them. (11:428)

John Ruskin, *Arabian Windows in Campo Santa Maria Mater Domini*, Plate 2 in *Examples of the Architecture of Venice* (11:320)

CAMPO SANTA MARIA MATER DOMINI

A most interesting little piazza surrounded by early Gothic houses, once of singular beauty: the arcade at its extremity, of fourth-order windows drawn in my folio work [*Arabian Windows in Campo Santa Maria Mater Domini*], is one of the earliest and loveliest of its kind in Venice. (11:392)

This group of windows is the only remnant of a small palace [Palazzetto Viaro Zane] modernized in all its other parts; but it is one of the richest fragments in the city, and a beautiful example of the fantastic arches which I believe to have been borrowed from the Arabs. I defer my special account of it, noting at present only what might otherwise have been supposed errors in the drawing, that two of the circular ornaments at the points of the arches are larger than the rest; that

Fourth-order windows of Palazzetto Viaro Zane in
Campo S. Maria Mater Domini (Photograph 2013)

Detail of windows and paterae, Casa degli Zane,
Campo S. Maria Mater Domini (Photograph 2013)

the lateral windows are broader than the three
intermediate ones; and that of the lateral windows
themselves, the one on the right is broader than
that on the left.

In nearly every group of windows in Venice,
belonging to this transitional or Arabic period,
the same thing takes place – one of the lateral
openings is larger than all the rest; and I have not
as yet been able to discover the reason for such an
arrangement, as these groups of windows appear to
have always lighted one room only. The tesselated
and fragmentary incrustations are of marble, the
capitals and shafts (I think) of Istrian stone, the
walls of brick, whether formerly incrusted or not
cannot now be discovered; the piece of balcony,
seen at the top of the plate, is of course modern.
(11:320)

In the houses at the side[5] is a group of second-
order windows with their intermediate crosses,
all complete, and well worth careful examination.
(11:392)

Casa degli Zane in Campo S. Maria Mater Domini
(Photograph 2013)

Lunette above the door of Ca' Bosso at Ponte S. Tomà
(Photograph 2013)

PONTE SAN TOMÀ (CA' BOSSO)

There is an interesting ancient doorway opening on the canal close to this bridge, probably of the twelfth century, and a good early Gothic door, opening upon the bridge itself.[6] (11:434)

The 13th-century arch of the water gate and entrance portal of Ca' Bosso on the rio di S. Tomà (Photograph 2013)

CAMPO SANTA MARGHERITA: PALAZZETTO FOSCOLO CORNER

A doorhead belonging to a small house of the thirteenth century Gothic, in the Campo Santa Margherita. The central shield, with its hovering angel and supporters, is cut out of one piece of stone; the rest of the tympanum is formed by small squares of cast brick, enclosed by narrow bars also of brick. There are seven patterns used for the squares ... and they are so arranged by the builder that whichever way the courses of them are read – laterally or upwards – two similar patterns shall never be in juxtaposition; and that no regular arrangement or recurrence of pattern in any definable disposition shall be traceable. At least I can myself discover none – the reader may try – every pattern in the drawing being in its proper place. The lintel and jambs of the door are of marble, and have Byzantine mouldings, correspondent to those of the doors of St. Mark's. It is very possible that they may be older than the brickwork. (11:341)

Palazzetto Foscolo Corner in Campo S. Margherita
(Photograph 1997)

PALAZZO CONTARINI DELLA PORTA DI FERRO

Palazzo Contarini della Porta di Ferro, near the Church of St. John and Paul: so called from the beautiful ironwork on a door, which was some time ago taken down by the proprietor and sold. Mr Rawdon Brown rescued some of the ornaments from the hands of the blacksmith who had bought them for old iron.

The head of the door is a very interesting stone arch of the early thirteenth century, already drawn in my folio work.[7]

In the interior court is a beautiful remnant of staircase, with a piece of balcony at the top, circa 1350, and one of the most richly and carefully wrought in Venice. The palace, judging by these remnants (all that are now left of it, except a single traceried window of the same date at the turn of the stair) must once have been among the most magnificent in Venice. (11:368)

Doorhead of Palazzetto Foscolo Corner
(Photograph 2013)

A 13th-century doorhead of Palazzo Contarini della Porta di Ferro (Photograph 2010)

Staircase and Gothic window, courtyard of Palazzo Contarini della Porta di Ferro (Photograph 2006)

Casa Porta di Ferro Contarini: Certainly the most graceful 14th century work I have found externally in Venice: at p.63 Gothic book [is] one of the arches of its balustrade, with one of the intermediate leafage groups, each foil of the spiral successively laid over the other some half an inch deep & beautifully modulated. (Notebook 'M', p.187)

John Ruskin, detail of the balustrade, Palazzo Contarini della Porta di Ferro, from Notebook 'Gothic Book', p.63. Ruskin Library, Lancaster

CHURCH OF THE CARMINI
(S. MARIA DEL CARMELO)

A most interesting church, of later thirteenth-century work but much altered and defaced. Its nave, in which the early shafts and capitals of the pure truncate form are unaltered, is very fine in effect; its lateral porch is quaint and beautiful, decorated with Byzantine circular sculptures and supported on two shafts, whose capitals are the most archaic examples of the pure Rose form that I know in Venice. (11:365)

The 13th-century Greek marble paterae on the lateral porch of the Carmini church (S. Maria del Carmelo) in Dorsoduro (Photograph 2013)[8]

CAMPIELLO DELLA CHIESA, ST LUCA (CA' MAGNO)

In the little Campiello St. Luca is a very precious Gothic door, rich in brickwork of the thirteenth century. (11:391)

It is an entrance to a courtyard; and must have been singularly beautiful before the sculpture on the pieces of inlaid stone was defaced. Neither the bearings nor design in the pointed arch, or circle above, are any more decipherable; but the brickwork remains entirely uninjured. It is composed of five kinds of bricks, all in regular

Doorhead of Ca' Magno, Campiello della Chiesa, S. Luca (Photograph 2013)

John Ruskin, ink drawing from Notebook 'House Book 2', p.49. Ruskin Library, Lancaster

lengths of about 10 inches: one quite plain, but either straight or curved according to the requirements of the design; another with a pattern of raised triangles on it; another with one of raised squares and circles alternately; another with a chain of small squares, and another with little oblique rhombs.

The sloping courses of bricks are gradually set at a less and less angle, so that the whole system radiates like the branches of a fir tree, becoming less and less inclined as it nears the ground. In order to be sure of my fact, I counted the courses of bricks, and measured their angles with the dripstone at five separate points from top to bottom ... Observe, especially, how valuable mere joints filled with mortar may become, when they are used by a man who knows what he is about. (11:344–5)

Palazzo Dandolo on the Grand Canal at S. Luca
(Photograph 2013)

PALAZZO DANDOLO ON THE GRAND CANAL

Between the Casa Loredan and Casa Bembo is a range of modern buildings, some of which occupy, I believe, the site of the palace once inhabited by the Doge Henry Dandolo [Doge of Venice 1192–1205]. Fragments of early architecture of the Byzantine school may still be traced in many places among their foundations, and two doors in the foundation of the Casa Bembo itself belong to the same group. There is only one existing palace, however, of any value on this spot, a very small but rich Gothic one of about 1300, with two groups of fourth-order windows in its second and third stories, and some Byzantine circular mouldings built into it above. This is still reported to have belonged to the family of Dandolo, and ought to be carefully preserved, as it is one of the most interesting and ancient Gothic palaces which yet remain. (11:370)

John Ruskin and John Hobbs, daguerreotype of the windows of Palazzo Zorzi Bon, *c*.1849, courtesy of K. and J. Jacobson

PALACE AT FONDAMENTA SAN SEVERO (PALAZZO ZORZI BON)

A palace that was to suffer a major loss of its beautiful marble revetment was the gothic Palazzo Zorzi Bon on the rio di San Severo, Castello. Before discovering its name, Ruskin referred to it in notebooks as 'my bacon palace', a nickname first used by his valet, John Hobbs, for the resemblance to streaky bacon of its 'rosso di Egitto' marble. In Notebook 'M' (1849–50) Ruskin noted, 'I regret the injury of this palace, more than all I have seen yet.' A daguerreotype of the façade windows was made in c.1849, from which he made the watercolour Windows of Palazzo Zorzi Bon on the Rio di San Severo, Venice.

It is on the canal behind the Palazzo Priuli: the most splendid deep red alabaster set in its window spandrils – along the main tier daguerreotyped – the marble is left in only one of the detached windows on the right – there it is the most vivid verd antique. The shafts of the main story are curious for the long capitals of the two next side, & short in centre. The shafts with the long capitals are of Verona marble. (Notebook 'M', pp 116–18)

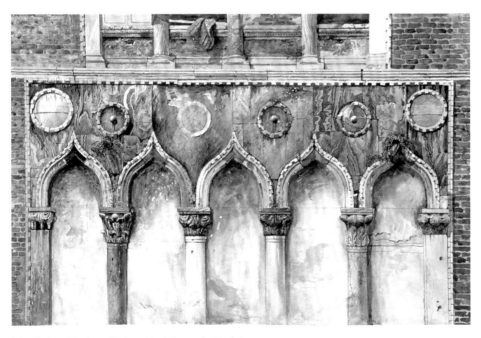

John Ruskin, *Windows of Palazzo Zorzi Bon on the Rio di San Severo, Venice*, *c*.1850, pencil, ink, watercolour and bodycolour, photograph courtesy of J.N. Bunney and S.E. Bunney

From the beginning of the thirteenth century there is found a singular increase of simplicity in all architectural ornamentation; the rich Byzantine capitals giving place to a pure and severe type hereafter to be described, and the rich sculptures vanishing from the walls, nothing but the marble facing remaining. One of the most interesting examples of this transitional state is a palace at San Severo, just behind the Casa Zorzi. This latter is a Renaissance building, utterly worthless in every respect, but known to the Venetian *ciceroni*; and by inquiring for it, and passing a little beyond it down the Fondamenta San Severo, the traveller will see, on the other side of the canal, a palace which the *ciceroni* never notice, but which is unique in Venice for the magnificence of the veined purple alabasters with which it has been decorated, and for the manly simplicity of the foliage of its capitals. Except in these it has no sculpture whatever, and its effect is dependent entirely upon colour. Disks of green serpentine are inlaid on the field of purple alabaster; and the pillars are alternately of red marble with white capitals, and of white marble with red capitals. Its windows appear of the third order; and the back of the palace, in a small and most picturesque court [Calle dell'Arco detta Bon], shows a group of windows which are, perhaps, the most superb examples of that order in Venice. But the windows to the front have, I think, been of the fifth order, and their cusps[9] have been cut away. (10:307–9)

The 'palace at San Severo' mentioned by Ruskin is Palazzo Zorzi Bon, next to Codussi's Palazzo Zorzi on the rio di S. Severo. Both palaces had originally belonged to the Zorzi family. The early Gothic building, now called Zorzi Bon, was let to a branch of the Bon family during the eighteenth century. Ruskin described it in The Stones as 'Palace at Fondamenta San Severo', referring to his watercolour drawing of its windows in a letter of 1877 to Count Zorzi (1846–1922) (see p.231).

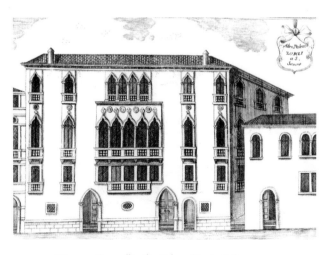

Vincenzo Coronelli, *Altro Palazzo Zorzi a S. Severo*, c.1709, engraving in *Singolarità di Venezia, i palazzi*, Museo Correr, Venice

Windows of Palazzo Zorzi Bon on the rio di S. Severo (Photograph 2013)

Fifth-order windows of Palazzo Gritti Badoer (Photograph 2012)

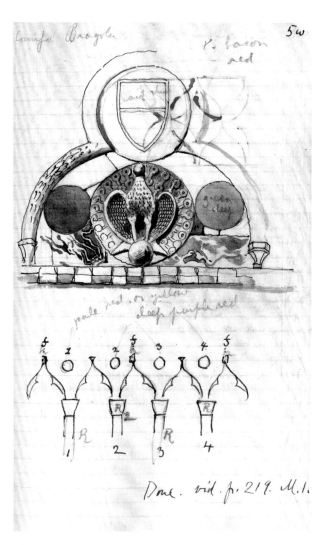

John Ruskin, *Palazzo [Gritti] Badoer*, Notebook 'Bit Book', p.78.
Ruskin Library, Lancaster

PALAZZO GRITTI BADOER IN
CAMPO SAN GIOVANNI IN BRAGORA
(CAMPO BANDIERA E MORO)

A magnificent example of the fourteenth-century
Gothic, circa 1310–1320, anterior to the Ducal
Palace, and showing beautiful ranges of the fifth-
order window with fragments of the original
balconies, and the usual lateral window larger than
any of the rest. In the centre of its arcade on the

first floor is the inlaid ornament drawn in Plate 8,
Vol. IX (9:11). The fresco painting on the walls[10]
is of later date; and I believe the heads which form
the finials have been inserted afterwards also, the
original windows having been pure fifth order.

The building is now a ruin, inhabited by the
lowest orders; the first floor, when I was last in
Venice, by a laundress. (11:363)

CHURCH OF THE CARITÀ:
ACCADEMIA DELLE BELLE ARTI

Once an interesting Gothic church of the fourteenth century, lately defaced.[11] The effect of its ancient façade may partly be guessed at from the pictures of Canaletto, but only guessed at; Canaletto being less to be trusted for renderings of details than the rudest and most ignorant painter of the thirteenth century. (11:365)

Notice above the door the two bas-reliefs of St. Leonard and St. Christopher, chiefly remarkable for their rude cutting at so late a date, 1377, but the niches under which they stand are unusual in their bent gables, and in the little crosses within circles which fill their cusps. (11:361)

Over the door are three of the most precious pieces of sculpture in Venice: her native work, dated, and belonging to the school of severe Gothic, which indicates the beginning of her Christian life in understanding of its real claims upon her. You see the infant sprawls on her knee in an ungainly manner; she herself sits with quiet maiden dignity, but in no manner of sentimental adoration ...

This is Venetian naturalism, showing their henceforward steady desire to represent things as they really (according to the workman's notions) might have existed. It begins first in this [fourteenth] century, separating itself from the Byzantine formalism – the movement being the same which was led by Giotto in Florence fifty

14th-century relief sculptures of the Madonna and Child, St Leonard and St Christopher at the entrance to the former Scuola di S. Maria della Carità, now the Accademia (Photograph 2014)

Relief sculpture of the Virgin and Child above entrance to the former Scuola di S. Maria della Carità (Photograph 2014)

Giovanni Antonio da Canal, called 'Canaletto', *Venice: Campo S. Vidal and S. Maria della Carità (The Stonemason's Yard)*, 1727–8, oil on canvas, National Gallery, London. Canaletto's picture shows the view towards the church and scuola of the Carità from Campo San Vidal. The campanile collapsed in 1744 and was not rebuilt

years earlier ... Accordingly, all the Venetian painting of any importance you are now to see in the Academy is subsequent to these sculptures. But these are fortunately dated – 1378 and 1384. Twenty years more will bring us out of the fourteenth century. And therefore, broadly, all the painter's art of Venice begins in the fifteenth. (24:149–50)

Church of S. Gregorio in Dorsoduro: view of the apse from the Grand Canal (Photograph 2013)

CHURCH OF SAN GREGORIO ON THE GRAND CANAL

An important church of the fourteenth century, now desecrated but still interesting. Its apse is on the little canal crossing from the Grand Canal to the Giudecca, beside the Church of the Salute, and is very characteristic of the rude ecclesiastical Gothic contemporary with the Ducal Palace. The entrance to its cloisters, from the Grand Canal, is somewhat later; a noble square door, with two windows on each side of it, the grandest examples in Venice of the late window of the fourth order. (11:388)

The west door of the church in Campo S. Gregorio (Photograph 2013)

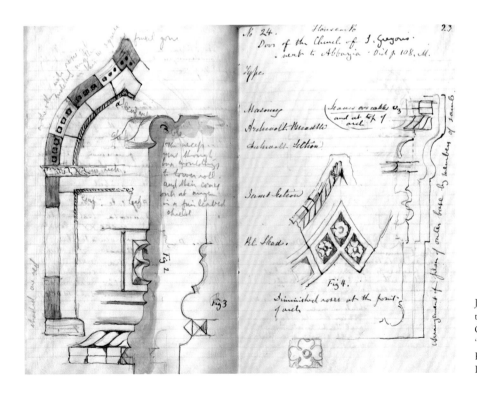

John Ruskin, 'Door of the Church of S. Gregorio', Notebook 'Door Book', p.23. Ruskin Library, Lancaster

PALAZZO PRIULI

A most important and beautiful early Gothic palace, at San Severo; the main entrance is from the Fondamenta San Severo, but the principal façade is on the other side, towards the canal. The entrance has been grievously defaced, having had winged lions filling the spandrils of its pointed arch, of which only feeble traces are now left; the façade has very early fourth-order windows in the lower story, and, above, the beautiful range of fifth-order windows drawn in the Plate, where the heads of the fourth-order range are also seen (note their inequality, the larger one at the flank). This palace has two most interesting traceried angle windows also, which, however, I believe are later than those on the façade. (11:399)

John Ruskin, *Windows of the Fifth Order from the Priuli Palace*, Plate 18 in *The Stones of Venice* II (10:310)

John Ruskin, *Part of the Palazzo Priuli, Venice*, c.1852, watercolour and bodycolour over graphite on wove paper. Presented by John Ruskin to the Ruskin Drawing School (University of Oxford) in 1875; transferred from the Ruskin Drawing School to the Ashmolean Museum, c.1949

Palazzo Bernardo on rio di S. Polo: view from Ponte Bernardo (Photograph 2014)

PALAZZO BERNARDO AT ST POLO

A glorious palace, on a narrow canal, in a part of Venice now inhabited by the lower orders only. It is rather late central Gothic, circa 1380–1400, but of the finest kind, and superb in its effect of colour when seen from the side ... taken as a whole I think that, after the Ducal Palace, this is the noblest in effect of all in Venice.[12] (11:364)

John Ruskin and John Hobbs, daguerreotype of Palazzo Bernardo at S. Polo, *c.*1850–52 (reversed image), Ruskin Library, Lancaster

PALAZZO GIOVANELLI
AT THE PONTE DI NOALE

A fine example of fifteenth-century Gothic, founded on the Ducal Palace. (11:384)

Gothic corner window of Palazzo Giovanelli on the rio di Noale, Cannaregio (Photograph 2009)

PALAZZO AGNUSDIO AND
PALAZZO ARIAN CICOGNA

When the Gothic feeling began more decidedly to establish itself, it evidently became a question with the Venetian builders how the intervals between the arches, now left blank by the abandonment of the Byzantine sculptures, should be enriched in accordance with the principles of the new school. Two most important examples are left of the experiments made at this period: one at the Ponte del Forner, at San Cassiano, a noble house [Ca' Agnusdio] in which the spandrils of the windows are filled by the emblems of the four Evangelists, sculptured in deep relief, and touching the edges of the arches with their expanded wings; the other now known as the Palazzo Cicogna near the church of San Sebastiano, in the quarter called 'of the Archangel Raphael', in which a large space of wall

'I think it has had narrow open Priuli [a reference to the windows of Palazzo Priuli] cusps now cut away' (Notebook 'Bit Book', p.31). Relief sculpture of St Mark the Evangelist, window on canal façade of Ca' Agnusdio (Photograph 2007)

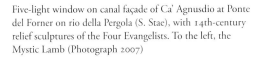

Five-light window on canal façade of Ca' Agnusdio at Ponte del Forner on rio della Pergola (S. Stae), with 14th-century relief sculptures of the Four Evangelists. To the left, the Mystic Lamb (Photograph 2007)

above the windows is occupied by an intricate but rude tracery of involved quatrefoils.

The question as to the mode of decorating the interval between the arches was suddenly and irrevocably determined by the builder of the Ducal Palace, who, as we have seen, taking his first idea from the traceries of the Frari, and arranging those traceries as best fitted his own purpose, designed the great arcade which thenceforward became the established model for every work of importance in Venice. (10:309)

Six-light window of Palazzo Arian Cicogna on the rio dell' Angelo Raffaele, Dorsoduro (Photograph 2008)

PALAZZO BARBARO ON THE GRAND CANAL, NEXT TO THE PALAZZO CAVALLI

These two buildings form the principal objects in the foreground of the view which almost every artist seizes on his first traverse of the Grand Canal, the Church of the Salute forming a most graceful distance. Neither is, however, of much value, except in general effect; but the Barbaro is the best, and the pointed arcade in its side wall, seen from the narrow canal between it and the Cavalli, is good Gothic of the earliest fourteenth-century type. (11:363)

The water gate of Palazzo Barbaro and angle of the façade between the Grand Canal and rio de l'Orso (Photograph 1999)

The early 15th-century Palazzo Barbaro on the Grand
Canal at San Vidal (Photograph 2014)

CASA D'ORO

In a letter to his father (21 September 1845), Ruskin had deplored the restorations being carried out at the Ca' d'Oro by the ballerina Marie Taglioni, who was responsible for ordering the demolition of the original staircase and the balconies overlooking the courtyard. The work was directed by the architect Giambattista Meduna, whose later restorations at St Mark's (1865–75) were to cause much controversy. Ruskin was determined to record as many details as he could before they disappeared forever. In his watercolour drawing of the palace he chose to leave blank the area that was being reconstructed, on the right-hand side of the façade.

... every hour is destructive of what I most value, and I must do what I can to save a little. On the Ca' d'Oro, the noblest Palace of the grand Canal, the stonemasons are hard at work, and of its once noble cornice there remains one fragment only. Had that gone, as in a day or two more it will, all knowledge of the contour of this noble building would have been lost for ever, for I can find no architectural drawings of anything here. (*Ruskin in Italy*, pp 208–9)

A noble pile of very quaint Gothic, once superb in general effect, but now destroyed by restorations. I saw the beautiful slabs of red marble, which formed the bases of its balconies, and were carved into noble spiral mouldings of strange sections, half a foot deep, dashed to pieces when I was last in Venice; its glorious interior staircase, by far the most interesting Gothic monument of the kind in Venice, had been carried away, piece by piece, and sold for waste

John Ruskin, *The Ca' d'Oro, Venice*, 1845, pencil, watercolour and bodycolour on toned paper, Ruskin Library, Lancaster

The 15th-century Ca' d'Oro on the Grand Canal
(Photograph 2008)

marble, two years before. Of what remains, the most beautiful portions are, or were, when I last saw them, the capitals of the windows in the upper story, most glorious sculpture of the fourteenth [sic] century. The fantastic window traceries are, I think, later; but the rest of the architecture of this palace is anomalous, and I cannot venture to give any decided opinion respecting it. Parts of its mouldings are quite Byzantine in character, but look somewhat like imitations. (11:370–71)

The Ca' d'Oro: capitals of the upper storey (Photograph 2014)

CHURCH OF SAN STEFANO

An interesting building of central Gothic, the best ecclesiastical example of it in Venice. The west entrance is much later than any of the rest, and is of the richest Renaissance Gothic, a little anterior to the Porta della Carta, and first-rate of its kind. The manner of the introduction of the figure of the angel at the top of the arch is full of beauty. Note the extravagant crockets and cusp finials as signs of decline. (11:433–4)

Church of S. Stefano: early 15th-century sculpture of an angel above the entrance portal (Photograph 2009)

CROCKETS AND FINIALS

Ruskin believed the increasingly florid decoration of the crockets and finials of the arch to be a corrupt form of Gothic, representing a decline in Venetian architecture from the late fourteenth century onwards. The theme of his discussion was 'Temperance and Intemperance in Curvature'. (11:8–12)

Crockets on the upper left arch of St Mark's, west side (Photograph 2014)

John Ruskin, *Temperance and Intemperance in Curvature* (detail), Fig.4, Plate 1 in *The Stones of Venice* III (11:8)

In the various forms assumed by the later Gothic of Venice, there are one or two features which, under other circumstances, would not have been signs of decline; but in the particular manner of their occurrence here, indicate the fatal weariness of decay. Of all these features the most distinctive are its crockets and finials.

There is not to be found a single crocket or finial upon any part of the Ducal Palace built during the fourteenth century; and although they occur on contemporary and on some much earlier buildings, they either indicate detached examples of schools not properly Venetian, or are signs of incipient decline.

The reason of this is that the finial is properly the ornament of gabled architecture; it is the compliance, in the minor features of the building,

The 15th-century Porta della Carta, gateway to the Ducal Palace,
and the north-west 'Judgment' angle (Photograph 2008)

Detail of the Porta della Carta (Photograph 2014)

with the spirit of its towers, ridged roof and spires. Venetian building is not gabled, but horizontal in its roofs and general masses; therefore the finial is a feature contradictory to its spirit, and is adopted only in that search for morbid excitement which is the infallible indication of decline. When it occurs earlier, it is on fragments of true gabled architecture, as, for instance, on the porch of the Carmini.

And not content with this exuberance in the external ornaments of the arch, the finial interferes with its traceries. The increased intricacy of these, as such, being a natural process in the development of Gothic, would have been no evil; but they are corrupted by the enrichment of the finial at the point of the cusp.

In the Porta della Carta, the vice reaches its climax. (11:11–14)

CHURCH OF SANTA MARIA DELL'ORTO

An interesting example of Renaissance Gothic, the traceries of the windows being very rich and quaint. (11:395)

The restoration of the Madonna dell'Orto church (begun 1969) was the first major project of a British private committee founded for the preservation of Italian monuments. The Italian Art and Archives Rescue Fund (IAARF) was formed in December 1966 in response to damage caused by the catastrophic floods of November 1966, which badly affected both Venice and Florence. It was chaired by Sir Ashley Clarke, who subsequently moved to Venice with his wife, Frances, in order to oversee operations. In 1971 the IAARF became the Venice in Peril Fund, chaired in London by John Julius Norwich.

Church of the Madonna dell'Orto (S. Maria dell'Orto) in Cannaregio (Photograph 2013)

Palazzo Corner Contarini dei Cavalli on the Grand Canal at
S. Luca (Photograph 2013)

PALAZZO CAVALLI, NEXT THE CASA GRIMANI, BUT ON THE OTHER SIDE OF THE NARROW CANAL

Good Gothic, founded on the Ducal Palace, circa 1380. The capitals of the first story are remarkably rich in the deep fillets at the necks. The crests, heads of sea-horses, inserted between the windows, appear to be later, but are very fine of their kind. (11:368)

... the best example of the florid capital I have yet found – the palace near Post Office ...[13] (Notebook 'M2', p.70)

Gothic windows and sea-horse on the façade of Palazzo Cavalli
(Photograph 2013)

The Giustinian palaces (left) and Ca' Foscari on the Grand Canal (Photograph 2013)

PALAZZO FOSCARI ON THE GRAND CANAL

The noblest example in Venice of the fifteenth-century Gothic, founded on the Ducal Palace, but lately restored and spoiled, all but the stonework of the main windows. The restoration was necessary, however: for, when I was in Venice in 1845, this palace was a foul ruin; its great hall a mass of mud, used as the back receptacle of a stonemason's yard;

and its rooms whitewashed, and scribbled over with indecent caricatures. It has since been partially strengthened and put in order; but as the Venetian municipality have now given it to the Austrians to be used as barracks, it will probably soon be reduced to its former condition.[14] The lower palaces at the side of this building are said by some to have belonged to the younger Foscari. (11:378)

PALAZZO GIUSTINIAN, NEXT TO THE CASA FOSCARI, ON THE GRAND CANAL

Lazari, I know not on what authority, says that this palace was built by the Giustiniani family before 1428.[15] It is one of those founded directly on the Ducal Palace, together with the Casa Foscari at its side: and there could have been no doubt of their date on this ground; but it would be interesting, after what we have seen of the progress of the Ducal Palace, to ascertain the exact year of the erection of any of these imitations. This palace contains some unusually rich detached windows, full of tracery. (11:388)

Window of Ca' Foscari (Photograph 2014)

Palazzo Dandolo-Mocenigo (Hotel Danieli): windows of the
piano nobile (Photograph 2014)

PALAZZO NANI-MOCENIGO
(NOW HOTEL DANIELI)

A glorious example of the central Gothic, nearly
contemporary with the finest parts of the Ducal
Palace. Though less impressive in effect than that
of the Casa Foscari or Casa Bernardo, it is of purer
architecture than either; and quite unique in the
delicacy of the form of the cusps in the central
group of windows, which are shaped like broad
scimitars, the upper foil of the windows being very
small. If the traveller will compare these windows
with the neighbouring traceries of the Ducal
Palace, he will easily perceive the peculiarity.
(11:395)

*From 1822 the second floor of the fifteenth-century
Palazzo Dandolo-Mocenigo was occupied by the Hotel
Danieli, where Ruskin and his parents stayed on their
first visit to Venice in 1835. The proprietor, Joseph
Dal Niel, acquired the rest of the building in 1840,
renovated it, and reopened the Danieli in 1845.*

CALLE DEI GIARDINI
(NOW THE VIA GARIBALDI), CASTELLO

Close to the gardens [the Giardini Pubblici] on the right is a door worth daguerreotyping; it has heads at the side of a richly crocketed pediment, like the tomb, but the heads carry niches, with octagonal canopies ... (Notebook 'M', p.59)

Late 14th-century entrance portal to the former Ospizio delle Putte in Via Garibaldi, Castello; low-relief sculpture of the Saviour blessing, with three saints (Photograph 2013)

FONDAMENTA S. ANNA, CASTELLO

A little beyond the gardens, at the Fondamenta St Anna, there are four low windows ... with three circles between; that on the left, six birds about a rose, very rich – on r[igh]t two beasts, in centre a flat sun about *IHS* like something in London, evidently later work [a fifteenth-century Eucharistic monogram]. Gutter above dogtoothed and bracketed. (Notebook 'M', p.60)

Gothic house in Fondamenta S. Anna, Castello (Photograph 2013)

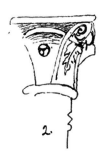

John Ruskin, Sketch of capital of house at Fondamenta S. Anna, Notebook 'M', p.60. Ruskin Library, Lancaster

Window and paterae of a house in
Fondamenta S. Anna (Photograph 2004)

Madonna degli Alberetti (*c.*1420–30), Istrian stone
sculpture, Campo S. Pietro di Castello (Photograph 2013)

CAMPO S. PIETRO DI CASTELLO

It may be useful to note a little Madonna in a
corner near the church of San Pietro di Castello,
under an arch ... (Notebook 'M', p.60)

CHURCH OF SS GIOVANNI E PAOLO

An impressive church, though none of its Gothic is comparable with that of the North, or with that of Verona. The western door is interesting as one of the last conditions of Gothic design passing into Renaissance, very rich and beautiful of its kind, especially the wreath of fruit and flowers which forms its principal moulding. (11:384)

Church of Santi Giovanni e Paolo: the west portal (Photograph 2014)

In his preface to the second edition (1855) of The Seven Lamps of Architecture, *Ruskin commented:* 'I have great respect for Venetian Gothic, but only as one among many early schools. My reason for devoting so much time to Venice was not that her architecture is the best in existence, but that it exemplifies, in the smallest compass, the most interesting facts of architectural history. The Gothic of Verona is far nobler than that of Venice, and that of Florence nobler than that of Verona.' (8:12–13)

Capitals and mouldings of the west portal, church of Santi Giovanni e Paolo (Photograph 2014)

PALAZZO PISANI (MORETTA) ON THE GRAND CANAL

The latest Venetian Gothic, just passing into Renaissance. The capitals of the first-floor windows are, however, singularly spirited and graceful, very daringly undercut, and worth careful examination. The Paul Veronese, once the glory of this palace, is, I believe, not likely to remain in Venice.[16] (11:398)

The 15th-century Palazzo Pisani Moretta on the Grand Canal
(Photograph 2014)

PALAZZO CONTARINI FASAN ON THE GRAND CANAL

The richest work of the fifteenth-century domestic Gothic in Venice, but notable more for riches than excellence of design. In one respect, however, it deserves to be regarded with attention, as showing how much beauty and dignity may be bestowed on a very small and unimportant dwelling-house by Gothic sculpture. Foolish criticisms upon it have appeared in English accounts of foreign buildings, objecting to it on the ground of its being 'ill-proportioned'; the simple fact being that there was no room in this part of the canal for a wider house, and that its builder made its rooms as comfortable as he could, and its windows and balconies of a convenient size for those who were to see through them, and stand on them, and left the 'proportions' outside to take care of themselves; which indeed they have very sufficiently done; for though the house thus honestly confesses its diminutiveness, it is nevertheless one of the principal ornaments of the very noblest reach of the Grand Canal, and would be nearly as great a loss, if it were destroyed, as the Church of La Salute itself. (11:368–9)

The traceried parapet is chiefly used in the Gothic of the North, from which the above example, in the Casa Contarini Fasan, is directly derived. It is, when well designed, the richest and most beautiful of all forms, and many of the best buildings of France and Germany are dependent for half their effect upon it; its only fault being a slight tendency to fantasticism. It was never frankly received in Venice, where the architects had unfortunately returned to the Renaissance forms before the flamboyant parapets were fully developed in the North; but, in the early stage of the Renaissance, a kind of pierced parapet was employed, founded on the old Byzantine interwoven traceries; that is to say, the slab of stone was pierced here and there with holes, and then an interwoven pattern traced on the surface round them. (11:286)

Palazzo Contarini Fasan (*c.*1470) on the Grand Canal (Photograph 2013)

Wheel-tracery on balconies of the 15th-century Palazzo Contarini Fasan (Photograph 2013)

Parapet of Ca' d'Oro (Photograph 2014)

ROOF PARAPETS

Of these roof parapets of Venice, the examples which remain differ from those of all other cities of Italy in their purely ornamental character.
They are not battlements, properly so called, still less machicolated cornices, such as crown the fortress palaces of the great mainland nobles; but merely adaptations of the light and crown-like ornaments which crest the walls of the Arabian mosque. Nor are even these generally used on the main walls of the palaces themselves. They occur on the Ducal Palace, on the Casa d'Oro and, some years back, were still standing on the Fondaco de' Turchi, but the majority of the Gothic palaces have the plain dog-tooth cornice under the tiled projecting roof; and the highly decorated parapet is employed only on the tops of walls which surround courts or gardens, and which, without such decoration, would have been utterly devoid of interest.

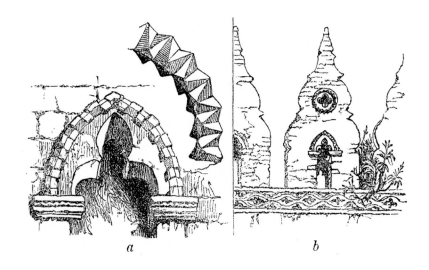

a   *b*

John Ruskin, *Roof Parapet of a House in the Calle del Bagatin*, Fig.23 (a) and (b) in *The Stones of Venice* II (10:282)

Terracotta crenellations on wall of Palazzo Marcello, rio del Gaffaro, Dorsoduro (Photograph 2013)

The figure [bottom of opposite page] represents part of a parapet in the Calle del Bagatin, between San Giovanni Gristostomo and San Canzian: the whole is of brick, and the mouldings particularly sharp and varied, the height of each separate pinnacle being about four feet, crowning a wall twelve or fifteen feet high. A piece of the moulding which surrounds the quatrefoil is given larger in the figure at *a*, together with the top of the small arch below, having the common Venetian dentil round it, and a delicate little moulding with dog-tooth ornament to carry the flanks of the arch. The moulding of the brick is, throughout, sharp and beautiful in the highest degree.

The parapets of the palaces themselves were lighter and more fantastic, consisting of narrow lance-like spires of marble, set between the broader pinnacles, which were in such cases generally carved into the form of a *fleur-de-lis*: the French word gives the reader the best idea of the form, though he must remember that this use of the lily for the parapets has nothing to do with France, but is the carrying out of the Byzantine system of floral ornamentation, which introduced the outline of the lily everywhere: so that I have found it convenient to call its most beautiful capitals, the lily capitals of St. Mark's. The decorations of the parapet were completed by attaching gilded balls of metal to the extremities of the leaves of the lilies, and of the intermediate spires, so as literally to form for the wall a diadem of silver touched upon the points with gold, the image being rendered still more distinct in the Casa d'Oro, by variation in the height of the pinnacles, the highest being in the centre of the front. (10:283)

PALAZZO BRAGADIN CARABBA

At Ponte del Teatro Malibran: a beautiful balcony with the trefoiled arch and cherubs' heads filling the spaces, a fine case of transition. The slab at the base dentiled instead of cabled, & fine lions at angles. (Notebook 'M', p.43)

Balcony of Palazzo Bragadin Carabba on the rio del Malibran (Photograph 2006)

CAMPO OF SAN BENEDETTO

Do not fail to see the superb, though partly ruinous, Gothic palace[17] fronting this little square. It is very late Gothic, just passing into Renaissance; unique in Venice, in masculine character, united with the delicacy of the incipient style. Observe especially the brackets of the balconies, the flower-work on the cornices, and the arabesques on the angles of the balconies themselves. (11:364)

Never imitate anything but natural forms, and those the noblest, in the completed parts. The degradation of the cinquecento manner of decoration was not owing to its naturalism, to its faithfulness of imitation, but to its imitation of ugly, i.e. unnatural things. So long as it restrained itself to sculpture of animals and flowers, it remained noble. The balcony from a house in the Campo St. Benedetto at Venice, shows one of the earliest occurrences of the cinquecento arabesque. (8:175)

John Ruskin, *Balcony in the Campo S. Benedetto*, engraving by R.P. Cuff, Plate 11 in *The Seven Lamps of Architecture* (8:175)

CORTE NUOVA ON THE RIO DELLA SENSA

Close to [the Scuola Vecchia della Misericordia] on the right-hand side of the canal, which is crossed by the wooden bridge, is one of the richest Gothic doors in Venice, remarkable for the appearance of antiquity in the general design and stiffness of its figures, though it bears its date, 1505.[18] Its extravagant crockets are almost the only features which, but for this written date, would at first have confessed its lateness; but on examination, the figures will be found as bad and spiritless as they are apparently archaic, and completely exhibiting the Renaissance palsy of imagination. The general effect is, however, excellent, the whole arrangement having been borrowed from earlier work. The action of the statue of the Madonna, who extends her robe to shelter a group of diminutive figures, representative of the Society for whose house the sculpture was executed,[19] may also be seen in most of the later Venetian figures of the Virgin which occupy similar situations. The image of Christ is placed in a medallion on her breast, thus fully, though conventionally, expressing the idea of self-support, which is so often partially indicated by the great religious painters in their representations of the infant Jesus. (11:394)

Entrance to Corte Nuova on Fondamenta della Misericordia, rio della Sensa, Cannaregio. Madonna of the Misericordia with kneeling friars, angels and saints: late 14th-century sculptures, with later decorative additions (Photograph 2013)

John Ruskin and John Hobbs, daguerreotype of the windows of Palazzo Grandiben at Ponte Erizzo, Arsenale, *c.*1849–50, courtesy of K. and J. Jacobson

PALAZZO GRANDIBEN AT PONTE ERIZZO, SAN MARTINO, ARSENALE

The uppermost of the three lower series in the Plate [*Windows of the Early Gothic Palaces*] shows this [fifth] order in its early purity; associated with intermediate decorations like those of the Byzantines, from a palace once belonging to the Erizzo family[20] near the Arsenal. The ornaments appear to be actually of Greek workmanship (except, perhaps, the two birds over the central arch, which are bolder and more free in treatment) and built into the Gothic fronts; showing, however, the early date of the whole by the manner of their insertion, corresponding exactly with that employed in the Byzantine palaces, and by the covering of the intermediate spaces with sheets of marble, which, however, instead of being laid over the entire wall, are now confined to the immediate spaces between and above the windows, and are bounded by a dentil moulding. (10:305)

Ruskin made a daguerreotype of the Veneto-Byzantine paterae and formelle above the five-light window of Palazzo Grandiben at Ponte Erizzo, near Arsenale, and used it as the basis for part of his drawing Windows of the Early Gothic Palaces *(see frontispiece to this book, the daguerreotype [above left] and the detail of his drawing [top of p.141]). He could scarcely have imagined that less than fifty years later his photograph would have become a unique record of that decorative complex in situ. Alberto Rizzi[21] has described as 'vandalous' the removal of ornamental reliefs from the Grandiben palace in 1894, when the valuable marbles were stripped from the façade and acquired by the antiquarian dealer Sig. Carrer, who sold them on to Baron Giorgio Franchetti (1865–1922). In 1896 Franchetti bought the Ca' d'Oro, where in due course these works, together with other artefacts from the façade of Palazzo Grandiben, reappeared as decorations set into the walls of the courtyard. In the late twentieth century, they were put in storage and replaced by the copies seen today.*

Window of the 15th-century Palazzo Grandiben at Ponte Erizzo, Arsenale (Photograph 2010)

John Ruskin, detail from *Windows of the Early Gothic Palaces*, photogravure from line engraving after a daguerreotype (*c.*1849–50), Plate 17 of *The Stones of Venice* II (10:302).

The section from Ruskin's drawing, a unique record drawn from his daguerreotype, shows the Palazzo Grandiben sculptures *in situ* before their removal in 1894

Courtyard window of Ca' d'Oro with copies of various *formelle* and paterae taken from Ca' Grandiben in the late 19th century (Photograph 2013)

Two *formelle* and a circular patera, 20th-century copies of the Veneto-Byzantine carvings taken from the façade of Ca' Grandiben in the late 19th century and installed above the courtyard window of Ca' d'Oro. The originals are in storage.

Left: a griffon with a bird on its back attacks a deer; below it, two lions rampant. *Centre*: storks drinking from a vase. *Right*: Tree of Life, with four birds. (Photograph 2014)

In the last paragraph of The Nature of Gothic, *Ruskin advised:*

Lastly, *read* the sculpture. Preparatory to reading it, you will have to discover whether it is legible (and, if legible, it is nearly certain to be worth reading). On a good building, the sculpture is always so set, and on such a scale, that at the ordinary distance from which the edifice is seen, the sculpture shall be thoroughly intelligible and interesting. In order to accomplish this, the uppermost statues will be ten or twelve feet high, and the upper ornamentation will be colossal, increasing in fineness as it descends, till on the foundation it will often be wrought as if for a precious cabinet in a king's chamber; but the spectator will not notice that the upper sculptures are colossal. He will merely feel that he can see them plainly, and make them all out at his ease.

And having ascertained this, let him set himself to read them. Thenceforward the criticism of the building is to be conducted precisely on the same principles as that of a book; and it must depend on the knowledge, feeling, and not a little on the industry and perseverance of the reader, whether, even in the case of the best works, he either perceive them to be great, or feel them to be entertaining. (10:269)

Two paterae and a *formella*, copies of the Veneto-Byzantine carvings taken from the façade of Ca' Grandiben in the late 19th-century and installed above the courtyard window of Ca' d'Oro. *Centre*: a lion attacks a deer; two lions stand on acanthus leaves (Photograph 2014)

THE DUCAL PALACE

A model of all perfection – the Doge's palace at Venice: its general arrangement, a hollow square; its principal façade, an oblong, elongated to the eye by a range of thirty-four small arches, and thirty-five columns, while it is separated by a richly-canopied window in the centre, into two massive divisions, whose height and length are nearly as four to five; the arcades which give it length being confined to the lower story, and the upper, between its broad windows, left a mighty surface of smooth marble, chequered with blocks of alternate rose-colour and white. It would be impossible, I believe, to invent a more magnificent arrangement of all that is in building most dignified and most fair.

The Seven Lamps of Architecture (8:111)

It is the central building of the world.

The Stones of Venice I (9:38)

THE FRONT OF THE DOGE'S PALACE at Venice is the purest and most chaste model that I can name of the fit application of colour to public buildings. The sculpture and mouldings are all white; but the wall surface is chequered with marble blocks of pale rose, the chequers being in no wise harmonised, or fitted to the forms of the windows; but looking as if the surface had been completed first, and the windows cut out of it. (8:183)

As soon as colour began to be used in broad and opposed fields, it was perceived that the mass of it destroyed its brilliancy, and it was tempered by chequering it with some other colour or colours in smaller quantities, mingled with minute portions of pure white ... Of all the chromatic decoration of the Gothic palaces, there is hardly a fragment left. Happily, in the pictures of Gentile Bellini, the fresco colouring of the Gothic palaces is recorded, as it still remained in his time; not with rigid

accuracy, but quite distinctly enough to enable us, by comparing it with the existing coloured designs in the manuscripts and glass of the period, to ascertain precisely what it must have been.

The walls were generally covered with chequers of very warm colour, a russet inclining to scarlet more or less relieved with white, black, and grey; as still seen in the only example which, having been executed in marble, has been perfectly preserved, the front of the Ducal Palace. This, however, owing to the nature of its materials, was a peculiarly simple example; the ground is white, crossed with double bars of pale red, and in the centre of each chequer there is a cross, alternately black with a red centre and red with a black centre where the arms cross. (11:25–7)

The Ducal Palace has two principal façades: one towards the sea, the other towards the Piazzetta. The seaward side, and, as far as the seventh main

The Ducal Palace (Photograph 1998)

The 'Eastern Windows' on the south façade of the Ducal Palace
(Photograph 2013)

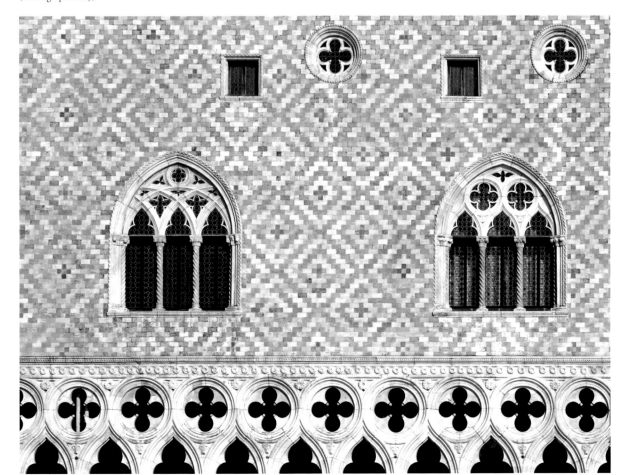

arch inclusive on the Piazzetta side, is work of the
early part of the fourteenth century, some of it
perhaps even earlier; while the rest of the Piazzetta
side is of the fifteenth. The difference in age has
been gravely disputed by the Venetian antiquaries,
who have examined many documents on the
subject, and quoted some which they never
examined. I have myself collated most of the
written documents, and one document more,
to which the Venetian antiquaries never thought
of referring: the masonry of the palace itself. That
masonry changes at the centre of the eighth arch
from the sea angle on the Piazzetta side. It has been
of comparatively small stones up to that point; the
fifteenth-century work instantly begins with larger
stones 'brought from Istria, a hundred miles away'.
The older work is of Istrian stone also but of
different quality. The ninth shaft from the sea in
the lower arcade, and the seventeenth, which is
above it, in the upper arcade, commence the series
of fifteenth-century shafts. These two are
somewhat thicker than the others, and carry the
party wall of the Sala del Scrutinio. (9:52–3)

The Gothic art of Venice was separated by the
building of the Ducal Palace into two distinct
periods; and in all the domestic edifices which
were raised for half a century after its completion,
their characteristic and chiefly effective portions
were more or less directly copied from it. The fact
is, that the Ducal Palace was the great work of
Venice at this period, itself the principal effort of
her imagination, employing her best architects in
its masonry, and her best painters in its decoration,
for a long series of years; and we must receive it as
a remarkable testimony to the influence which it
possessed over the minds of those who saw it in its
progress, that, while in the other cities of Italy
every palace and church was rising in some original
and daily more daring form, the majesty of this
single building was able to give pause to the Gothic
imagination in its full career; stayed the restlessness
of innovation in an instant, and forbade the powers
which had created it thenceforth to exert

The Ducal Palace: view from the campanile of St Mark's,
looking east (Photograph 2009)

themselves in new directions, or endeavour to
summon an image more attractive. (10:328)

The Ducal Palace is arranged somewhat in the form
of a hollow square, of which one side faces the
Piazzetta, and another the quay called the Riva de'
Schiavoni; the third is on the dark canal called the
'Rio del Palazzo', and the fourth joins the Church
of St. Mark.

Of this fourth side, therefore, nothing can be
seen. Of the other three sides we shall have to speak
constantly; and they will be respectively called, that
towards the Piazzetta, the 'Piazzetta Façade'; that
towards the Riva de' Schiavoni, the 'Sea Façade'; and
that towards the Rio del Palazzo, the 'Rio Façade'.
This Rio, or canal, is usually looked upon by the
traveller with great respect, or even horror, because
it passes under the Bridge of Sighs. It is, however,
one of the principal thoroughfares of the city; and
the bridge and its canal together occupy, in the
mind of a Venetian, very much the position of Fleet
Street and Temple Bar in that of a Londoner – at
least, at the time when Temple Bar was occasionally
decorated with human heads. (10:328–31)

We must now proceed to obtain some rough idea of
the appearance and distribution of the palace itself;
but its arrangement will be better understood by
supposing ourselves raised some hundred and fifty
feet above the point in the lagoon in front of it, so
as to get a general view of the Sea Façade and Rio

Façade (the latter in very steep perspective), and to look down into its interior court. In this drawing we have merely to notice that, of the two bridges seen on the right, the uppermost, above the black canal, is the Bridge of Sighs; the lower one is the Ponte della Paglia, the regular thoroughfare from quay to quay, and, I believe, called the Bridge of Straw, because the boats which brought straw from the mainland used to sell it at this place.

The corner of the palace, rising above this bridge, and formed by the meeting of the Sea Façade and Rio Façade, will always be called the Vine angle, because it is decorated by a sculpture of the drunkenness of Noah. The angle opposite will be called the Fig-tree angle, because it is decorated

by a sculpture of the Fall of Man. The long and narrow range of building, of which the roof is seen in perspective behind this angle, is the part of the palace fronting the Piazzetta; and the angle under the pinnacle most to the left of the two which terminate it will be called, for a reason presently to be stated, the Judgment angle. Within the square formed by the building is seen its interior court (with one of its wells), terminated by small and fantastic buildings of the Renaissance period, which face the Giants' Stair, of which the extremity is seen sloping down on the left. (10:331–2)

In the bird's-eye view [below], it will be noticed that the two windows on the right are lower than

John Ruskin, *The Ducal Palace, Bird's-eye View*, woodcut, Fig.37 in *The Stones of Venice* II (10:331)

The west and south façades of the Ducal Palace, seen from
the Molo (Photograph 1998)

the other four of the façade. In this arrangement
there is one of the most remarkable instances
I know of the daring sacrifice of symmetry to
convenience, which was noticed as one of the chief
noblenesses of the Gothic schools. (10:333–4)

In nearly the centre of the Sea Façade, and between
the first and second windows of the Great Council
Chamber, is a large window to the ground,
opening on a balcony, which is one of the chief
ornaments of the palace, and will be called in
future the 'Sea Balcony'. (10:335)

The façade which looks on the Piazzetta is very
nearly like this to the Sea, but the greater part
of it was built in the fifteenth century when people
had become studious of their symmetries. Its side

windows are all on the same level. Two light the
west end of the Great Council Chamber, one lights
a small room anciently called the Quarantia Civile
Nuova; the other three, and the central one, with
a balcony like that to the Sea, light another large
chamber, called Sala del Scrutinio, or 'Hall of
Inquiry', which extends to the extremity of the
palace above the Porta della Carta.

We have seen that there were three principal
styles of Venetian architecture: Byzantine, Gothic,
and Renaissance.

The Ducal Palace, which was the great work
of Venice, was built successively in the three styles.
There was a Byzantine Ducal Palace, a Gothic
Ducal Palace, and a Renaissance Ducal Palace.
The second superseded the first totally: a few stones
of it (if indeed so much) are all that is left. But the

Venice enthroned as Justice, 14th-century relief sculpture on the west (Piazzetta) façade (Photograph 2009)

figure sculptures above the capitals. These, observe, are the very corner-stones of the edifice, and in them we may expect to find the most important evidences of the feeling, as well as of the skill, of the builder. If he has anything to say to us of the purpose with which he built the palace, it is sure to be said here; if there was any lesson which he wished principally to teach to those for whom he built, here it is sure to be inculcated; if there was any sentiment which they themselves desired to have expressed in the principal edifice of their city, this is the place in which we may be sure of finding it legibly inscribed.

Now the first two angles, of the Vine and Fig-tree, belong to the old, or true Gothic, palace; the third angle belongs to the Renaissance imitation of it: therefore, at the first two angles, it is the Gothic spirit which is going to speak to us; and, at the third, the Renaissance spirit.

third superseded the second in part only, and the existing building is formed by the union of the two. (10:336)

The great façade which fronts the spectator looks southward. Hence the two traceried windows lower than the rest, and to the right of the spectator, may be conveniently distinguished as the 'Eastern Windows'. There are two others like them, filled with tracery, and at the same level, which look upon the narrow canal between the Ponte della Paglia and the Bridge of Sighs: these we may conveniently call the 'Canal Windows'. The reader will observe a vertical line in this dark side of the palace, separating its nearer and plainer wall from a long four-storied range of rich architecture. This more distant range is entirely Renaissance. (10:332–3)

The first point to which the reader's attention ought to be directed is the choice of subject in the great

The south-west 'Fig-tree' angle of the Ducal Palace, with 14th-century sculptures of St Michael (above) and Adam and Eve (Photograph 2014)

The most characteristic sentiment of all that we traced in the working of the Gothic heart, was the frank confession of its own weakness; and I must anticipate, for a moment, the results of our enquiry in subsequent chapters, so far as to state that the principal element in the Renaissance spirit is its firm confidence in its own wisdom.

Hear then, the two spirits speak for themselves.

The first main sculpture of the Gothic palace is on what I have called the angle of the Fig-tree:

Its subject is the FALL OF MAN

The second sculpture is on the angle of the Vine:

Its subject is the DRUNKENNESS OF NOAH

The Renaissance sculpture is on the Judgment angle:

Its subject is the JUDGMENT OF SOLOMON

It is impossible to overstate, or to regard with too much admiration, the significance of this single fact. It is as if the palace had been built at various epochs, and preserved uninjured to this day, for the sole purpose of teaching us the difference in the temper of the two schools. (10:358–9)

THE FIG-TREE ANGLE: THE FALL OF MAN

I have called the sculpture on the Fig-tree angle the principal one, because it is at the central bend of the palace, where it turns to the Piazzetta (the façade upon the Piazzetta being, as we saw above, the more important one in ancient times). The great capital, which sustains this Fig-tree angle, is also by far more elaborate than the head of the pilaster under the Vine angle, marking the pre-eminence of the former in the architect's mind. It is impossible to say which was first executed, but that of the Fig-tree angle is somewhat rougher in execution, and more stiff in the design of the figures, so I rather suppose it to have been the earliest completed.

Adam and Eve, 14th-century sculptures on the south-west 'Fig-tree' angle of the Ducal Palace (Photograph 2009)

Adam and the fig-tree (Photograph 2014)

The figures of Adam and Eve, sculptured on each side of the Fig-tree angle, are more stiff than those of Noah and his sons, but are better fitted for their architectural service; and the trunk of the tree, with the angular body of the serpent writhed around it, is more nobly treated as a terminal group of lines than that of the vine.

In both the subjects, of the Fall and the Drunkenness, the tree, which forms the chiefly decorative portion of the sculpture – fig in the

Adam (detail) on the south-west angle of the Ducal Palace
(Photograph 2014)

tempted the sculptor to greater effort, he has passed the proper limits of his art, and cut the upper stems so delicately that half of them have been broken away by the casualties to which the situation of the sculpture necessarily exposes it.

While it may be assumed as a law that fine modulation of surface in light becomes quickly invisible as the object retires, there are a softness and mystery given to the harder markings, which enable them to be safely used as media of expression. There is an exquisite example of this use, in the head of the Adam of the Ducal Palace. It is only at the height of 17 or 18 feet above the eye; nevertheless, the sculptor felt it was no use to trouble himself about drawing the corners of the mouth, or the lines of the lips, delicately, at that distance; his object has been to mark them clearly, and to prevent accidental shadows from concealing them or altering their expression. The lips are cut thin and sharp, so that their line cannot be mistaken, and a good deep drill-hole struck into the angle of the mouth; the eye is anxious and questioning, and one is surprised, from below, to perceive a kind of darkness in the iris of it, neither like colour, nor like a circular furrow. The expedient can only be discovered by ascending to the level of the head: it is one which would have been quite inadmissible except in distant work, six drill-holes cut into the iris, round a central one for the pupil. (9:297)

THE VINE ANGLE: THE DRUNKENNESS OF NOAH

Although half of the beauty of the composition is destroyed by the breaking away of its central masses, there is still enough in the distribution of the variously bending leaves, and in the placing of the birds on the lighter branches, to prove to us the power of the designer. [It is] a remarkable instance of the Gothic Naturalism; and, indeed, it is almost impossible for the copying of nature to be carried farther than in the fibres of the marble branches, and the careful finishing of the tendrils: note especially the peculiar expression of the knotty

one case, vine in the other – was a necessary adjunct. Its trunk, in both sculptures, forms the true outer angle of the palace; boldly cut separate from the stonework behind, and branching out above the figures so as to enwrap each side of the angle, for several feet, with its deep foliage. Nothing can be more masterly or superb than the sweep of this foliage, the broad leaves lapping round the budding fruit, and sheltering from sight, beneath their shadows, birds of the most graceful form and delicate plumage. The branches are, however, so strong, and the masses of stone hewn into leafage so large, that, notwithstanding the depth of the undercutting, the work remains nearly uninjured; not so at the Vine angle, where the natural delicacy of the vine-leaf and tendril having

The Drunkenness of Noah, 14th-century sculpture on the south-east angle of the Ducal Palace (Photograph 2007)

Head of Noah with foliage and birds on the 'Vine' angle (Photograph 2007)

joints of the vine in the light branch which rises highest. Yet only half the finish of the work can be seen: for in several cases the sculptor has shown the under sides of the leaves turned boldly to the light, and has literally carved every rib and vein upon them in relief; not merely the main ribs which sustain the lobes of the leaf, and actually project in nature, but the irregular and sinuous veins which chequer the membraneous tissues between them, and which the sculptor has represented conventionally as relieved like the others, in order to give the vine-leaf its peculiar tessellated effect upon the eye. (10:360–61)

As must always be the case in early sculpture, the figures are much inferior to the leafage; yet so skilful in many respects that it was a long time before I could persuade myself that they had

Detail of tree stem, foliage and birds on the 'Vine' angle (Photograph 1998)

The head of the Noah on the Ducal Palace, evidently worked in emulation of this statue, has the same profusion of flowing hair and beard, but wrought in smaller and harder curls; and the veins on the arms and breast are more sharply drawn, the sculptor being evidently more practised in keen and fine lines of vegetation than in those of the figure; so that, which is most remarkable n a workman of this early period, he has failed in telling his story plainly, regret and wonder being so equally marked on the features of all the three brothers that it is impossible to say which is intended for Ham.

It may be observed, as further evidence of the date of the group, that, in the figures of all the three youths, the feet are protected simply by a bandage arranged in crossed folds round the ankle and lower

Sons of Noah on the *rio* façade of the Ducal Palace
(Photograph 2014)

Son of Noah on the *rio* façade of the Ducal Palace
(Photograph 2014)

indeed been wrought in the first half of the fourteenth century. Fortunately, the date is inscribed upon a monument in the Church of San Simeone Grande, bearing a recumbent statue of the saint, of far finer workmanship in every respect than those figures of the Ducal Palace, yet so like them, that I think there can be no question that the head of Noah was wrought by the sculptor of the palace in emulation of that of the statue of St. Simeon ... this monument [in S. Simeone Grande] bears date 1317.[22]

part of the limb; a feature of dress which will be found in nearly every piece of figure sculpture in Venice from the year 1300 to 1380, and of which the traveller may see an example within three hundred yards of this very group, in the bas-reliefs on the tomb of the Doge Andrea Dandolo (in St. Mark's) who died in 1354. (10:361–3)

THE JUDGMENT ANGLE: THE JUDGMENT OF SOLOMON

The Renaissance sculptor of the figures of the Judgment of Solomon has very nearly copied the fig-tree from this angle, placing its trunk between the executioner and the mother, who leans forward to stay his hand. But, though the whole group is much more free in design than those of the earlier palace, and in many ways excellent in itself, so that it always strikes the eye of a careless observer more than the others, it is of immeasurably inferior spirit in the workmanship; the leaves of the tree, though far more studiously varied in flow than those of the fig-tree from which they are partially copied, have none of its truth to nature; they are ill set on the stems, bluntly defined on the edges, and their curves are not those of growing leaves, but of wrinkled drapery.

Above these sculptures are set, in the upper arcade, the statues of the archangels Raphael, Michael, and Gabriel ... the figure of Gabriel, which is by much the most beautiful feature of the Renaissance portion of the palace, has only in its hand the Annunciation lily.

Such are the subjects of the main sculptures decorating the angles of the palace; notable, observe, for their simple expression of two feelings, the consciousness of human frailty and the dependence upon Divine guidance and protection: this being, of course, the general purpose of the introduction of the angels. (10:363–4)

The Judgment of Solomon on the north-west 'Judgment' angle of the Ducal Palace (Photograph 2014)

The Archangel Gabriel, 15th-century sculpture above the north-west 'Judgment' angle of the Ducal Palace (Photograph 2008)

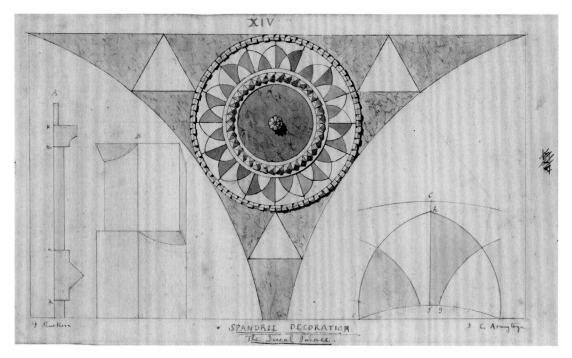

John Ruskin, *Spandril Decoration – the Ducal Palace*, pencil, ink and watercolour, engraved by J.C. Armytage, Ruskin Library, Lancaster

SPANDRIL DECORATION

The mass of the building being of Istrian stone, a depth of about two inches is left within the mouldings of the arches, rough hewn, to receive the slabs of fine marble composing the patterns. I cannot say whether the design was never completed, or the marbles have since been removed, but there are now only two spandrils retaining their fillings, and vestiges of them in a third.

The two complete spandrils are on the sea façade. The white portions are all white marble, the dentil band surrounding the circle is in coarse sugary marble, which I believe to be Greek, and never found in Venice, to my recollection, except in work at least anterior to the fifteenth century. The shaded fields charged with the three white triangles are of red Verona marble; the inner disc is green serpentine, and the dark pieces of the radiating leaves are grey marble.

This decoration by discs, or shield-like ornaments, is a marked characteristic of Venetian architecture in its earlier ages, and is carried into later times by the Byzantine Renaissance, already distinguished from the more corrupt forms of Renaissance … here we have, on the Ducal Palace, the most characteristic of all, because likest to the shield, which was probably the origin of the same ornament among the Arabs, and assuredly among the Greeks. (9:460)

It was evidently intended that all the spandrils of this building should be decorated in this manner, but only two of them seem to have been completed. (9:352)

The Ponte della Paglia and part of the south façade of the Ducal Palace (Photograph 1997)

Spandrel and capital on the south façade of the Ducal Palace
(Photograph 2013)

CAPITALS

The palace has seventeen main arches on the sea façade; eighteen on the Piazzetta side, which in all are, of course, carried by thirty-six pillars; and these pillars I shall always number from right to left, from the angle of the palace at the Ponte della Paglia to that next the Porta della Carta. I number them in this succession because I thus have the earliest shafts first numbered. So counted, the 1st, the 18th and the 36th are the great supports of the angles of the palace; and the first of the fifteenth century series, being, as above stated, the 9th from the sea on the Piazzetta side, is the 26th of the entire series, and will always in future be so numbered, so that all numbers above twenty-six indicate fifteenth century work, and all below it, fourteenth century, with some exceptional cases of restoration.

Then the copied capitals are: the 28th, copied from the 7th; the 29th from the 9th; the 30th from the 10th; the 31st from the 8th; the 33rd from the 12th; and the 34th from the 11th; the others being dull inventions of the fifteenth century, except the 30th, which is very nobly designed. (9:54)

We have next to examine the course of divinity and of natural history embodied by the old sculptor in the great series of capitals which support the lower arcade of the palace; and which, being at a height of little more than eight feet above the eye, might be read like the pages of a book by those (the noblest men in Venice) who habitually walked beneath the shadow of this great arcade at the time of their first meeting each other for morning converse.

The principal sculptures of the capitals consist of personifications of the Virtues and Vices, the favourite subjects of decorative art at this period in all the cities of Italy; and there is so much that is significant in the various modes of their distinction and general representation, more especially with reference to their occurrence as expressions of praise to the dead in sepulchral architecture, hereafter to be examined, that I believe the reader may both happily and profitably rest for a little

while beneath the first vault of the arcade, to review the manner in which these symbols of the virtues were first invented by the Christian imagination, and the evidence they generally furnish of the state of religious feeling in those by whom they were recognized. (10:365)

There are, in all, thirty-six great pillars supporting the lower story; and these are to be counted from right to left, because then the more ancient of them come first ... thus arranged, the first, which is not a shaft, but a pilaster, will be the support of the Vine angle; the eighteenth will be the great shaft of the Fig-tree angle; and the thirty-sixth, that of the Judgment angle.

All their capitals, except that of the first, are octagonal, and are decorated by sixteen leaves, differently enriched in every capital, but arranged in the same way: eight of them rising to the angles, and there forming volutes; and eight others set between them on the sides, rising halfway up the bell of the capital; there nodding forward and showing above them, rising out of their luxuriance, the groups or single figures which we have to examine. In some instances, the intermediate or lower leaves are reduced to eight sprays of foliage; and the capital is left dependent for its effect on the bold position of the figures. (10:386)

In the mid-nineteenth century the Ducal Palace was in a bad state of repair. Early in 1852, Ruskin commissioned a series of plaster casts of some of the fourteenth-century capitals, and presented them to the South Kensington Museum (now the Victoria and Albert Museum, where they are preserved). Casts made from the sculptures of The Drunkenness of Noah *on the south-east 'Vine' angle are displayed at the Ruskin Gallery (the Guild of St George Collection) in Sheffield. During an extensive restoration (1876–89) certain arcade columns and forty-two capitals were removed from the ground-floor arcades and upper loggia of the south and west façades of the palace. They were taken inside, and replaced by the nineteenth-century copies seen today. In 1994 a thorough cleaning*

John Ruskin, *Leafage of the Venetian Capitals*, Plate 20 in *The Stones of Venice* II (10:431)

and consolidation of thirteen of the fourteenth- and fifteenth-century capitals was financed by the Venice in Peril Fund: these are permanently displayed in the Museo dell'Opera of the Ducal Palace.

Ruskin described the sculptures on each of the thirty-six octagonal capitals on the ground-level portico, numbering them 1–36, beginning from the south-east 'Vine' angle at the Ponte della Paglia. A selection of details is reproduced here.

In referring to the figures on the octagonal capitals, I shall call the outer side, fronting either the Sea or the Piazzetta, the first side; and so count round from left to right; the fourth side being thus, of course, the innermost. (10:386)

FOURTH CAPITAL Has three children.[23] The eastern one is defaced; the one in front holds a small bird, whose plumage is beautifully indicated in its right [*sic*] hand; and with its left [*sic*] holds up half a walnut, showing the nut inside; the third holds a fresh fig, cut through, showing the seeds.

The hair of all three children is differently worked: the first has luxuriant flowing hair, and a double chin; the second, light flowing hair falling in pointed locks on the forehead; the third, crisp curling hair, deep cut with drill holes.

This capital has been copied on the Renaissance side of the palace [see thirty-fifth capital on the Piazzetta side], only with such changes in the ideal of the children as the workman thought expedient and natural. It is highly interesting to compare the child of the fourteenth century with the child of the fifteenth century. The early heads are full of youthful life, playful, humane, affectionate, beaming with sensation and vivacity, but with much manliness and firmness also, not a little cunning, and some cruelty perhaps, beneath all; the features small and hard, and the eyes keen. There is the making of rough and great men in them. But the children of the fifteenth century are dull smooth-faced dunces, without a single meaning line in the fatness of their stolid cheeks; and although, in the vulgar sense, as handsome as the other children are ugly, capable of becoming nothing but perfumed coxcombs. (10:388)

Fourth capital on the south (sea) portico, original 14th-century sculpture of children (Photograph 2014)

John Ruskin, *Capital from the Lower Arcade of the Doge's Palace, Venice*, Plate V in *The Seven Lamps of Architecture* (8:122)

Eleventh capital of birds, original 14th-century sculpture on the south façade (Photograph 2011)

ELEVENTH CAPITAL Its decoration is composed of eight birds, arranged as shown in Plate V of the *Seven Lamps,* which, however, was sketched from the Renaissance capital. These birds are all varied in form and action, but not so as to require special description. (10:406)

Eleventh capital, on the Piazzetta side, Renaissance copy (15th century) of the 14th-century sculpture of birds (Photograph 2011)

FIFTEENTH CAPITAL Its leafage is handled a good deal as that described of the Bartolomeo Bon third-order capitals. Its breast ribs ripple beautifully. All is exquisite in lobing and undulation; but it has a late look: though its flower band is pure. (Notebook 'M2', p.102)

The pillar to which it belongs is thicker than the rest, as well as the one over it in the upper arcade. The sculpture of this capital is also much coarser, and seems to me later than that of the rest; and it has no inscription, which is embarrassing, as its subjects have had much meaning, but I believe [Pietro] Selvatico is right in supposing it to have been intended for a general illustration of idleness. (10:410)

Sixth side A man with a very thoughtful face, laying his hand upon the leaves of the capital. (10:410)

Seventh side A lady with crown, strangely set with bunch or brush shaped ornaments, and with the beautiful rose. Both these last figures lay their hands on the leaves out of which they rise most beautifully: and the [side] 7 especially lays her hand right over the edge, and underneath, most sweetly, as if lifting a veil. (Notebook 'M', p.172)

Fifteenth capital, sixth side (Photograph 2004)

Fifteenth capital, seventh side: original 14th-century capital on the south portico – 'A crowned lady with a rose in her hand' (10:409–10) (Photograph 2006)

John Ruskin, page from Notebook 'Palace Book', p.34. Ruskin Library, Lancaster

Eighteenth capital, second side: *The Planets and the Creation of Man: Jupiter*, original 14th-century sculpture from the corner capital, now in the Museo dell'Opera (Photograph 1994)

EIGHTEENTH CAPITAL Sea Angle. This is the most glorious capital of the palace. It shows first with peculiar delicacy the essential mark of this design, that the central rib of the angle leaf, after it has thrown off the lateral divisions, runs up itself as straight as an arrow till close under its nod, thus opposing all the wavy lines and giving spring to the whole. And further the last upper pointed lobe of its breast leaves, sweeping alternately to right and left lies over and shuts down the top of the meeting wave of the angle leaf lateral lobes; while it falls at the same time under the feet or the drapery of the figures. This is seen in the dag[uerreotype] of the Luna side. It is marvellously beautiful. (Notebook 'M2', pp 102–3)

The most interesting and beautiful of the palace. It represents the planets, and the sun and moon, in those divisions of the zodiac known to astrologers as their 'houses'; and perhaps indicates, by the position in which they are placed, the period of the year at which this great cornerstone was laid. The inscriptions above have been in quaint Latin rhyme, but are now decipherable only in fragments, and that with the more difficulty because the rusty iron bar that binds the abacus has broken away, in its expansion, nearly all the upper portions of the stone, and with them the signs of contraction, which are of great importance.

It should be premised that, in modern astrology, the houses of the planets are thus arranged:

The house of the Sun is Leo
The house of the Moon is Cancer
The house of Mars is Aries and Scorpio
The house of Venus is Taurus and Libra
The house of Mercury is Gemini and Virgo
The house of Jupiter is Sagittarius and Pisces
The house of Saturn is Capricorn
The house of Herschel is [Uranus] Aquarius

The Herschel planet being of course unknown to the old astrologers, we have only the other six planetary powers, together with the sun; and Aquarius is assigned to Saturn as his house. I could not find Capricorn at all; but this sign may have been broken away, as the whole capital is grievously defaced. The eighth side of the capital, which the Herschel planet would now have occupied, bears a sculpture of the Creation of Man: it is the most conspicuous side, the one set diagonally across the angle; or the eighth in our usual mode of reading the capitals, from which I shall not depart.

Eighteenth capital, seventh side: The Moon, original 14th-century sculpture from the corner capital, now in the Museo dell'Opera (Photograph 2013)

Second side Jupiter, in his houses Sagittarius and Pisces, represented throned, with an upper dress disposed in radiating folds about his neck, and hanging down upon his breast, ornamented by small pendent trefoiled studs or bosses. He wears the drooping bonnet and long gloves; but the folds about the neck, shot forth to express the rays of the star, are the most remarkable characteristic of the figure. He raises his sceptre in his left hand over Sagittarius, represented as the centaur Chiron; and holds two thunnies in his right. Something rough, like a third fish, has been broken away below them; the more easily because this part of the group is entirely undercut, and the two fish glitter in the light, relieved on the deep gloom below the leaves. (10:413)

Third side Mars, in his houses Aries and Scorpio. Represented as a very ugly knight in chain mail, seated sideways on the ram, whose horns are broken away, and having a large scorpion in his left hand … The knight carries a shield, on which fire and water are sculptured, and bears a banner upon his lance, with the word 'DEFEROSUM', which puzzled me for some time. It should be read, I believe, 'De ferro sum'; which would be good Venetian Latin for 'I am of iron'. (10:414)

Fourth side The sun, in his house Leo. Represented under the figure of Apollo, sitting on the Lion, with rays shooting from his head, and the world in his hand. (10:414)

Seventh side The Moon, in her house Cancer. This sculpture, which is turned towards the Piazzetta, is the most picturesque of the series. The moon is represented as a woman in a boat upon the sea, who raises the crescent in her right hand, and with her left draws a crab out of the waves, up the boat's side. The moon was, I believe, represented in Egyptian sculpture as in a boat; but I rather think the Venetian was not aware of this, and that he meant to express the peculiar sweetness of the moonlight at Venice, as seen across the lagoons.

Eighteenth capital, fourth side: The Sun, original 14th-century sculpture from the corner capital, now in the Museo dell'Opera (Photograph 2014)

Eighteenth capital, third side: Mars, original 14th-century sculpture from the corner capital, now in the Museo dell'Opera (Photograph 1994)

Whether this was intended by putting the planet in the boat may be questionable, but assuredly the idea was meant to be conveyed by the dress of the figure. For all the draperies of the other figures on this capital, as well as on the rest of the façade, are disposed in severe but full folds, showing little of the forms beneath them; but the moon's drapery *ripples* down to her feet, so as exactly to suggest the trembling of the moonlight on the waves. (10:415)

I imagine the whole of this capital, therefore – the principal one of the old palace – to have been intended to signify, first, the formation of the planets for the service of man upon the earth; secondly, the entire subjection of the fates and fortune of man to the will of God, as determined from the time when the earth and stars were made, and, in fact, written in the volume of the stars themselves.

In the workmanship and grouping of its foliage, this capital is, on the whole, the finest I know in Europe. The sculptor has put his whole strength into it. I trust that it will appear among the other Venetian casts lately taken for the Crystal Palace; but if not, I have myself cast all its figures and two of its leaves. (10:412–16)

Nineteenth capital, sixth side: *Sculptor Saints and Disciples: S. Nicostrato*, original 14th-century sculpture from the west (Piazzetta) side, now in the Museo dell'Opera (Photograph 1994)

NINETEENTH CAPITAL This is, of course, the second counting from the Sea, on the Piazzetta side of the palace, calling that of the Fig-tree angle the first.

It is the most important capital, as a piece of evidence in point of dates, in the whole palace. Great pains have been taken with it, and in some portion of the accompanying furniture or ornaments of each of its figures, a small piece of coloured marble has been inlaid, with peculiar significance: for the capital represents the arts of sculpture and architecture, and the inlaying of the coloured stones (which are far too small to be effective at a distance and are found in this one capital only of the whole series) is merely an expression of the architect's feeling of the essential importance of this art of inlaying, and of the value of colour generally in his own art.

Sixth side A crowned figure, with hammer and chisel, employed *on a little range of windows of the fifth order*, having roses set, instead of orbicular ornaments, between the spandrils, with a rich cornice, and a band of purple marble inserted above. This sculpture assures us of the date of the fifth-order window, which it shows to have been universal in the early fourteenth century. There

John Ruskin, detail of the nineteenth capital, Notebook 'Palace Book'. p.20. Ruskin Library, Lancaster

Twenty-fourth capital: *The History of Marriage*; side 1: 'Meeting at the balcony'; side 2: 'Betrothal'; side 8: 'Death of a child'. (Photograph 2009)

are also five arches in the block on which the sculptor is working, marking the frequency of the number five in the window groups of the time.

It would be difficult to find a more interesting expression of the devotional spirit in which all great work was undertaken at this time. (10:417–18)

Has a crown also – hammer and chisel, employed on the very valuable miniature of a balustrade drawn real size and very carefully. These are from entire arches to the piece: of which only the half of course is given, with the entire central leaf plinth. The depth back is seen in the section at side: and the arches are all finished sharp to that depth. The red marble is only let in about 1/2 an inch. (Notebook 'Palace Book', p.21)

TWENTY-FOURTH CAPITAL This belongs to the large shaft which sustains the great party wall of the Sala del Gran Consiglio. The shaft is thicker than the rest; but the capital, though ancient, is coarse and somewhat inferior in design to the others of the series. It represents the history of marriage: the lover first seeing his mistress at a window, then addressing her, bringing her presents; then the bridal, the birth and the death of a child. But I have not been able to examine these sculptures properly, because the pillar is encumbered by the railing which surrounds the two guns set before the Austrian guardhouse. (10:422)

THIRTY-FIFTH CAPITAL Has children, with birds or fruit, pretty in features, and utterly inexpressive, like the cherubs of the eighteenth century. (10:425)

A 19th-century photograph showing the barricaded south-west angle of the Ducal Palace, with Austrian guns (the twenty-fourth capital is further to the left)

Thirty-fifth capital on the west (Piazzetta) side: *Childhood*, Renaissance version of the fourth capital on the south side (Photograph 2004)

Thirty-sixth capital under the 'Judgment' angle, with *The Lawgivers*, 15th-century sculptures (Photograph 2008)

THIRTY-SIXTH CAPITAL This is the last of the Piazzetta façade, the elaborate one under the Judgment angle. Its foliage is copied from the eighteenth at the opposite side, with an endeavour on the part of the Renaissance sculptor to refine upon it, by which he has merely lost some of its truth and force. This capital will, however, be always thought, at first, the most beautiful of the whole series, and indeed it is very noble; its groups of figures most carefully studied, very graceful, and much more pleasing than those of the earlier work, though with less real power in them; and its foliage is only inferior to that of the magnificent Fig-tree angle. It represents on its front or first side, Justice enthroned, seated on two lions; and on the seven other sides examples of acts of justice or good government, or figures of lawgivers.

Seventh side Moses receiving the law. Moses kneels on a rock, whence springs a beautifully fancied tree, with clusters of three berries in the centre of three leaves, sharp and quaint, like fine Northern Gothic. The half figure of the Deity comes out of the abacus, the arm meeting that of Moses, both at full stretch, with the stone tablets between.

In June 2004 a vandal attacked this capital with a hammer, smashing the hands and arms of the figures of God and Moses, as well as the tablet of the law. Similarly damaged were the statues of St Francis and St Mark on the façade of the Redentore church on the island of Giudecca. The works have been well restored.

The reader will observe that this capital is of peculiar interest in its relation to the much disputed question of the character of the later government of Venice. It is the assertion by that government of its belief that Justice only could be the foundation of its stability; as these stones of Justice and Judgment are the foundation of its halls of council. (10:425–7)

Thirty-sixth capital under the 'Judgment' angle: Moses receiving the Ten Commandments, 15th-century sculpture (Photograph 2006)

John Ruskin, *The Ducal Palace: Renaissance Capitals of the Loggia*, lithograph by Thomas Shotter Boys, Plate 15 in *Examples of the Architecture of Venice* (11.348)

It is foolish to carve what is to be seen forty feet off with the delicacy which the eye demands within two yards; not merely because such delicacy is lost in the distance, but because it is a great deal worse than lost: the delicate work has actually worse effect in the distance than rough work. This is a fact well known to painters, and, for the most part, acknowledged by the critics of painters, namely, that there is a certain distance for which a picture is painted; and that the finish, which is delightful if that distance be small, is actually injurious if the distance be great; and, moreover, that there is a particular method of handling which none but consummate artists reach, which has its effect at the intended distance, and is altogether hieroglyphical and unintelligible at any other.

On my first careful examination of the capitals of the upper arcade of the Ducal Palace at Venice I was induced, by their singular inferiority of workmanship, to suppose them inferior to those of the lower arcade. It was not till I discovered that some of those which I thought the worst above, were the best when seen from below, that I obtained the key to this marvellous system of adaptation; a system which I afterwards found carried out in every building of the great times which I had opportunity of examining. (9:292–3)

I trust that, in a few months, casts of many portions will be within the reach of the inhabitants of London, and that they will be able to judge for themselves of their perfect, pure, unlaboured naturalism.

This early sculpture of the Ducal Palace, then, represents the state of Gothic work in Venice at its central and proudest period, i.e. circa 1350. After this time, all is decline – of what nature and by what steps we shall inquire in the ensuing chapter: for as this investigation, though still referring to Gothic architecture, introduces us to the first symptoms of the Renaissance influence, I have considered it as properly belonging to the third division of our subject. (10:432–3)

Sometimes when walking at evening on the Lido, whence the great chain of the Alps, crested with silver clouds, might be seen rising above the front of the Ducal Palace, I used to feel as much in awe in gazing on the building as on the hills, and could believe that God had done a greater work in breathing into the narrowness of dust the mighty spirits by whom its haughty walls had been raised, and its burning legends written, than in lifting the rocks of granite higher than the clouds of heaven, and veiling them with their various mantle of purple flower and shadowy pine. (10:438–9)

The upper loggia of the Ducal Palace, facing south
(Photograph 1993)

View towards the Dogana and Santa Maria della Salute,
with the island of Giudecca and the Redentore church
beyond (Photograph 1994)

previous pages: View from the campanile of St Mark's
Square, looking north (Photograph 1998)

RENAISSANCE

Venice, as she was once the most religious, was in her fall the most
corrupt of European states; and as she was in her strength the centre of
the pure currents of Christian architecture, so she is in her decline the
source of the Renaissance. It was the originality and splendour of the
Palaces of Vicenza and Venice which gave this school its eminence in the
eyes of Europe; and the dying city, magnificent in her dissipation, and
graceful in her follies, obtained wider worship in her decrepitude than
in her youth, and sank from the midst of her admirers into the grave.

It is in Venice, therefore, and in Venice only that effectual blows can
be struck at this pestilent art of the Renaissance. Destroy its claims to
admiration there, and it can assert them nowhere else.

The Stones of Venice I (9:46–7)

RENAISSANCE ARCHITECTURE IS THE SCHOOL which
has conducted men's inventive and constructive
faculties from the Grand Canal to Gower Street;
from the marble shaft, and the lancet arch, and
the wreathed leafage, and the glowing and melting
harmony of gold and azure, to the square cavity
in the brick wall. We have now to consider the
causes and the steps of this change; and, as we
endeavoured above to investigate the nature of
Gothic, here to investigate also the nature of
Renaissance.

Although Renaissance architecture assumes
very different forms among different nations, it
may be conveniently referred to three heads: Early
Renaissance, consisting of the first corruptions
introduced into the Gothic schools; Central or
Roman Renaissance, which is the perfectly formed
style; and Grotesque Renaissance, which is the
corruption of the Renaissance itself.

Philippe de Commynes,[1] writing of his entry into
Venice in 1495, says:

They placed me between the two Ambassadors
(the middle being the most honourable place
in Italy), and I was conducted through the
principal street, which they call the Grand
Canal, and it is so wide that galleys frequently
cross one another; indeed I have seen vessels of
four hundred tons or more ride at anchor just
by the houses. It is the fairest and best-built
street, I think, in the world, and goes quite
through the city; the houses are very large and
lofty, and built of stone; the old ones are all
painted; those of about a hundred years standing
are faced with white marble from Istria, which is
about a hundred miles from Venice, and inlaid
with porphyry and serpentine …. It is the most
triumphant city that I have ever seen, the most

respectful to all ambassadors and strangers, governed with the greatest wisdom, and serving God with the most solemnity.[2]

This passage is of peculiar interest, for two reasons. Observe, first, the impression of Commynes respecting the religion of Venice: of which, as I have above said, the forms still remained with some glimmering of life in them, and were the evidence of what the real life had been in former times. But observe, secondly, the impression instantly made on Commynes' mind by the distinction between the older palaces and those built 'within this last hundred years; which all have their fronts of white marble brought from Istria, a hundred miles away, and besides, many a large piece of porphyry and serpentine upon their fronts' ...

There had indeed come a change over Venetian architecture in the fifteenth century; and a change of some importance to us moderns: we English owe to it our St. Paul's Cathedral, and Europe in general owes to it the utter degradation or destruction of her schools of architecture, never since revived. But that the reader may understand this, it is necessary that he should have some general idea of the connection of the architecture of Venice with that of the rest of Europe, from its origin forwards.

All European architecture, bad and good, old and new, is derived from Greece through Rome, and coloured and perfected from the East. The history of architecture is nothing but the tracing of the various modes and directions of this derivation. Understand this once for all: if you hold fast this great connecting clue, you may string all the types of successive architectural invention upon it like so many beads. (9:33–4)

ARSENAL

Its gateway is a curiously picturesque example of Renaissance workmanship, admirably sharp and expressive in its ornamental sculpture; it is in many parts like some of the best Byzantine work. The Greek lions in front of it appear to me to deserve more praise than they have received; though they are awkwardly balanced between conventional and imitative representation, having neither the severity proper to the one, nor the veracity necessary for the other. (11:362)

Greek lion to the left of gateway to the Arsenale (Photograph 2006)

Renaissance gateway, dating from 1460, to the Arsenale
(Photograph 2005)

CHURCH OF SAN GIOBBE

Its principal entrance is a very fine example
of early Renaissance sculpture. Note in it,
especially, its beautiful use of the flower of
the convolvulus. There are said to be still more
beautiful examples of the same period, in the
interior. The cloister, though much defaced,
is of the Gothic period, and worth a glance.
(11:380)

Entrance portal to the mid 15th-century church of S. Giobbe in
Cannaregio; the church was rebuilt between 1450 and 1493
(Photograph 2013)

Greek lion to the right of gateway to the Arsenale
(Photograph 2009)

The entrance door of the church ought to be seen by afternoon sunlight. There is no work in Venice more characteristic of the fine middle Renaissance. Its freedom and softness of leafage are very far carried; the skulls of cattle, with serpents through the eyeholes for ornaments, on the capitals, are true symbols of the sculptor's mind. The bas-relief above is St. Francis of Assisi and St. Job, but of little merit. (24:437)

CHURCH OF SAN MICHELE IN ISOLA

On the island between Venice and Murano. The little Cappella Emiliana at the side of it has been much admired, but it would be difficult to find a building more feelingless or ridiculous. It is more like a German summer-house, or angle turret, than a chapel, and may be briefly described as a bee-hive set on a low hexagonal tower, with dashes of

Above and below: S. Giobbe: details of the portal by Pietro Lombardo and assistants (Photographs 2013)

Church of S. Michele in Isola and the Cappella Emiliana. The church, begun in 1468, was designed by Mauro Codussi; the Cappella Emiliana was built by Guglielmo de' Grigi between 1528 and 1543 (Photograph 2013)

Giovanni Pividor, *Church of S. Michele in Isola*, mid-19th-century drawing, Museo Correr, Venice

stonework about its windows like the flourishes of an idle penman.

The cloister of this church is pretty; and the attached cemetery is worth entering, for the sake of feeling the strangeness of the quiet sleeping ground in the midst of the sea. (11:392–3)

MONUMENT TO BARTOLOMEO COLLEONI

The statue of Bartolomeo Colleoni in the little square beside the church [of SS Giovanni e Paolo] is certainly one of the noblest works in Italy. I have never seen anything approaching it in animation, in vigour of portraiture, or nobleness of line. (11:384)

His equestrian statue … is the finest I have ever seen: the set of it is the most living, muscular and resolute conceivable: the limbs straight so as to come out far from the horse's belly when seen in front; the armour of the foot turned down at the point over the stirrup, so as to give it a grasp and weight; the left shoulder flung forward so that the arm holding the bridle takes something of the action of holding a shield; the right arm drawn back with the truncheon as in Turner's Jason; the consequence of throwing the left shoulder so far forward is necessarily to render that side, when seen too far behind, a little

heavy; but the face, which looks over that shoulder forward, is superb, the very type of soldierly resolution; a little verging on fierceness, but in the profile seen from the right side it becomes almost mild; the expression depends mainly on the dark undercutting of the eyes. (11:19)

Do not let me be misunderstood when I speak generally of the evil spirit of the Renaissance. The reader may look through all I have written, from first to last, and he will not find one word but of the most profound reverence for those mighty men who could wear the Renaissance armour of proof, and yet not feel it encumber their living limbs: Leonardo and Michael Angelo, Ghirlandajo and Masaccio, Titian and Tintoret. But I speak of the Renaissance as an evil time, because, when it

Campo SS Giovanni e Paolo with equestrian monument to Bartolomeo Colleoni by Andrea del Verrocchio (1435–88) (Photograph 2009)

Equestrian monument to Bartolomeo Colleoni by Andrea del Verrocchio in Campo SS Giovanni e Paolo; begun in 1483 and completed by Alessandro Leopardi after Verrocchio's death in 1488 (Photographs 2008)

saw those men go burning forth into the battle, it mistook their armour for their strength; and forthwith encumbered with the painful panoply every stripling who ought to have gone forth only with his own choice of three smooth stones out of the brook.

    This, then, the reader must always keep in mind when he is examining for himself any examples of cinquecento work. When it has been done by a truly great man, whose life and strength could not be oppressed, and who turned to good account the whole science of his day, nothing is more exquisite. I do not believe, for instance, that there is a more glorious work of sculpture existing in the world than that equestrian statue of Bartolomeo Colleoni, by Verrocchio, of which I hope, before these pages are printed, there will be a cast in England. (11:18–19)

Scuola Grande di S. Giovanni Evangelista: marble screen and portal of the courtyard (1481) by Pietro Lombardo (Photograph 2013)

SCUOLA DI SAN GIOVANNI (EVANGELISTA)

A fine example of the Byzantine Renaissance, mixed with remnants of good late Gothic. The little exterior cortile is sweet in feeling. (11:388)

Above right: Detail of the portal (Photograph 2013)

Right: A 15th-century stone angel by Pietro and Tullio Lombardo above the courtyard screen (Photograph 2013)

Church of S. Maria dei Miracoli in Cannaregio, built 1481–9 by Pietro Lombardo (Photograph 2011)

S. Maria dei Miracoli: marble incrustation on the façade (Photograph 1998)

Carved door panel on the south side of the church (Photograph 2011)

CHURCH OF SANTA MARIA DEI MIRACOLI

The most interesting and finished example in Venice of the Byzantine Renaissance, and one of the most important in Italy of the Cinquecento Style. (11:393)

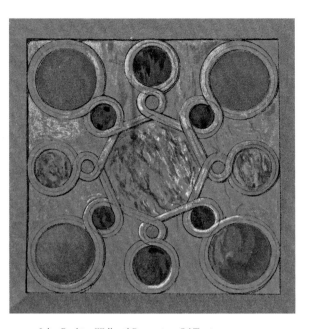

John Ruskin, *Wall-veil Decoration, Ca' Trevisan*,
chromolithograph, Plate 1 *The Stones of Venice* I (9:33)

John Ruskin, *Wall-veil Decoration, Ca' Dario*,
chromolithograph, Plate 1 *The Stones of Venice* I (9:33)

EARLY RENAISSANCE MARBLE DECORATION

There having been three principal styles of
architecture in Venice: The Greek or Byzantine,
the Gothic, and the Renaissance, it will be shown
that the Renaissance itself is divided into three
correspondent families: Renaissance engrafted on
Byzantine, which is earliest and best; Renaissance
engrafted on Gothic, which is second, and second
best; Renaissance on Renaissance, which is double
darkness, and worst of all.

The palaces in which Renaissance is engrafted
on Byzantine are those noticed by Commynes:
they are characterized by an ornamentation very
closely resembling, and in some cases identical
with, early Byzantine work; namely groups of
coloured marble circles enclosed in interlacing
bands [i.e. *opus Alexandrinum*].

The upper figure is from Ca' Trevisan, and it is
very interesting in its proportions. If we take five
circles in geometrical proportion, each diameter
being two-thirds of the diameter next above it, and
arrange the circles so proportioned in contact with

each other in the manner shown in the plate, we
shall find that an increase, quite imperceptible in
the diameter of the circles in the angles, will enable
us to inscribe the whole in a square. The lines so
described will then run in the centre of the white
bands. I cannot be certain that this is the actual
construction of the Trevisan design because it is
on a high wall surface, where I could not get at
its measurements; but I found this construction
exactly coincides with the lines of my eye-sketch.
(9:425)

The lower figure in the Plate is from the
front of the Ca' Dario, and probably struck the
eye of Commynes in its first brightness. [Pietro]
Selvatico indeed considers both the Ca' Trevisan
and the Ca' Dario as buildings of the sixteenth
century. I defer the discussion of the question at
present, but have, I believe, sufficient reason for
assuming the Ca' Dario to have been built about
1486, and the Ca' Trevisan not much later.
(9:425–6)

CASA DARIO

The question of the date of the Casa Dario and Casa Trevisan was deferred until I could obtain from my friend Mr. Rawdon Brown, to whom the former palace once belonged, some more distinct data respecting this subject than I possessed myself.

Speaking first of the Casa Dario, he says:

Fontana [G. Fontana in *Venezia monumentale*, 1845] dates it from about the year 1450, and considers it the earliest specimen of the architecture founded by Pietro Lombardo, and followed by his sons, Tullio and Antonio. In a Sanuto autograph miscellany, purchased by me long ago, and which I gave to St. Mark's Library, are two letters from Giovanni Dario, dated 10th and 11th July, 1485, in the neighbourhood of Adrianople; where the Turkish camp found itself, and Bajazet II received presents from the Soldan of Egypt, from the Schah of the Indies (query Grand Mogul), and from the King of Hungary: of these matters, Dario's letters give many curious details. Then, in the printed Malipiero Annals, page 136 (which err, I think, by a year), the Secretary Dario's negotiations at the Porte are alluded to; and in date of 1484 he is stated to have returned to Venice, having quarrelled with the Venetian bailiff at Constantinople; the annalist adds that 'Giovanni Dario was a native of Candia, and that the Republic was so well satisfied with him for having concluded peace with Bajazet, that he received, as a gift from his country, an estate at Noventa, in the Paduan territory, worth 1500 ducats in cash for the dower of one of his daughters.' These largesses probably enabled him to build his house about the year 1486, and are doubtless hinted at in the inscription, which I restored a.d. 1837;[3] it had no date, and ran thus: URBIS. GENIO. JOANNES. DARIVS. In the Venetian history of Paolo Morosini, page 594, it is also mentioned, that Giovanni Dario was, moreover,

Ca' Dario on the Grand Canal, built *c.*1487 and attributed to Pietro Lombardo (Photograph 1998). At the time of writing, the Ca' Dario is undergoing a long restoration programme, with the façade still under scaffolding

the Secretary who concluded the peace between Mahomet, the conqueror of Constantinople, and Venice, a.d. 1478; but, unless he built his house by proxy, that date has nothing to do with it; and in my mind, the fact of the present, and the inscription, warrant one's dating it 1486 and not 1450. (11:255–6)

Decoration of the façade of Ca' Dario on the Grand Canal
(Photograph 1997)

Domes of St Mark's and the upper storey of Ca' Trevisan Cappello on the rio di Canonica; the details illustrated on pp 181 and 185 are on the left- and right-hand sides of the façade (Photograph 1999)

CASA TREVISAN

A most curious and delicate piece of inlaid design is introduced into a band which is almost exactly copied from the church of Theotocos at Constantinople, and correspondent with others in St. Mark's. There is also much Byzantine feeling in the treatment of the animals, especially in the two birds of the lower compartment, while the peculiar curves of the cinquecento leafage are visible in the leaves above. The dove, alighted with the olive-branch plucked off, is opposed to the raven with restless expanded wings. Beneath are evidently the two sacrifices 'of every clean fowl and every clean beast'. The colour is given with green and white marbles, the dove relieved on a ground of greyish green, and all is exquisitely finished. (9:425)

In the inlaid design of the dove with the olive branch from the Casa Trevisan, it is impossible for anything to go beyond the precision with which the olive leaves are cut out of the white marble; and, in some wreaths of laurel below, the rippled edge of each leaf is as finely and easily drawn, as if by a delicate pencil. (11:32)

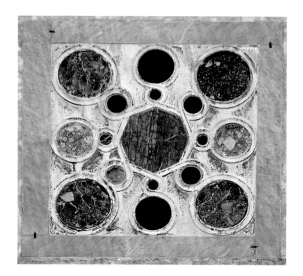

Ca' Trevisan, detail of the façade, with *opus Alexandrinum*
decoration (Photograph 2013)

John Ruskin, *Wall-veil Decoration, Ca' Trevisan*, Plate 20
The Stones of Venice I (9:425)

Ca' Trevisan, inlaid marble decoration on the early
16th-century façade (Photograph 2012)

PALAZZO MANZONI (PALAZZO CONTARINI POLIGNAC) ON THE GRAND CANAL, NEAR THE CHURCH OF THE CARITÀ

A perfect and very rich example of Byzantine Renaissance: its warm yellow marbles are magnificent. (11:391)

So soon as the classical enthusiasm required the banishment of Gothic forms, it was natural that the Venetian mind should turn back with affection to the Byzantine models in which the round arches and simple shafts, necessitated by recent law, were presented under a form consecrated by the usage of their ancestors. And, accordingly, the first distinct school of architecture which arose under the new dynasty was one in which the method of inlaying marble, and the general forms of shaft and arch, were adopted from the buildings of the twelfth century and applied with the utmost possible refinements of modern skill. Both at Verona and Venice the resulting architecture is exceedingly beautiful. At Verona it is, indeed, less Byzantine, but possesses a character of richness and tenderness almost peculiar to that city. At Venice it is more severe, but yet adorned with sculpture which, for sharpness of touch and delicacy of minute form, cannot be rivalled, and rendered especially brilliant by the introduction of those inlaid circles of coloured marble, serpentine and porphyry, by which Philippe de Commynes was so much struck on his first entrance into the city. (9:20)

Paterae in porphyry and serpentine on the façade of Palazzo Contarini Polignac at S. Vio (Photograph 2003)

The late 15th-century Palazzo Contarini Polignac on the Grand Canal at S. Vio (Photograph 2008). Originally named Palazzo Contarini dal Zaffo, and later Palazzo Manzoni, the building is now known as Palazzo Contarini Polignac. In 1871, at Ruskin's commission, the palace was drawn by his former pupil John Wharlton Bunney (see p.227).

SCUOLA GRANDE DI SAN MARCO

One of the two most refined buildings in Venice which combine Byzantine and Renaissance characteristics ...

The two most refined buildings in this style in Venice are the small Church of the Miracoli, and the Scuola di San Marco beside the church of St John and St Paul. The noblest is the Rio Façade of the Ducal Palace. The Casa Dario, and Casa Manzoni on the Grand Canal, are exquisite examples of the school, as applied to domestic architecture. (11:20–21)

The Scuola Grande di San Marco and the rio dei Mendicanti
(Photograph 2012)

Detail of the façade of the Scuola Grande di San Marco,
with *trompe-l'oeil* decoration (Photograph 2014)

PALAZZO CORNER SPINELLI ON THE GRAND CANAL

A graceful and interesting example of the early Renaissance, remarkable for its pretty circular balconies. (11:369)

On the whole, the finest Renaissance palace in Venice. Giocondine, but late, with Newgate lower story, but very fine in the irregular insertion of its six windows, obtaining an entresol: note how poor it would be in comparison if the entresol windows were not put quite out of traceable relation to the balconies above. There, the lateral circular ones, unique, as also the window traceries and the projecting stair for landing, useful in the effect of this palace, but a bad innovation. (24:441)

Above and left: Palazzo Corner Spinelli on the Grand Canal, designed by Mauro Codussi and built *c.*1490–1510 (Photographs 2013)

RIO FAÇADE OF THE DUCAL PALACE

The Rio façade of the Ducal Palace, though very sparing in colour, is yet, as an example of finished masonry in a vast building, one of the finest things not only in Venice, but in the world. It differs from other work of the Byzantine Renaissance, in being on a very large scale; and it still retains one pure Gothic character which adds not a little to its nobleness, that of perpetual variety. There is hardly one window of it, or one panel, that is like another; and this continual change so increases its apparent size by confusing the eye, that, though presenting no bold features, or striking masses of any kind, there are few things in Italy more impressive than the vision of it overhead, as the gondola glides from beneath the Bridge of Sighs. (11:32–3)

The canal or *rio* façade of the Ducal Palace, built *c*.1485 by
Mauro Codussi, on the rio del Palazzo (Photograph 2013)

Detail of rustication on the *rio* façade of the Ducal Palace
(Photograph 2013)

In passing along the Rio del Palazzo the traveller ought especially to observe the base of the Renaissance building, formed by alternately depressed and raised pyramids, the depressed portions being casts of the projecting ones, which are truncated on the summits. The work cannot be called rustication, for it is cut as sharply and delicately as a piece of ivory, but it thoroughly answers the end which rustication proposes, and misses: it gives the base of the building a look of crystalline hardness, actually resembling, and that very closely, the appearance presented by the fracture of a piece of cap quartz; while yet the light and shade of its alternate recesses and projections are so varied as to produce the utmost possible degree of delight to the eye attainable by a geometric pattern so simple. (11:256–7)

The school of architecture which we have just been examining is, as we have seen above, redeemed from severe condemnation by its careful and noble use of inlaid marbles as means of colour. From that time forward, this art has been unknown or despised; the frescoes of the swift and daring Venetian painters long contended with the inlaid marbles, outvying them with colour, indeed more glorious than theirs, but fugitive as the hues of woods in autumn; and, at last, as the art itself of painting in this mighty manner failed from among men, the modern decorative system established itself, which united the meaningless of the veined marble with the evanescence of the fresco, and completed the harmony by falsehood. (11:35–6)

PALAZZO CONTARINI DELLE FIGURE

In the reach of the Canal between the Casa Foscari and the Rialto, there are several palaces of which the Casa Contarini, called 'delle Figure', is remarkable for the association of the Byzantine principles of colour with the severest lines of the Roman pediment, gradually superseding the round arch. The precision of chiselling and delicacy of proportion in the ornament and general lines of these palaces cannot be too highly praised and I believe that the traveller in Venice in general gives them rather too little attention than too much. But while I would ask him to stay his gondola beside each of them long enough to examine their every line, I must also warn him to observe most carefully the peculiar feebleness and want of soul in the conception of their ornament, which mark them as belonging to a period of decline; as well as the absurd mode of introduction of their pieces of coloured marble: these, instead of being simply and naturally inserted in the masonry, are placed in small circular or oblong frames of sculpture, like mirrors or pictures, and are represented as suspended by ribbons against the wall; a pair of wings being generally fastened on to the circular tablets, as if to relieve the ribbons and knots from their weight, and the whole series tied under the chin of a little cherub at the top, who is nailed against the façade like a hawk on a barn door.

But chiefly let him notice, in the Casa Contarini delle Figure, one most strange incident, seeming to have been permitted, like the choice of the subjects at the three angles of the Ducal Palace, in order to teach us by a single lesson, the true nature of the style in which it occurs. In the intervals of the windows of the first story, certain shields and torches are attached, in the form of trophies, to the stems of two trees whose boughs have been cut off, and only one or two of their faded leaves left, scarcely observable, but delicately sculptured here and there, beneath the insertions of the severed boughs.

It is as if the workman had intended to leave us an image of the expiring naturalism of the

Palazzo Contarini delle Figure: details of the façade
(Photographs 2013)

Gothic school. I had not seen this sculpture when I wrote the passage referring to its period, in the first volume of this work: 'Autumn came – the leaves were shed – and the eye was directed to the extremities of the delicate branches. The Renaissance frosts came, and all perished!'

And the hues of this autumn of the early Renaissance are the last which appear in architecture. The winter which succeeded was colourless as it was cold; and although the Venetian painters struggled long against its influence, the numbness of the architecture prevailed over them at last, and the exteriors of all the latter palaces were built only in barren stone. As at this point of our inquiry, therefore, we must bid farewell to colour. (11:21–2)

PALAZZO MINELLI[4]

In the Corte del Maltese, at St. Paternian.[5] It has a spiral external staircase, very picturesque, but of the fifteenth century, and without merit. (11:393)

Exterior spiral staircase of Palazzo Minelli (Contarini dal Bòvolo), c.1497–99 (Photograph 2002)

The 16th-century Palazzo Contarini delle Figure on the Grand Canal, by Antonio Scarpagnino (Photograph 1998)

FONDACO DEI TEDESCHI

A huge and ugly building near the Rialto, rendered, however, peculiarly interesting by remnants of the frescoes by Giorgione with which it was once concerned.[6] When we have passed under the Rialto, ascending the Grand Canal, the first building on the right is that called the Fondaco dei Tedeschi. A huge, blank, five-storied pile, on whose walls the first glance detects nothing but the signs of poverty and ruin. They have been covered with stucco, which for the most part is now peeled away from the brick beneath, and stains of rusty red, and sickly grey and black hang down in dark streams from the cornices, or spread in mossy patches hither and thither between its casements. Among this grisly painting where the stucco is still left, the eye may here and there discern other lines faint shades of that noble grey which nothing can give but the pencil of a great colourist, and subdued fragments of purple and scarlet, dying into rusty wash from the iron bolts that hold the walls together. This is all that is left of the work of Titian and Giorgione. (11:378)

The Fondaco dei Tedeschi on the Grand Canal. Formerly a trading centre for German merchants in Venice, it was rebuilt between 1505 and 1508 following its destruction in a fire. From 1939 it became the headquarters of the main Post Office, which was closed in 2010 after the building was sold for redevelopment (Photograph 2009)

PROCURATIE VECCHIE

A graceful series of buildings, of late fifteenth
century design, forming the northern side
of St. Mark's Place, but of no particular
interest. (11:399)

The Procuratie Vecchie, Piazza S. Marco
(Photograph 2014)

CHURCH OF SANTA MARIA FORMOSA

There is now but one landmark to guide the steps of the traveller to the place where the white cloud rested, and the shrine was built to St. Mary the Beautiful. Yet this spot is still worth his pilgrimage, for he may receive a lesson upon it, though a painful one. Let him first fill his mind with the fair images of the ancient festival, and then seek that landmark, the tower of the modern church, built upon the place where the daughters of Venice knelt yearly; and let him look at the head that is carved on the base of the tower, still dedicated to St. Mary the Beautiful.

A head – huge, inhuman and monstrous – leering in bestial degradation, too foul to be either pictured or described, or to be beheld for more than an instant; yet let it be endured for that

Church of S. Maria Formosa: grotesque head at base of the campanile (Photograph 2009)

instant; for in that head is embodied the type of the evil spirit to which Venice was abandoned in the fourth period of her decline; and it is well that we should see and feel the full horror of it on this spot, and know what pestilence it was that came and breathed upon her beauty; until it melted away like the white cloud from the ancient field of Santa Maria Formosa.

This head is one of the many hundreds which disgrace the latest buildings of the city, all more or less agreeing in their expression of sneering mockery, in most cases enhanced by thrusting out the tongue. Most of them occur upon the bridges, which were among the very last works undertaken by the republic, several, for instance, upon the Bridge of Sighs; and they are evidences of a delight in the contemplation of bestial vice and the expression of low sarcasm, which is, I believe, the most hopeless state into which the human mind can fall. The spirit of idiotic mockery is, as I have said, the most striking characteristic of the last period of the Renaissance, which, in consequence of the character thus imparted to its sculpture, I have called grotesque.

This façade, whose architect is unknown,[7] consists of a pediment, sustained on four Corinthian pilasters, and is, I believe, the earliest in Venice which appears entirely destitute of every religious symbol, sculpture, or inscription; unless the cardinal's hat upon the shield in the centre of the pediment be considered a religious symbol. The entire façade is nothing else than a monument to the Admiral Vincent Cappello. Two tablets, one between each pair of flanking pillars, record his acts and honours; and, on the corresponding spaces upon the base of the church, are two circular trophies, composed of halberts, arrows, flags, tridents, helmets, and lances: sculptures which are just as valueless in a military as in an ecclesiastical point of view; for, being all copied from the forms

Monument to Admiral Vincenzo Cappello above the portal of the west façade of S. Maria Formosa (Photograph 2014)

of Roman arms and armour, they cannot even be referred to for information respecting the costume of the period. Over the door, as the chief ornament of the façade, exactly in the spot which in the 'barbarous' St. Mark's is occupied by the figure of Christ, is the statue of Vincenzo Cappello, in Roman armour. He died in 1542; and we have, therefore, the latter part of the sixteenth century fixed as the period when, in Venice, churches were first built to the glory of Man, instead of the glory of God. (11:145–6)

SCUOLA GRANDE DI SAN ROCCO

The Scuola di San Rocco is one of the most
interesting examples of Renaissance work in Venice.
Its fluted pillars are surrounded each by a wreath,
one of vine, another of laurel, another of oak, not
indeed arranged with the fantasticism of early
Gothic; but especially the laurel, reminding one
strongly of the laurel sprays, powerful as well as
beautiful, of Veronese and Tintoret. Their stems are
curiously and richly interlaced – the last vestige of
the Byzantine wreathed work – and the vine leaves
are ribbed on the surfaces, I think, nearly as fine as
those of the Noah [on the south-east 'Vine' angle
of the Ducal Palace], though more injured by time.
The capitals are far the richest Renaissance in
Venice, less corrupt and more masculine in plan,
than any other, and truly suggestive of support,
though of course showing the tendency to error in
this respect; and finally, at the angles of the pure
Attic bases, on the square plinth, are set couchant
animals; one, an elephant four inches high, very
curiously and cleverly cut, and all these details
worked with a spirit, finish, fancy, and affection
quite worthy of the middle ages. But they have all

Scuola Grande di S. Rocco: detail of the façade
(Photograph 2014)

Scuola Grande di S. Rocco: wreath of vine leaves on
fluted pillar (Photograph 2008)

the marked fault of being utterly detached from the
architecture. The wreaths round the columns look
as if they would drop off the next moment, and
the animals at the bases produce exactly the effect
of mice who had got there by accident: one feels
them ridiculously diminutive and utterly useless.

The effect of diminutiveness is, I think, chiefly
owing to there being no other groups of figures
near them to accustom the eye to the proportion,
and to the needless choice of the largest animals,
elephants, bears, and lions, to occupy a position
so completely insignificant, and to be expressed
on so contemptible a scale – not in a bas-relief or
pictorial piece of sculpture, but as independent
figures. The whole building is a most curious
illustration of the appointed fate of the Renaissance
architects – to caricature whatever they imitated,
and misapply whatever they learned. (9:471)

Scuola Grande di S. Rocco: capital above
fluted pillar (Photograph 2013)

Scuola Grande di S. Rocco: carved elephant at base
of pillar (Photograph 2013)

PALAZZO VENDRAMIN CALERGHI

How curious the return in the Renaissance time to the earliest types – not only as we have seen in the rich ornament of vine leaves etc. at Scuola di San Rocco, but in the Italian window itself: the circle between two rounds ... In the Vendramin Calerghi the brackets which carry the cornice are placed exactly above the circle of the tracery, where the tracery is weakest: this idea of putting a bracket leaning against a tracery is to me, of all the vile things I have seen of renaissance, the vilest. The vulgar musical instruments and hanging ribands of the Calerghi are in ornamental just what this construction is in mechanical science. (Notebook 'M2', p.111)

Palazzo Vendramin Calergi: detail of the façade
(Photograph 2013)

Palazzo Vendramin Calergi on the Grand Canal
(Photograph 2014)

RIO DE
MARGHERITA

Late 15th-century statue of a warrior in Istrian stone on
façade of Ca' Civran-Guoro, rio di S. Margherita, near
the church of the Carmini (Photograph 2013)

HOUSE OF OTHELLO AT THE CARMINI

The researches of Mr Brown into the origin of the play of 'Othello' have, I think, determined that Shakespeare wrote on definite historical grounds; and that Othello may be in many points identified with Christopher Moro, the lieutenant of the republic at Cyprus in 1508. His palace was standing till very lately, a Gothic building of the fourteenth century, of which Mr Brown possesses a drawing. It is now destroyed, and a modern square-windowed house built on its site. A statue, said to be a portrait of Moro, but a most paltry work, is set in a niche in the modern wall. (11:397)

LIBRERIA VECCHIA

A graceful building of the central Renaissance, designed by Sansovino, 1536, and much admired by all architects of the school. It was continued by Scamozzi, down the whole side of St. Mark's Place, adding another story above it, which modern critics blame as destroying the 'eurithmia', never considering that had the two low stories of the Library been continued along the entire length of the Piazza, they would have looked so low that the entire dignity of the square would have been lost. As it is, the Library is left in its originally good proportions, and the larger mass of the Procuratie

Libreria Vecchia on the west side of the Piazzetta di S. Marco: detail of the façade (Photograph 2014)

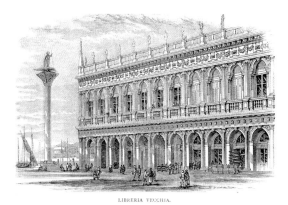

LIBRERIA VECCHIA.

Libreria Vecchia, wood engraving, 1869, Biblioteca Marciana, Venice

Nuove forms a more majestic, though less graceful, side for the great square.

But the real faults of the building are not in the number of stories, but in the design of the parts. It is one of the grossest examples of the base Renaissance habit of turning keystones into brackets, throwing them out in bold projection (not less than a foot and a half) beyond the mouldings of the arch; a practice utterly barbarous, inasmuch as it evidently tends to dislocate the entire arch, if any real weight were laid on the extremity of the keystone; and it is also a very characteristic example of the vulgar and painful mode of filling spandrils by naked figures in alto-rilievo, leaning against the arch on each side, and appearing as if they were continually in danger of slipping off. Many of these figures have, however, some merit in themselves; and the whole building is graceful and effective of its kind. (11:389)

Antonio Visentini (engraved after Canaletto, *c.*1735), *View of Piazza San Marco with the Church of San Geminiano*

The Ala Napoleonica at the west end of Piazza S. Marco
(Photograph 1997)

The continuation of the Procuratie Nuove, at the western extremity of St. Mark's Place (together with various apartments in the great line of the Procuratie Nuove), forms the 'Royal Palace', the residence of the Emperor when at Venice. This building is entirely modern, built in 1810, in imitation of the Procuratie Nuove, and on the site of Sansovino's Church of San Geminiano. (11:390)

The church of S. Geminiano was demolished by Napoleon in 1807 to create space for a ballroom. The west wing of the Piazza became known as the Ala Napoleonica and now houses part of the collection of the Museo Correr.

PALAZZO GRIMANI ON THE GRAND CANAL

Of all the buildings in Venice, later in date than the final additions to the Ducal Palace, the noblest is, beyond all question, that which, having been condemned by its proprietor, not many years ago, to be pulled down and sold for the value of its materials, was rescued by the Austrian government, and appropriated – the government officers having no other use for it – to the business of the Post Office; though still known to the gondolier by its ancient name, the Casa Grimani. It is composed of three stories of the Corinthian order, at once simple, delicate and sublime; but on so colossal a scale, that the three-storied palaces on its right and left only reach to the cornice which marks the level

John Ruskin, *The Grand Canal, Venice*, pencil on paper, frontispiece to *The Stones of Venice* I

of its first floor. Yet it is not at first perceived to be so vast; and it is only when some expedient is employed to hide it from the eye, that by the sudden dwarfing of the whole reach of the Grand Canal, which it commands, we become aware that it is to the majesty of the Casa Grimani that the Rialto itself, and the whole group of neighbouring buildings, owe the greater part of their impressiveness. Nor is the finish of its details less notable than the grandeur of their scale. There is not an erring line, nor a mistaken proportion, throughout its noble front; and the exceeding fineness of the chiselling gives an appearance of lightness to the vast blocks of stone out of whose perfect union that front is composed. The decoration is sparing but delicate: the first story only simpler

Palazzo Grimani on the Grand Canal at S. Luca, designed mid-16th century by Michele Sanmicheli and completed by Gian Giacomo de' Grigi. It was bought by the State in 1806 and became the Post Office until 1872. It is now the headquarters of the Court of Appeal (Photograph 2008)

than the rest, in that it has pilasters instead of shafts, but all with Corinthian capitals, rich in leafage, and fluted delicately; the rest of the walls flat and smooth, and their mouldings sharp and shallow, so that the bold shafts look like crystals of beryl running through a rock of quartz.

This palace is the principal type at Venice, and one of the best in Europe, of the central architecture of the Renaissance schools; that carefully studied and perfectly executed architecture to which those schools owe their principal claims to our respect, and which became the model of most of the important works subsequently produced by civilized nations. I have called it the Roman Renaissance because it is founded, both in its principles of superimposition and in the style of its ornament, upon the architecture of classic Rome at its best period. The revival of Latin literature both led to its adoption and directed its form; and the most important example of it which exists is the modern Roman basilica of St Peter's. It had, at its Renaissance or new birth, no resemblance either to Greek, Gothic, or Byzantine forms, except in retaining the use of the round arch, vault and dome; in the treatment of all details it was exclusively Latin, the last links of connexion with medieval tradition having been broken by its builders in their enthusiasm for classical art, and the forms of true Greek or Athenium architecture being still unknown to them. The study of these noble Greek forms has induced various modifications of the Renaissance in our own times; but the conditions which are found most applicable to the uses of modern life are still Roman, and the entire style may most fitly be expressed by the term 'Roman Renaissance'. (11:45)

CHURCH OF THE REDENTORE

On the opposite side of the broad canal of the Giudecca [from the church of Santa Maria della Salute] is a small church, celebrated among Renaissance architects as of Palladian design, but which would hardly attract the notice of the general observer, unless on account of the pictures by John Bellini which it contains, in order to see which the traveller may perhaps remember having been taken across the Giudecca to the church of the 'Redentore'. But he ought carefully to compare these two buildings with each other, the one built 'to the Virgin', the other 'to the Redeemer' (also a votive offering after the cessation of the plague of 1576): the one, the most conspicuous church in Venice, its dome, the principal one by which she is first discerned, rising out of the distant sea; the other, small and contemptible, on a suburban island, and only becoming an object of interest because it contains three small pictures! (10:443)

Church of the Redentore, designed by Andrea Palladio and built 1577–92, on the island of Giudecca (Photograph 1993)

The church of S. Giorgio Maggiore on the island of San Giorgio:
begun 1566 by Andrea Palladio; completed 1610 by Simone
Sorella (Photograph 2009)

CHURCH OF SAN GIORGIO MAGGIORE

A building which owes its interesting effect chiefly to its isolated position, being seen over a great space of lagoon. The traveller should especially notice in its façade the manner in which the central Renaissance architects (of whose style this church is a renowned example) endeavoured to fit the laws they had established to the requirements of their age. Churches were required with aisles and clerestories, that is to say, with a high central nave and lower wings; and the question was, how to face this form with pillars of one proportion. The noble Romanesque architects built story above story, as at Pisa and Lucca; but the base Palladian architects dared not do this. They must needs retain some image of the Greek temple; but the Greek temple was all of one height, a low gable roof being borne on ranges of equal pillars. So the Palladian builders raised first a Greek temple with pilasters for shafts; and, through the middle of its roof, or horizontal beam, that is to say, of the cornice which externally represented this beam, they lifted another temple on pedestals, adding these barbarous appendages to the shafts, which otherwise would not have been high enough; fragments of the divided cornice or tie-beam being left between the shafts, and the great door of the church thrust in between the pedestals.

It is impossible to conceive a design more gross, more barbarous, more childish in conception, more servile in plagiarism, more insipid in result, more contemptible under every point of rational regard. Observe also that when Palladio had got his pediment at the top of the church, he did not know what to do with it; he had no idea of decorating it except by a round hole in the middle. (The traveller should compare, both in construction and decoration, the Church of the Redentore with this of San Giorgio.) Now, dark penetration is often a most precious assistance to a building dependent upon colour for its effect; for a cavity is the only means in the architect's power of obtaining certain and vigorous shadow; and for this purpose, a circular penetration, surrounded by a deep russet marble moulding, is beautifully used in the centre of the white field on the side of the Portico of St. Mark's. But Palladio had given up colour, and pierced his pediment with a circular cavity, merely because he had not wit enough to fill it with sculpture. The interior of the church is like a large assembly room, and would have been undeserving of a moment's attention, but that it contains some most precious pictures. (11:381–2)

BRIDGE OF THE RIALTO

The best building raised in the time of the Grotesque Renaissance; very noble in its simplicity, in its proportions, and in its masonry. Note especially the grand way in which the oblique archstones rest on the butments of the bridge, safe, palpably both to the sense and eye: note also the sculpture of the Annunciation on the southern side of it; how beautifully arranged, so as to give more lightness and grace to the arch – the dove flying

The Rialto Bridge, anon. 19th-century engraving, Museo Correr, Venice

Rialto Bridge, south side: relief sculpture of the angel of the
Annunciation by Agostino Rubini, c.1590 (Photograph 2006)

towards the Madonna, forming the keystone – and
thus the whole action of the figures being parallel
to the curve of the arch, while all the masonry is
at right angles to it. Note, finally, one circumstance
which gives peculiar firmness to the figure of the
angel, and associates itself with the general
expression of strength in the whole building;
namely, that the sole of the advanced foot is set
perfectly level, as if placed on the ground, instead
of being thrown back behind like a heron's, as in
most modern figures of this kind.

The bridge was built by Antonio da Ponte, in
1588. It was anciently of wood, with a drawbridge
in the centre, a representation of which may
be seen in one of Carpaccio's pictures[8] at the
Accademia delle Belle Arti: and the traveller should
observe that the interesting effect, both of this and
the Bridge of Sighs, depends in great part on their
both being more than bridges: the one a covered
passage, the other a row of shops, sustained on an
arch. No such effect can be produced merely by the
masonry of the roadway itself. (11:400)

Rialto Bridge, south side: relief sculpture of the Virgin
Annunciate by Agostino Rubini, c.1590 (Photograph 2006)

Dove of the Annunciation on the keystone of the Rialto Bridge
(Photograph 2007)

PONTE DE' SOSPIRI

The well-known 'Bridge of Sighs', a work of no merit, and of a late period, owing the interest it possesses chiefly to its pretty name, and to the ignorant sentimentalism of Byron.[9] (11:433)

Ponte dei Sospiri on the rio del Palazzo (Photograph 2014)

CHURCH OF SANTA MARIA DELLA SALUTE ON THE GRAND CANAL

One of the earliest buildings of the Grotesque Renaissance, rendered impressive by its position, size, and general proportions. These latter are exceedingly good; the grace of the whole building being chiefly dependent on the inequality of size in its cupolas, and pretty grouping of the two campaniles behind them. It is to be generally observed that the proportions of buildings have nothing whatever to do with the style or general merits of their architecture. An architect trained in the worst schools and utterly devoid of all meaning or purpose in his work, may yet have such a natural gift of massing and grouping as will render all his structures effective when seen from a distance: such a gift is very general with the late Italian builders, so that many of the most

Cumaean Sibyl above the portal of S. Maria della Salute (Photograph 2013)

Church of Santa Maria della Salute on the Grand Canal, designed by Baldassare Longhena and built 1631–81 (Photograph 2013)

contemptible edifices in the country have good stage effect so long as we do not approach them. The Church of the Salute is further assisted by the beautiful flight of steps in front of it down to the canal; and its façade is rich and beautiful of its kind, and was chosen by Turner for the principal object in his well-known view of the Grand Canal [*Venice: the Grand Canal*, 1840]. The principal faults of the building are the meagre windows in the sides of the cupola, and the ridiculous disguise of the buttresses under the form of colossal scrolls; the buttresses themselves being originally a hypocrisy, for the cupola is stated by Lazari to be of timber, and therefore needs none. (11:428)

S. Maria della Salute: part of the façade, with Eritrean and Cumaean Sibyls above the portal; the sculptures by Francesco Cavrioli were installed in 1660 (Photograph 2014)

Istrian stone volutes and sculptures on the church of S. Maria della Salute (Photographs 2013–14)

PALAZZO PESARO ON THE GRAND CANAL

The most powerful and impressive in effect of all the palaces of the Grotesque Renaissance. The heads upon its foundation are very characteristic of the period, but there is more genius in them than usual. Some of the mingled expressions of faces and grinning casques are very clever. (11:398)

Palazzo Pesaro on the Grand Canal, designed by Baldassare Longhena, completed after 1682 by Antonio Gaspari (Photograph 2014)

Palazzo Pesaro: rustication and casques on the waterline (Photograph 2014)

CHURCH OF THE OSPEDALETTO

The most monstrous example of the Grotesque Renaissance which there is in Venice; the sculptures on its façade representing masses of diseased figures and swollen fruit.

It is almost worth devoting an hour to the successive examination of five buildings, as illustrative of the last degradation of the Renaissance. S. Moisè is the most clumsy, S. Maria Zobenigo the most impious, S. Eustachio the most ridiculous, the Ospedaletto the most monstrous, and the head at S. Maria Formosa the most foul. (11:397)

Detail of the façade of the church of the Ospedaletto (S. Maria dei Derelitti), rebuilt 1674 by Baldassare Longhena (Photograph 2006)

CHURCH OF SANTA MARIA ZOBENIGO
(SANTA MARIA DEL GIGLIO)

The Church of Santa Maria Zobenigo is entirely dedicated to the Barbaro family; the only religious symbols with which it is invested being statues of angels blowing brazen trumpets, intended to express the spreading of the fame of the Barbaro family in heaven. At the top of the church is Venice crowned, between Justice and Temperance, Justice holding a pair of grocer's scales, of iron, swinging in the wind. There is a two-necked stone eagle (the Barbaro crest), with a copper crown, in the centre of the pediment. A huge statue of a Barbaro in armour, with a fantastic head-dress, over the central

Statue of Francesco Barbaro, 17th-century sculpture attributed to Heinrich Meyring, on the façade of the church of S. Maria Zobenigo (del Giglio), constructed 1670–80 to a design by Giuseppe Benoni; the façade (1680–83) was erected by Giuseppe Sardi (Photograph 2009)

Right: Angel representing Fame (Photograph 2013)

door; and four Barbaros in niches, two on each side of it, strutting statues, in the common stage postures of the period – Jo. Maria Barbaro, sapiens ordinum; Marinus Barbaro, Senator (reading a speech in a Ciceronian attitude); Franc. Barbaro, legatus in classe (in armour, with high-heeled boots, and looking resolutely fierce); and Carolus Barbaro, sapiens ordinum: the decorations of the façade being completed by two trophies, consisting of drums, trumpets, flags and cannon; and six plans, sculptured in relief, of the towns of Zara, Candia, Padua, Rome, Corfu, and Spalatro.

When the traveller has sufficiently considered the meaning of this façade, he ought to visit the Church of St. Eustachio [church of San Stae on the Grand Canal], remarkable for the dramatic effect of the group of sculpture on its façade, and then the Church of the Ospedaletto, noticing, on his way, the heads on the foundations of the Palazzo Corner della Regina, and the Palazzo Pesaro, and any other heads carved on the modern bridges, closing with those on the Bridge of Sighs. He will then have obtained a perfect idea of the style and feeling of the Grotesque Renaissance. (11:149–50)

Map of Corfu: low-relief carving
on façade of S. Maria del Giglio
(Photograph 2013)

Church of San Stae: group of angels above the portal by Giuseppe
Torretto, c.1710 (Photograph 2013)

Church of San Moisè: detail of the 17th-century façade, with sculptures by Heinrich Meyring (Photograph 2013)

CHURCH OF SAN MOISÈ

Notable as one of the basest examples of the basest school of the Renaissance. (11:394)

The churches raised throughout this period are so grossly debased, that even the Italian critics of the present day, who are partially awakened to the true state of art in Italy, though blind as yet to its true cause, exhaust their terms of reproach upon these last efforts of the Renaissance builders. The two churches of S. Moisè and S. Maria Zobenigo, which are among the most remarkable in Venice for their manifestation of insolent atheism, are characterized by Lazari, the one as 'culmine d'ogni follia architettonica' [the height of all architectural folly], the other as 'orrido ammasso di pietra d'Istria' [a hideous mass of Istrian stone], with added expressions of contempt, as just as it is unmitigated.

Now both these churches, which I should like the reader to visit in succession, if possible, after that of S. Maria Formosa, agree with that church, and with each other, in being totally destitute of

Church of S. Moisè, near Piazza S. Marco, designed by Alessandro Tremignon, 1668 (Photograph 2013)

religious symbols, and entirely dedicated to the honour of two Venetian families. In San Moisè, a bust of Vincenzo Fini is set on a tall narrow pyramid above the central door, with this marvellous inscription:

OMNE FASTIGVM
VIRTVTE IMPLET
VINCENTIVS FINI

It is very difficult to translate this; for 'fastigium', besides its general sense, has a particular one in architecture, and refers to the part of the building occupied by the bust; but the main meaning of it is that Vincenzo Fini fills all height with his virtue. The inscription goes on into further praise, but this example is enough. Over the two lateral doors are two other laudatory inscriptions of younger members of the Fini family, the dates of death of the three heroes being 1660, 1685, and 1726, marking thus the period of consummate degradation. (11:147–9)

PALAZZO CORNER DELLA REGINA

A late Renaissance building of no merit or interest. (11:369)

Palazzo Corner della Regina on the Grand Canal, designed by Domenico Rossi, begun 1724 (Photograph 2014)

Palazzo Corner della Regina: detail of the façade (Photograph 2013)

Church of S. Simeone Piccolo on the Grand Canal, designed by
Giovanni Antonio Scalfarotto, begun 1718 (Photograph 1998)

CHURCH OF SAN SIMEONE PICCOLO

One of the ugliest churches in Venice or elsewhere.
Its black dome, like an unusual species of
gasometer, is the admiration of modern Italian
architects. (11:433)

*The copper covering on the dome turned black
soon after the church's completion, as can be seen
in Canaletto's* Venice: The Upper Reaches of
the Grand Canal with S. Simeone Piccolo *(1738)
at the National Gallery, London. In 1870 the dome
was re-covered in copper, which developed the
greenish colour seen today. A restoration of the
church was completed in 2012.*

We have seen above that the whole mass of the architecture founded on Greek and Roman models, which we have been in the habit of building for the last three centuries, is utterly devoid of all life, virtue, honourableness, or power of doing good. It is base, unnatural, unfruitful, unenjoyable, and impious ... an architecture invented, as it seems, to make plagiarists of its architects, slaves of its workmen, and Sybarites of its inhabitants; an architecture in which intellect is idle, invention impossible, but in which all luxury is gratified, and all insolence fortified; the first thing we have to do is to cast it out, and shake the dust of it from our feet for ever. (11:227)

I believe it to be possible for us, not only to equal, but far to surpass, in some respects, any Gothic yet seen in Northern countries. In the introduction of figure sculpture, we must indeed, for the present, remain utterly inferior, for we have no figures to study from. No architectural sculpture was ever good for anything which did not represent the dress and persons of the people living at the time; and our modern dress will not form decorations for spandrils and niches. But in floral sculpture we may go far beyond what has yet been done, as well as in refinement of inlaid work and general execution. For, although the glory of Gothic architecture is to receive the rudest work, it refuses not the best; and, when once we have been content to admit the handling of the simplest workman, we shall soon be rewarded by finding many of our simple workmen become cunning ones: and, with the help of modern wealth and science, we may do things like Giotto's campanile, instead of like our own rude cathedrals; but better than Giotto's campanile, insomuch as we may adopt the pure and perfect forms of the Northern Gothic, and work them out with the Italian refinement. It is hardly possible at present to imagine what may be the splendour of buildings designed in the forms of English and French thirteenth-century surface Gothic, and wrought out with the refinement of Italian art in the details, and with a deliberate resolution, since we cannot have figure sculpture, to display in them the beauty of every flower and herb of the English fields, each by each; doing as much for every tree that roots itself in our rocks, and every blossom that drinks our summer rains, as our ancestors did for the oak, the ivy, and the rose. Let this be the object of our ambition, and let us begin to approach it, not ambitiously, but in all humility; accepting help from the feeblest hands; and the London of the nineteenth century may yet become as Venice without her despotism, and as Florence without her dispeace. (11:228–30)

AFTER 'THE STONES'

As I re-read the description I gave, thirty years since, of St. Mark's Church – much more as I remember, forty since, and before, the first happy hour spent in trying to paint a piece of it, with my six-o'clock breakfast on the little café table beside me on the pavement in the morning shadow, I am struck almost into silence by wonder at my own pert little Protestant mind, which never thought for a moment of asking what the Church had been built for!

St Mark's Rest, 1877 (24:277)

THE STONES OF VENICE *was published in three volumes between 1851 and 1853, followed by volumes III and IV of* Modern Painters.

In 1854 Effie left Ruskin, and their marriage was annulled.[1] Four years later Ruskin met the young Rose La Touche,[2] his pupil in drawing, with whom he was later to fall deeply in love. In 1864 his father, John James Ruskin, died; two years later, when Rose was seventeen, Ruskin proposed marriage and was asked to wait for three years.

In 1869 Ruskin was appointed first Slade Professor of Art at Oxford, and during a summer spent in Switzerland and Italy made short visits to Venice, followed by a longer stay in the summer of 1870, when he returned to the Hotel Danieli. Publication of a monthly pamphlet of letters, Fors Clavigera: Letters to the Workmen and Labourers of Great Britain, *began in 1871, continuing until Ruskin's illness in 1878 and then published intermittently until 1884. In 1871 Ruskin had purchased Brantwood,[3] a house near Coniston in the Lake District; and in the same year he founded the Guild of St George,[4] a utopian instrument of social reform, formally established in*

1878 and still active today as a charitable educational trust. Ruskin's increasingly heavy workload and publishing commitments, the temporary loss of his Evangelical Protestant faith and a growing sense of disappointment that his message in The Stones of Venice *had not – in spite of the book's continuing success – been widely understood, meant that his involvement with Venice was not properly resumed until he returned to the city for a long working visit in 1876.*

Letter from Ruskin to his American friend, Charles Eliot Norton:[5]

Denmark Hill, May 1857 – And so you are going to Venice, and this letter will I hope be read by you by the little square sliding frame of the gondola window. For I hope you hold to your true gondola, with black felze [the small covered cabin on a gondola], eschewing all French and English substitutions of pleasure-boat and awning. I have no doubt – one day, that the

John Wharlton Bunney, *The West Front of St Mark's*, 1877–82,
oil on canvas, Guild of St George Collection, Museums Sheffield

gondolas will be white instead of black,
at the rate they carry on their reforms at
Venice …

I went through so much hard, dry,
mechanical toil there, that I quite lost,
before I left it, the charm of the place.
Analysis is an abominable business: I
am quite sure that people who work out
subjects thoroughly are disagreeable
wretches. One only feels as one should
when one doesn't know much about the
matter. If I could give you for a few
minutes, as you are floating up the canal
just now, the kind of feeling I had when
I had just done my work, when Venice
presented itself to me merely as so many
'mouldings', and I had few associations with
any building but those of more or less pain
and puzzle and provocation: Pain of frost-

bitten finger and chilled throat as I
examined or drew the window-sills in the
wintry air; Puzzlement from said window-
sills which didn't agree with the doorsteps,
or back of house which didn't agree with
front; and Provocation, from every sort of
soul or thing in Venice at once – from my
gondoliers, who were always wanting to
go home, and thought it stupid to be tied
to a post in the Grand Canal all day long,
and disagreeable to have to row to Lido
afterwards; from my cook, who was always
trying to catch lobsters on the doorsteps,
and never caught any; from my valet-de-
place, who was always taking me to see
nothing, and waiting by appointment at
the wrong place; from my English servant,
whom I caught smoking genteelly on St.
Mark's Place, and expected to bring home

to his mother quite an abandoned character; from my tame fish, who splashed the water all over my room, and spoiled my drawings; from my little sea-horses, who wouldn't coil their tails about sticks when I asked them; from a fisherman outside my window who used to pound his crabs alive for bait every morning, just when I wanted to study morning light on the Madonna della Salute; from the sacristans of all the churches, who used never to be at home when I wanted them; from the bells of all the churches, which used always to ring most when I was at work in the steeples; from the tides, which never were up, or down, at the hour they ought to have been; from the wind, which used to blow my sketches into the canal, and one day blew my gondolier after them; from the rain, which came through the roof of the Scuola di San Rocco; from the sun, which blistered Tintoret's Bacchus and Ariadne every afternoon at the Ducal Palace; and from the Ducal Palace itself, worst of all, which wouldn't be found out, nor tell me how it was built. (I believe this sentence had a beginning somewhere, which wants an end somewhere; but I haven't any end for it, so it must go on as it is.)

There was only one place in Venice which I never lost the feeling of joy in – at least the pleasure which is better than joy – and that was just halfway between the end of the Giudecca and St. George of the Seaweed,[6] at sunset. If you tie your boat to one of the posts there, you can see the Euganeans, where the sun goes down, and all the Alps and Venice behind you by the rosy sunlight: there is no other spot so beautiful ... I have got all the right feeling back, now, however; and hope to write a word or two about Venice yet, when I have got the mouldings well out of my head – and the Mud. (9:xxvii–xxix)

From Praeterita, *Ruskin's autobiography and his last book, written between 1885 and 1889:*

The two chapters closing the first, and beginning the second volume of 'The Stones of Venice' were written, I see on re-reading, in the melancholy experience of 1852, with honest effort to tell every traveller what was really to be seen. They do not attempt to recall my own joys of 1835 and 1841, when there was not even beginning of railway bridges; when everything, muddy Brenta, vulgar villa, dusty causeway, sandy beach, was equally rich in rapture, on the morning that brought us in sight of Venice; and the black knot of gondolas in the canal at Mestre, more beautiful to me than a sunrise full of clouds all scarlet and gold ...

My Venice, like Turner's, had been chiefly created for us by Byron; but for me, there was also still the pure childish passion of pleasure in seeing boats float in clear water. The beginning of everything was in seeing the gondola-beak come actually inside the door at Danieli's, when the tide was up, and the water two feet deep at the foot of the stairs; and then, all along the canal sides, actual marble walls rising out of the salt sea, with hosts of little brown crabs on them, and Titians inside ... I find a sentence in diary of 8th May [1841] which seems inconsistent with what I have said of the centres of my life's work:

'Thank God I am here; it is the Paradise of cities.' (35:294–6)

In September 1876 Ruskin returned to Venice for an eight-month working visit, initially staying at the Grand Hotel (Ca' Ferro) on the Grand Canal. In spite of suffering periods of depression, principally caused by grief following the death of Rose La Touche in the previous year, he began work on his Guide to the Principal Pictures in the Academy *(1877) and* St Mark's Rest *(1877–84), having originally intended to write a revised edition of* The Stones of Venice. *He was also commissioning artists such as Angelo Alessandri, John Wharlton Bunney,[7] Raffaele Carloforti[8] and Thomas Rooke to make pictorial architectural records in oil and watercolour.*

John Wharlton Bunney, *The Palazzo Manzoni on the Grand Canal*, 1871, watercolour and body colour, Guild of St George Collection, Museums Sheffield

In November, he met Count Alvise Piero Zorzi, member of an ancient Venetian family, who had studied art at the Accademia and was deeply concerned with the protection of Venice's heritage. Zorzi was campaigning against insensitive restorations in the city, in particular those being carried out at St Mark's. During a ten-year project between 1865 and 1875 the south side of the Basilica had been drastically reconstructed under the direction of G.B. Meduna, and now the west front was threatened with a major intervention. The draft of Zorzi's authoritative pamphlet on the subject, Osservazioni intorno ai ristauri interni ed esterni della Basilica di S. Marco (*Observations on the internal and external restorations of the Basilica*

of St Mark's, Venice, 1877), was discussed by Zorzi and Ruskin at an evening meeting arranged by Raffaele Carloforti, at Ruskin's hotel, and thereafter the two men met regularly. An account of their collaboration, recorded in Zorzi's diary, was published in August/September 1906 in the Cornhill Magazine. Osservazioni *was published in Venice in April 1877, with a prefatory letter by Ruskin, to whom the work was dedicated.*

During this visit Ruskin commissioned the artist J.W. Bunney, his former pupil at the Working Men's College and resident in Venice since 1870, to paint a detailed picture of the west façade of St Mark's for the Guild of St George.[9] In February 1877 Ruskin moved to La Calcina, *a small lodging-house on the Zattere in the sestiere of Dorsoduro.*

Ruskin to his publisher, George Allen:[10]

> *Venice, 10th September 1876* – I got here on Thursday in great comfort; and find things much less grievous than I feared; and have set to work fairly on the new *Stones of Venice*,[11] which will have all the 'eloquent' bits in the second and third volume served up like pickled walnuts, in sauce of a very different flavour – perhaps brandy cherries would be a better symbol of what I hope the book will be ... Bunney is doing good work too, which pleases me ... (37:208)

The kind of work that John Bunney carried out in Venice for Ruskin is typified by his watercolour drawing of the Palazzo Manzoni, a building that Ruskin was particularly anxious to have recorded. At the time the building was occupied by the Pompieri, the Venetian fire brigade, as indicated by the sign over the water entrance door. The following note from Bunney's journal of 1871 refers to this picture:

> *12th February 1871* – This morning I took a gondola & went with the drawings I am going to send away [to Ruskin] to Mr. Rawdon Brown, Casa della Vida [Palazzo Gussoni Grimani della Vida on the Grand Canal], to show them to him, he being a great friend of Mr Ruskin's, and he has been very polite & kind to me at different times. He was much pleased with them, & told me that he had heard many persons, one an artist, say how much they were astonished at what they called my wonderful skill in drawing, how I had carried away to my house the real corner of St. Marco. With the others I showed him the unfinished drawing of the palace on the Grand Canal, known generally as the Manzoni Palace [now Palazzo Contarini Polignac]. Mr. R.B. has found out lately the original name &

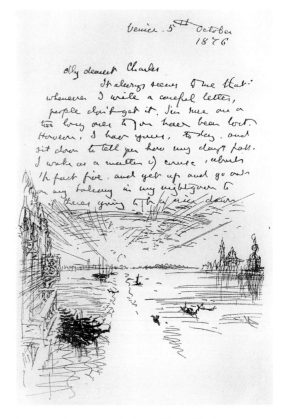

Facsimile of a letter from Ruskin to Charles Eliot Norton, 1876 (37:210)

who built it. The proper name is *Langaren*, spelt as pronounced by him. This Langaren 'was one of the most eminent lawyers in 15 century, and the University of Padua wanted him to hold the chair of law at that place, but the money they had to give was not sufficient for his salary, and so not wishing to lose him, the state of Venice gave the proceeds of the tax on *prostitution* to make up the sum, and with this as part of his pay he or his son erected this beautiful house, giving the Elder Lombardi, the architect, the commission in 1480'.[12]

Ruskin to Charles Eliot Norton:

> *Venice, 5th October 1876* – It always seems to me that whenever I write a careful letter,

people don't get it. I'm sure one or two long ones to you have been lost. However, I have yours, today, and sit down to tell you how my days pass. I wake as a matter of course, about half-past five, and get up and go out on my balcony in my nightgown to see if there's going to be a nice dawn.

That's the view I have from it [see opposite facsimile of letter showing the view from the balcony of Ca' Ferro, then the Grand Hotel] with the pretty traceried balcony of the Contarini Fasan next-door ...

At half-past seven the gondola is waiting and takes me to the bridge before St. John and Paul [church of SS Giovanni e Paolo],

where I give an hour of my very best day's work to painting the school of Mark and vista of Canal to Murano. It's a great Canaletto view, and I'm painting it against him.[13]

I am rowed back to breakfast at nine, and, till half-past ten, think over and write what little I can of my new fourth vol. of Stones of Venice [*St Mark's Rest*].

I strike work at two or a little after – go home, read letters – and dine at three; lie on sofa and read any vicious book I can find to amuse me – to prevent St. Ursula having it all her own way.[14] Am greatly amused with the life of Casa [Casanova's *Histoire de ma vie*] at present ... At half-past four, gondola again

John Ruskin, *Moonlight on Venice from the Lagoon*, 1849, photogravure from the watercolour, Plate J, *The Stones of Venice* II (10:415)

– I am floated, half asleep, to Murano – or the Armenians – or San Giorgio in Alga[15] – wake up, and make some little evening sketch, by way of diary. Then take oar myself – and row into the dark or moonlight ... (36:210–11)

Ruskin to his cousin Joan Severn:[16]

13th February [1877] – The Grand Hotel was really *too* expensive; I was getting quite ruined, so I came away to a little inn[17] fronting the Giudecca, and commanding sunrise and sunset both, where I have two rooms for six francs a day instead of one for twelve. Also, which I find a great advantage, look along the water instead of down on it, and get perfectly picturesque view of boats instead of masthead ones, and I think I shall be comfy. (24:xxxvi)

Ruskin to Joan Severn:

16th February [1877] – I am taken up at present – as if I had not enough to do of my own, with a pamphlet by my new friend Count Zorzi, in defence of St. Mark's – the best thing I ever saw written on architecture but by myself: and it is more furious than me![18]

Ruskin to Count Zorzi:

[Venice] 1877 – Carissimo Conte Zorzi – That is all the Italian I know, pretty nearly, and I must trust your sweet secretary[19] to interpret my letter to-day ... *Indeed* there are most grave reasons for the changes I am making in my letter [the preface to Zorzi's pamphlet on St Mark's]. You have been thinking, my dear friend, too much of the Prefecture of Venice – and not enough of the Soul of Europe. It is neither your part nor mine becomingly to play the part of police officers detecting petty theft. We

are antiquaries and artists, defending a monument of Christianity ... (35:220)

Extracts from Ruskin's letter of 1877 to Count Zorzi, published as the preface to Zorzi's Osservazioni:

My Dear Friend – I have no words in my rough English, nor with any less passionate than Dante's could I tell you with what thankfulness of heart I see a Venetian noble at last rising to defend the beauty of his native city, and the divinity of her monuments, from the ruin of attempted restoration ...

St. Mark's was the most rich in associations, the most marvellous in beauty, the most perfect in preservation, of all the eleventh-century buildings in Europe; and of St. Mark's, precisely the most lovely portions were those which have now been destroyed.

Their mosaics especially were of such exquisite intricacy of deep golden glow between the courses of small pillars, that those two upper arches [on the south side of the Basilica] had an effect as of peacocks' feathers in the sun, when their green and purple glitters through and through with light. But now they have the look of a peacock's feather that has been dipped in white paint.

What changes have been made in the other stones, or what damage done to the surfaces of those which remain, I do not know: but this I know, that in old time I looked every day at this [south] side of St. Mark's, wondering whether I ever should be able to paint anything so lovely; and that now, not only would any good colourist refuse to paint it as a principal subject, but he would feel that he could not introduce that portion of the building into any picture without spoiling it. It would not, indeed, have been possible, unless with Aladdin's lamp, to make a new St. Mark's as beautiful

John Ruskin, *The North West
Porch of St. Marks*, 1877, pencil,
watercolour and bodycolour.
Ruskin Library, Lancaster

as the old, for the like of the old marbles
cannot, I believe, be obtained from any now
known quarry. So that last year, lecturing in
my schools at Oxford [actually at the
London Institution] on the geology of
architecture, I took these very marbles of St.
Mark's for principal illustration, and to my
bitter sorrow, was able to hold in my hand,
and show to my scholars, pieces of the white
and purple veined alabasters, more than a
foot square, bought here in Venice out of the
wrecks of restoration.

I cannot enough thank you for the
admirable care and completeness with which
you have exposed the folly of thus throwing
away the priceless marbles of the original
structure, and explained to your readers
every point relating to the beauty and
durability of such materials. Your analysis
of the value of colours produced by age, is
new in art literature, and cannot possibly
be better done. It may be interesting to
you to know, with reference to this subject,
that the Gothic palace at San Severo[20] next
to the Renaissance, Lombard palace (both,
I think, belonging once to your own ancient
family) was radiant with the same veined

purple alabasters as St Mark's; I was
then a youth, and, in my love of geology,
I painted them literally vein for vein – a
nd, fortunately, have preserved the drawing.
That palace is now stripped into a defaced
wall; I have the drawing now here from
England, and by the time your book is
published all those true Venetians who
love their city may compare it with the
existing ruin.[21]

And if any question is made of your
statement of the destruction of the colours
of the south side of St. Mark's, I can produce
an exact coloured drawing of that also, in
old time – but it belongs to the schools of
Oxford, to which I presented it as the most
beautiful example of Byzantine colours
I could give.[22]

Is this, to the people of the lagoons, no
loss? To us foreigners, it is *total* loss. We can
build models of St. Mark's for ourselves, in
England, or in America. We came to Venice
to see *that* St. Mark's whose pillars had
trembled with Crusaders' shouts, seven
hundred years ago ... we came to kneel on
the pavement where the Doge Selvo walked
barefoot to receive his crown: and we find

it torn up to be replaced by the vile advertisement of a mosaic manufactory![23]

But now I must be mute, for shame, knowing as I do that English influence and example are at the root of many of these mischiefs; unless, indeed, I venture partly to answer the question which will occur to the readers whom you convince, – what means of preservation ought to be used for a building which it is impossible to restore. The single principle is, that after any operation whatsoever necessary for the safety of the building, every external stone should be set back in its actual place: if any are added to strengthen the walls, the new stones, instead of being made to resemble the old ones, should be left blank of sculpture, and every one should have the date of its insertion engraved upon it. The future antiquary would then still be able to study the history of architecture on the authentic building; in my own work it now takes me at least half the time I have to study a building, to find out first what pieces of it are genuine.

And now I leave the cause in your hands, dear Count. If, by your intercession, the façade to the Square, and mosaics of the porch, can yet be saved, every true artist in Europe will bring you tribute of honour, and future Venice, of never-ending gratitude ...[24]

Ruskin to Joan Severn:

Easter Monday [1877] ... I am at work on a drawing of the richest portico of St. Mark's – a thing to be done before my eyes fail me, if Heaven please, and well.[25]

Letter to the Editor of the Liverpool Daily Post, *published on 9 June 1877:*

Venice, 15th April 1877 – My Dear Sir: It is impossible for any one to know the horror and contempt with which I regard modern restoration – but it is so great that it simply paralyzes me in despair ... things are worse here than in England: you have little there left to lose – here, every hour is ruining buildings of inestimable beauty and historical value – simply to keep stone-layers at work ... (34:531)

From Count Zorzi's diary (later published as 'Ruskin in Venice' in the Cornhill Magazine, *August/ September 1906):*

Meanwhile the printing was advancing. I was growing impatient, as I was most anxious that the book [*Osservazioni*] should be published on St. Mark's Day ... the terrible book finally saw the light on St. Mark's Day, April 25th 1877, and the very first person who went to buy a copy at Ongania's, the publishers, was the Director of the restorations then going on at St. Mark's [architect Giovanni Battista Meduna (1800–80)]. I cannot describe the joy of Mr. Ruskin, of my artist friends, and of all the lovers of the 'most beautiful building in the world', as Mr. Ruskin called the Basilica, at the publication. Everyone was enthusiastic about Ruskin's splendid letter. Journalists, friends and acquaintances stopped to congratulate me in the street or wrote their felicitations ...

Together with Raffaele Carloforti I accompanied Ruskin to the station on May 23rd. After he had embraced us, he stepped back a few paces amid all the crowd of travellers, and taking off and waving his hat, he bowed his head and sent us the last adieu. When I got home my heart was full; I felt so sure that I should never see him again.[26]

In 1877 the Society for the Protection of Ancient Buildings ('Anti-Scrape') was founded by the artist, designer and poet William Morris (1834–96). In 1878 Ruskin suffered a mental breakdown, and in the same year a much-publicised court case took place in London after a libel suit brought by the American artist James Whistler (1834–1903), following an article by Ruskin in Fors Clavigera.[27]

Brantwood, 29th January '78 – My silence has been only in sadness. When I left Venice, I found myself (measuring my strength and sight on the Alps) far more exhausted than I knew – and was forced to rest utterly through great part of the summer, throwing all my intended work in England out of tune, and at last preventing my return to Venice.

What was the use of writing to tell you this? When I received your book on San Moisè,[28] though I entirely agreed with you, I was sorry that you had divided your strength, and appeared as a general caviller, and objector, instead of champion of St. Mark's alone ... In my own country, all is going wrong too – and my battle here is not only with those who would pull down churches, but who would pull down England – church, people, and God – if they could rake sixpence out of the ruin ... If only I could be in two places at once! It always seems as if one *ought* to be. But I am sure that my business at present is in England. Only believe me, as much as there in Venice, your affectionate friend ... (37:241)

From 'Ruskin in Venice' by Count Zorzi:

Meanwhile the 'restorations' went on in Venice ... and the ignorant proprietors of most beautiful ancient houses allowed them to be demolished and replaced by ugly modern buildings. Window frames, doors, balconies, staircases, well-heads, etc., found their way to the antiquaries' shops and then emigrated ...[29]

From a letter by William Morris to the Editor of the Daily News*:*

31st October 1879 – Sir, I have just received information, on the accuracy of which I can rely, that the restoration of the west front of St. Mark's at Venice, which has long been vaguely threatened, is to be taken in hand at once. A commission is called for next month, to examine its state and to determine whether it is to be pulled down immediately or to be allowed to stand till next year ... Surely it can never be too late to pull down St. Mark's at Venice, the wonder of the civilized world?[30]

Zorzi's publication on St Mark's led to a debate in Italy that aroused intense interest and controversy in other countries. The campaign from England, led by William Morris and the Society for the Protection of Ancient Buildings, resulted in a circular petition, sent in 1879 to the Italian Minister of Public Works and signed by over a thousand people, including Gladstone, Disraeli and Robert Browning. Ruskin, his health diminished by a severe mental breakdown in 1878, signed the petition but withdrew from the public debate, believing that the Basilica could not be saved by protest alone. Instead, he concentrated his energies on raising funds to ensure that his pupils and employees continued to make visual and written records of the city's architecture. By the time the petition arrived in Italy, the immediate restoration plans had already been reconsidered and withdrawn.

Ruskin to Mr F.W. Pullen, Secretary to the Ruskin Society of Manchester:

29th November 1879 – I am very glad to have your most satisfactory letter, and as gladly give you authority to receive subscriptions for drawings and sculptures of St. Mark's. Mr. Bunney's large painting of the whole west façade,[31] ordered by me a year and a half ago, and in steady progress ever since, is to be completed this spring. It was a £500 commission for the Guild [of St George], but I don't want to have to pay it with Guild capital. I have the power of getting casts, also, in places where nobody else can, and have now energy enough to give directions, but can no more pay for them out of my own pocket. (24:423)

Ruskin to William Morris:

27th May 1880 – I am old, ill, and liable any
day to be struck crazy if I get into a passion.
And, therefore, while I can still lecture – if
I choose – on rattlesnakes' tails, I can't on
anything I care about. Nor do I care to
say on this matter more than I have done,
especially since I know that the modern mob
will trample to-morrow what it spares to-day.
You younger men must found a new dynasty
– the old things *are* passed away ... (37:315)

From Ruskin's Circular Respecting Memorial
Studies of St. Mark's, Venice *(1879–80):*[32]

My friends have expressed much surprise at my
absence from the public meetings called in defence
of St. Mark's. They cannot, however, be too clearly
certified that I am now entirely unable to take part
in exciting business, or even, without grave danger,
to allow my mind to dwell on the subjects which,
having once been dearest to it, are now the sources
of acutest pain. The illness which all but killed me
two years ago [his breakdown in 1878] was not
brought on by overwork, but by grief at the course
of public affairs in England, and of affairs, public
and private alike, in Venice ...

The principles of that architecture [of St.
Mark's] are analyzed at length in the second
volume of the 'Stones of Venice', and the whole
façade described there with the best care I could,
in hope of directing the attention of English
architects to the forms of Greek sculpture which
enrich it. The words have been occasionally read
for the sound of them; and perhaps, when the
building is destroyed, may some day, with
amazement, be perceived to have been true ...

There will yet, I doubt not, be time to obtain
perfect record of all that is to be destroyed. I have
entirely honest and able draughtmanship at my
command;[33] my own resignation of my Oxford
Professorship [early in 1879] has given me leisure;
and all that I want from the antiquarian sympathy

of England is so much instant help as may permit
me, while yet in available vigour of body and
mind, to get the records made under my own
overseeship, and registered for sufficient and true.
The casts and drawings which I mean to have
made will be preserved in a consistent series in my
Museum [of the Guild of St George] at Sheffield,
where I have freehold ground enough to build a
perfectly lighted gallery for their reception.
(24:412–16)

*In 1879 Ruskin's watercolour of the north-west porch
of St Mark's was exhibited at the winter exhibition of
the Royal Society of Painters in Water Colours (Old
Water Colour Society) in the hope of attracting public
attention to the plight of St Mark's. In a postscript to
the* Circular *he listed ten photographs, which he had
commissioned in Venice in 1877 and which were
exhibited there in the following year to support the
appeal for funds.*[34]

*Count Zorzi continued to campaign for Venice,
sending his publications to Ruskin in England.
Following his protest against the demolition of the
cloister of the church of San Francesco da Paola in
Castello, which was destroyed by the Municipality
in 1885, Zorzi resigned his job at the Museo Correr
to become the director of the archaeological collection
at Cividale in the Friuli. He later returned to Venice
as Inspector of Monuments.*

From 'Ruskin in Venice' by Count Zorzi:

Mr. Ruskin returned to Venice, with his servant
Baxter and Mr. Detmar Blow [1867–1939,
architect], in 1888; and it is a source of grief and
regret to me that circumstances prevented our
meeting on this, his last visit. Instead of going to
the Calcina, he took some small rooms on the
highest floor of the Hotel Europa. He was ill, and
during the first days of his stay he did not even go
out; later he visited the Ducal Palace, St. Mark's
and other churches; but never on foot: he always
went out now in a gondola. At St. Mark's he made
the acquaintance of the late engineer Signor Pietro

Saccardo,[35] who had succeeded Signor Meduna in the direction of the restorations. On this occasion the Rev. Alexander Robertson, minister of the Scotch Church, visited Mr. Ruskin frequently at his hotel.[36]

On this last visit to Venice, Ruskin was very happy to learn that the Italian Government was maintaining its own school of mosaic workers in connection with the church, and was spending a great deal for the conservation of St. Mark's; and that, as he was told, the restorations were being carried out in harmony with the proposals made. He thought that the influence of the resident English, and of the strangers who passed through the city contributed to its welfare. Thus he departed in the confidence that our campaign had produced its effect, and that the work he had done for the 'Paradise of Cities' had been blessed by God.[37]

Ruskin to the painter and copyist Angelo Alessandri:[38]

Venice, October 1888 – Dearest Alessandri, – I was just going to bring you this note and enclosure when you came in with the dear Signor Boni [1859–1925, Director of Works at the Ducal Palace]. I am in more pain at going away than I can tell you, but there have been symptoms of illness threatening me now for some time which I cannot conquer – but by getting away from the elements of imagination which haunt me here. I am at least thankful to have seen what noble work you are doing – and to have heard Boni for that happy hour. (37:608)

The final entries from Ruskin's 'Diary for Continental Journey', 1888:

September 28th. Friday. Among the kindest people in the world –

September 30th. Sunday. – but I don't know what is going to become of me.

October 10th. VENICE. And less still here ...[39]

From 'Ruskin in Venice' by Count Zorzi:

When Ruskin died, Venice, on the proposal of Professor Alessandri and Cavalier Bordiga,[40] voted a memorial stone to be placed in the Calcina on the Zattere, where he had found the quiet needed for his beloved studies. For me at Cividale it was left to say that such a stone was not enough – that the city ought to vote a majestic monument with a statue and an inscription whereby the passing generation should record for generations to come the benefits Ruskin had conferred on Venice by his writings ...

Let us hope that my fellow-citizens may see their way to act on the proposal. Nevertheless, in his own works Ruskin created for himself a monument high above any envy, any ingratitude; enduring superior to the ruin of centuries and oblivion.[41]

Memorial plaque on the façade of the rebuilt Pensione Calcina on the Zattere[42] (Photograph 2008)

Stained glass memorial window to John Ruskin in St George's Anglican Church, Campo S. Vio. One of seven memorial windows made for the church by the Whitefriars Glass Company in London, the Ruskin window was installed in Venice during the first decade of the 20th century. In 2008 the windows were restored with funds contributed by the Venice in Peril Fund, in response to the 400th Anniversary Appeal of St George's, launched in 2005. (Photograph 2008)

NOTES

CHRONOLOGY (pp 12–14)

1 In 1836 Ruskin had fallen in love with Adèle Domecq, daughter of his father's Spanish partner in the sherry-importing firm of Ruskin, Telford and Domecq. The news of her engagement in 1839 caused a breakdown of health and the temporary interruption of his Oxford studies.

2 *Modern Painters*, originally entitled *Turner and the Ancients*, extended to a work of five volumes on the principles of art, written over seventeen years. Volume V was published in 1860.

BEFORE 'THE STONES' (pp 28–37)

1 Henry Telford, Kentish landowner, and a partner in the firm of Ruskin, Telford and Domecq.

2 Samuel Rogers (1763–1855), poet, and friend of Wordsworth, Scott and Byron. *Italy: A Poem* was illustrated with vignette engravings after Samuel Prout, Thomas Stothard and J.M.W. Turner (1775–1851).

3 John Hobbs, known as 'George' to distinguish him from Ruskin and Ruskin's father, was secretary-valet to Ruskin from 1841 to 1854. He copied much of the manuscript of the first and second volumes of *The Stones of Venice*, and learned to operate Ruskin's daguerreotype equipment.

4 Then at the Ca' Giustinian, opposite the Dogana.

5 The long railway bridge across the lagoon, connecting Venice to the mainland at Mestre, was officially opened in 1846.

6 H.I. Shapiro (ed.), *Ruskin in Italy: Letters to his Parents 1845*, Oxford, 1972, pp 198–9.

7 The Austrian Emperor's colours: a black double-headed eagle on a yellow background.

8 Shapiro, *Ruskin in Italy*, pp 201–2.

9 Shapiro, *Ruskin in Italy*, p.203.

10 Shapiro, *Ruskin in Italy*, p.207.

11 Shapiro, *Ruskin in Italy*, p.218.

12 Shapiro, *Ruskin in Italy*, p.220.

13 In late October 1845 he wrote to his father that he had 'paid twenty napoleons for Daguerreotypes alone'. Stephen Wildman notes that this expenditure amounted to almost £20 at the time and about £1,400 today. S. Wildman, *Ruskin and the Daguerreotype*, exh. cat., Ruskin Library, Lancaster, 2006.

14 *Praeterita*, Ruskin's unfinished autobiography and his last work, was published in sections over a period of four years (1885–9). During that time Ruskin was suffering intermittent and serious breakdowns of mental health, despite which *Praeterita* recalls some of the happier experiences and episodes in his life and work. For this reason it is not always reliable as a factual account.

15 Henry Liddell (1811–98), Ruskin's tutor in Greek at Christ Church, and father of Alice Liddell, the child who inspired Lewis Carroll's *Alice's Adventures in Wonderland* and *Through the Looking Glass*. Liddell became Dean of Christ Church (1855–91) and Vice-Chancellor of Oxford University (1870–74).

16 Louis-Jacques Mandé Daguerre (1787–1851), French artist and physicist, and inventor of the

daguerreotype photographic process, which used silver iodide as a light-sensitive substance to produce positive pictures on a silver-coated metal plate after an exposure of several minutes. Following immersion in a salt or sodium sulphate solution, the plate was toned with gold chloride and polished. Without a correcting mirror mechanism in the camera, the image appeared in reverse.

17 Not the first: in March 1840, in the previous year, an exhibition of daguerreotypes had been given at the Royal Society in London.

18 Jacopo Robusti, called 'Tintoretto' (1518–94), Venetian painter. 'Tintoret swept me away at once into the *mare maggiore* [the wider sea] of the schools of painting which crowned the power and perished in the fall of Venice' (35:372).

19 M. Lutyens (ed.), *Effie in Venice: Unpublished Letters of Mrs John Ruskin written from Venice between 1849 and 1852*, London, 1965, p.146 (letter of 24 February 1850).

20 In later life Ruskin was to revise his opinion, expressing growing doubts about the mechanical process. Lecturing in Oxford in 1870, he stated that photographs 'supersede no single quality nor use of fine art ... they are invaluable for some kind of facts, and for giving transcripts of drawings by great masters ... they are not true, though they seem so'. (20:165) However, he continued to commission photographs until the end of his working life.

21 Rawdon Lubbock Brown (1806–83), English scholar, resident in Venice from 1833, who worked on Venetian State papers in the city's archives until the end of his life. He befriended John and Effie Ruskin in 1849, and assisted Ruskin at all times in his researches for *The Stones of Venice*.

22 J.L. Bradley (ed.), *Ruskin's Letters from Venice: 1851–1852*, New Haven, 1955, p.1.

23 In rooms at the Casa Wetzlar on the Grand Canal, now the Gritti Palace Hotel. John and Effie had 'a room for [Ruskin] to write in ... and a kind of hall dining room; a beautiful drawing room, double bedroom and dressing room – three servants' rooms and kitchen; on the grand canal with south aspect – nearly opposite the Salute, and on first floor; for about 17 pounds a month' (letter to his father, 10:xxviii–xxix). When the lease expired, the Ruskins moved to lodgings in Piazza San Marco.

24 Bradley, *Ruskin's Letters*, p.36.

25 Bradley, *Ruskin's Letters*, p.39.

26 Bradley, *Ruskin's Letters*, pp 40–41.

27 Bradley, *Ruskin's Letters*, p.49.

28 Bradley, *Ruskin's Letters*, p.52.

29 Lord Dufferin (1826–1902) was to become Viceroy of India and Ambassador at St Petersburg, Constantinople, Rome and Paris.

30 Bradley, *Ruskin's Letters*, pp 54–5.

31 Bradley, *Ruskin's Letters*, p.67. Ruskin discussed the tides in *Stones* II (10:12–14) and in the Appendix of the same volume (10:443–4).

32 Ruskin always referred to S. Giorgio in Alga as 'St George of the Seaweed', noting in *Stones* that the church was 'unimportant in itself, but the most beautiful view of Venice at sunset is from a point at about two-thirds of the distance from the city to the island'. In 1877 he added: 'From the island itself, now, the nearer view is spoiled by loathsome mud-castings and machines. But all is spoiled from what it was. The campanile, good early Gothic, had its top knocked off to get space for an observatory in the siege.' (11:381).

33 Bradley, *Ruskin's Letters*, p.75.

34 Bradley, *Ruskin's Letters*, p.138.

BYZANTINE (pp 43–85)

1 M. Vickers, 'Wandering stones: Venice, Constantinople and Athens', in K.L. Selig and E. Sears (eds), *The Verbal and the Visual: Essays in Honour of William S. Heckscher*, New York, 1990, p.228.

2 Joseph Woods (1776–1864), English architect.

3 A reference to the remains of the frescoes by Titian and Giorgione that had once decorated the upper façade of the Fondaco dei Tedeschi. A fragment of the Giorgione fresco is preserved at Palazzo Grimani, near S. Maria Formosa.

4 The leafage balls on the outer arch can still be identified, but the details of their carving have deteriorated badly since Ruskin's day. The casts can be seen at the Ruskin Gallery, Sheffield, Guild of St George Collection. In *Ruskin and St Mark's* (London, 1984), John Unrau writes: 'Did [Ruskin] foresee the day when his casts might also become the best three-dimensional record of those superb carvings?'

5 *Procession of the Holy Cross in Piazza San Marco* (1496) by Gentile Bellini, Accademia Galleries, Venice.

6 The Pillars of Acre, so-called, were not in fact included in *Examples of the Architecture of Venice*, but were the subject of numerous daguerreotypes in Ruskin's collection and were frequently drawn by him (see pp 40, 67). More daguerreotypes were made of the pillars than of any other Venetian subject in his collection.

7 G. Saccardo, 'I Pilastri Acritani', *Archivio Veneto*, vol.34, 1887, pp 285–309.

8 Saccardo, 'I Pilastri Acritani'.

9 N. Firatli and R.M. Harrison, 'Excavations at Saraçhane in Istanbul', *Dumbarton Oaks Papers*, Washington, DC, vols 19–22, 1965–8.

10 R.M. Harrison, 'Solomon's Temple and excavations in Byzantium', *New Scientist*, 10 February 1983, pp 388–9; and *A Temple for Byzantium*, Texas, 1989; Firatli and Harrison, 'Excavations at Saraçhane in Istanbul'; Vickers, 'Wandering Stones'.

11 A seventy-six-line poem preserved in the *Palatine Anthology*, a medieval collection of epigrams.

12 I Kings vii: 17–20 (King James Version). Pietro Selvatico Estense (1803–80), architect and President of the Accademia, in *Sulla architettura e sulla scultura in Venezia*, Venice, 1847, citing the biblical text and quoted by Ruskin in *Stones* II (10:164–5).

13 M. Vickers, 'The use of the royal cubit in country house design', in L. Schmidt, C. Keller, R. Jaeger and P. Burman (eds) *Looking Forwards: The Country House in Contemporary Research and Conservation*, Cottbus, 2001.

14 Harrison, *A Temple for Byzantium*.

15 For Ruskin the colour purple symbolised royalty and divinity, as well as Kinghood and its Sorrow, as noted by Michael Wheeler, *Ruskin's God*, Cambridge, 2006, p.241.

16 A clearly visible example of this symbol can be seen at the Casa degli Zane in Campo Santa Maria Mater Domini (see pp. 82, 105).

GOTHIC (pp 89–169)

1 G. Piamonte, *Venezia vista dall'acqua*, Venice, 1968; E. Arslan, *Gothic Architecture in Venice*, London, 1972; and A. Rizzi, *Scultura esterna a Venezia*, Venice, 1987.

2 A hard biscuit manufactured by Huntley & Palmer from the 1830s.

3 At the time of writing an extensive restoration of the palace is approaching completion. The photograph of the whole building, reproduced here, was taken in 2006 before the works began. The detail of the Veneto-Byzantine paterae and *formelle* was taken in May 2014, after cleaning.

4 Beheaded for treason in 1355.

5 The Casa degli Zane. Ruskin daguerreotyped this house in *c.*1850, writing in his notes on Campo Santa Maria Domini, 'The beautiful 2nd order house daged. The cross on the left has hand in centre between sun and moon' (Notebook 'M2', p.69). In 1961 the daguerreotype was acquired by the Museum of the History of Science, Oxford.

6 In Notebook 'Bit Book' (*c.*1850), p.35, Ruskin recorded, 'Door daguerred with lozenge centre at Ponte St Tomà'.

7 Plate 6 in *Examples of the Architecture of Venice* (11:340).

8 In 2005 the Venice in Peril Fund financed the cleaning and restoration of the six paterae of the front and lateral porches of the Carmini church (S. Maria del Carmelo).

9 Visible in the early eighteenth-century engraving by Vincenzo Coronelli, illustrated on p.112, and entitled 'The other Palazzo Zorzi at S. Severo', *Singolarità di Venezia*, Venice, 1709.

10 No longer visible, though certain sections have been reconstructed.

11 The church of the Carità was extensively remodelled in the eighteenth century after the fall of its campanile.

12 Ruskin's daguerreotype of the building is held at the Ruskin Library, Lancaster.

13 Palazzo Contarini dei Cavalli is at the junction of the Grand Canal and the rio di S. Luca. When Ruskin knew it, Palazzo Grimani, to the left of Palazzo Cavalli, was the headquarters of the Venice Post Office.

14 Ca' Foscari was to become, from 1868, the headquarters of the University of Venice, since when the building has undergone several major restorations.

15 Vincenzo Lazari and Pietro Selvatico, *Guida di Venezia e delle isole circonvicine*, Venice, 1852. Building of the Giustiniani palace commenced in the 1450s.

16 *The Family of Darius at the Feet of Alexander after the Battle of Issus* (1565–70) by Paolo Veronese. The

painting was purchased by the British government in 1857, and hangs in the National Gallery, London.

17 Palazzo Pesaro degli Orfei, now known as Palazzo Fortuny, and open as a museum and exhibition space.

18 The year 1505 was the date of installation, not of the work itself, which is of the fifteenth century with later decorative additions.

19 The Scuola Vecchia della Misericordia, founded in 1308, and the seat of the confraternity of the Misericordia, one of the many charitable and religious institutions for the laity.

20 In fact, the palace of the Grandiben family, at Ponte Erizzo, rio di S. Martino, Castello 4003.

21 Rizzi, *Scultura Esterna a Venezia*, pp 31–2, 579, 625–6.

22 In 1876 Ruskin commissioned a watercolour, *The Recumbent Statue of San Simeone in the Church of S. Simeone Grande*, for the Guild of St George from Raffaele Carloforti, which can be seen at the Ruskin Gallery (Guild of St George Collection), Sheffield.

23 Only three sides of the fourth capital were visible to Ruskin at the time, the inner sides being walled up.

RENAISSANCE (pp 173–221)

1 Philippe de Commynes (1446–1511), Flemish-born French chronicler and diplomat. The last part of his *Mémoires* concerns the Italian expedition of Charles VIII of France.

2 Book VI, chapter 18 of the *Mémoires*. The passage is given in French in *The Stones of Venice* I (9:32–3).

3 Rawdon Brown had purchased the Ca' Dario for £480, restoring it to its former condition and selling it.

4 Palazzo Contarini dal Bòvolo near Campo Manin. In 1499 the spiral staircase was augmented to the 15th-century Palazzo Contarini by Giovanni Candi. *Bòvolo* means 'snail-shell' in Venetian dialect.

5 The church of S. Paternian, together with its ancient pentagonal campanile, was demolished in 1871 and the square was renamed in memory of Daniele Manin (1804–57), lawyer, Venetian patriot and leader of the 1848–9 uprising against Austrian rule.

6 The remains of one of the early sixteenth-century frescoes, *La Nuda* by Giorgione, are preserved in Palazzo Grimani (S. Maria Formosa).

7 Mauro Codussi remodelled the church in 1492–1504, leaving it unfinished. The west façade dates

from 1542 and the campo façade from 1604; both were benefactions of the Cappello family.

8 *The Miracle of the True Cross* by Vittore Carpaccio, 1494, Accademia Galleries, Venice.

9 'I stood in Venice on the Bridge of Sighs / A palace and a prison on each hand' are the first lines of the fourth canto of Byron's *Childe Harold's Pilgrimage* (1812–18). Towards the end of his life Ruskin recalled in *Praeterita* that 'My Venice, like Turner's, had been chiefly created for us by Byron' (32:295).

AFTER 'THE STONES' (pp 224–235)

1 In 1855 Effie married the artist John Everett Millais.

2 Rose La Touche (1849–75) was aged nine when Ruskin agreed to give drawing lessons to her and her elder sister Emily at the request of their mother, Maria La Touche. As Rose grew up, an intense but ultimately unhappy relationship developed between the older man and the young girl, with misunderstandings on both sides. Rose, who was sickly, suffered from religious mania and died in a sanatorium at the age of twenty-six.

3 Brantwood, overlooking Coniston Water in the Lake District, was bought by Ruskin in 1871 and became his home from 1872 until his death in 1900. The house and garden were saved for the nation by J.H. Whitehouse (founder of Bembridge School on the Isle of Wight and the Birmingham Ruskin Society), who purchased the property and established the Brantwood Trust in 1951 to preserve the house and its contents. Filled with Ruskin's watercolours, furniture and personal memorabilia, Brantwood is now in the care of the Ruskin Foundation and is kept open as a museum and exhibition space for most of the year.

4 The Guild of St George, initially known as the St George's Fund, was founded by Ruskin in 1871 with his own money, and its aims were outlined in *Fors Clavigera* (27:9). The Guild was formally established in 1878 with premises at Walkley in Sheffield, and in 1890 moved to Meersbrook Park, Sheffield, opening as the Ruskin Museum. The Guild of St George's Collection is now cared for by the Ruskin Collection at Museums Sheffield.

5 Charles Eliot Norton (1827–1908), American scholar, who became Ruskin's trusted friend, intimate correspondent, and ultimately his literary executor.

Norton was involved in the launch of the *Atlantic Monthly* with James Russell Lowell, and established his scholarly career with a book on Dante's *Vita Nuova*, becoming Harvard Professor of Fine Arts in 1875. His anxiety to protect Ruskin's reputation after the latter's death led to the destruction of some of Ruskin's letters, particularly those relating to Rose La Touche.

6 The island of San Giorgio in Alga, to the south-west of the Giudecca. (See pp 35, 36.)

7 John Wharlton Bunney (1828–82), artist, had been Ruskin's pupil in drawing at the Working Men's College in London. With Ruskin's help, Bunney and his wife moved to Italy immediately after their marriage in 1863. Bunney worked for several years between Florence and Verona, and in 1870 established his studio in Venice. Ruskin commissioned many works from him, including the 1871 watercolour drawing of the Palazzo Manzoni reproduced on p.227. Bunney died suddenly in Venice in 1882 after completing a major work, *The West Front of St Mark's* (see p.225), having recorded in his journal some 565 working sessions on the picture. 'His name', wrote Ruskin, 'will remain ineffaceably connected with the history of all efforts recently made in Italy for preservation of true record of her national monuments.'

8 Raffaele Carloforti (1853–1901), artist and copyist, was befriended by Ruskin in the 1870s, probably in Assisi. Ruskin supported his later studies at the Accademia delle Belle Arti in Venice, and commissioned many works for the Guild of St George. Carloforti introduced Ruskin to Count Zorzi in November 1876.

9 For accounts of the works at St Mark's, see Unrau, *Ruskin and St Mark's*, London, 1984; Pemble, *Venice Rediscovered*, Oxford, 1995; and Hewison, *Ruskin on Venice*, London, 2009.

10 George Allen (1832–1907). Formerly Ruskin's pupil at the Working Men's College in London, where Ruskin gave weekly drawing lessons in the 1850s, Allen became general assistant and engraver of plates for Ruskin, who paid for his instruction. From 1871 he took over the publication and distribution of Ruskin's works from Smith, Elder & Co.

11 *St Mark's Rest* was published in six parts between 1877 and 1884, and later in a collected volume. Its subtitle was *The history of Venice, written for the help of the few travellers who still care for her monuments.*

12 Extract courtesy of the executors of M.J.H. Bunney.

13 A reference to Canaletto's *The Church of Santi Giovanni e Paolo with the Scuola di San Marco*, 1725 (Gemäldegalerie, Dresden). Ruskin's drawing of the Scuola Grande di San Marco (1876) is reproduced as the frontispiece to *The Stones of Venice* III (*Works* 11).

14 Preoccupied with the memory of Rose La Touche, who had died in 1875, Ruskin was spending long hours in the Accademia copying Carpaccio's *The Dream of St Ursula*, a painting he associated with Rose. St Ursula was believed to have died a virgin after requesting her suitor to wait for three years before marriage. Ruskin's copy of the picture is reproduced in *Fors Clavigera* (28:344).

15 The Armenian monastery on the island of San Lazzaro or the island of San Giorgio in Alga in the southern lagoon.

16 Joan Severn, *née* Agnew (1846–1924), Ruskin's distant cousin, had joined the family as companion to his mother, Margaret, after the death of John James Ruskin in 1864. She and her husband, Arthur Severn, continued to live with and care for Ruskin until the end of his life.

17 In 1877 the Calcina on the Zattere was a small inn with connecting lodgings. It was completely rebuilt in 1905 and a memorial plaque to Ruskin was placed on the façade of the new building. (See p.235.)

18 For an account of restorations at St Mark's see *Works* 24: pp lviii–lxiii. See also Clegg, *Ruskin and Venice*, 1978, pp 183–7; Unrau, *Ruskin and St Mark's*, 1984, pp 191–205; Pemble, *Venice Rediscovered*, 1995, pp 145–55; and Hewison, *Ruskin on Venice*, 2009, pp 345–397.

19 Eugenia Szczepanowska was engaged to Zorzi and later became his wife. She was fluent in English, and acted as interpreter and translator for Ruskin and Zorzi.

20 The early gothic Palazzo Zorzi Bon on the rio di S. Severo, next to Codussi's Renaissance Palazzo Zorzi.

21 Ruskin's watercolour of Palazzo Zorzi Bon (see p.111) was made after he had daguerreotyped the window during his 1849–50 visit. In 1877, recognising its value as a record of subsequently destroyed incrustation, he arranged for the drawing to be sent out from England to provide visual evidence in support of Zorzi's argument. He left the picture in Venice in the safekeeping of John Bunney, whose journal of May 1877 records that

Ruskin asked him to take care of a number of his books and architectural drawings.

22 *The South Side of St. Mark's: Sketch after Rain*, Ashmolean Museum, Oxford (see p.40).

23 Salviati & Company, founded in 1859, and later the partly British-owned glass-manufacturing firm, Compagnia Venezia Murano, had supplied the glass for new mosaics in a modern design.

24 A.P. Zorzi, *Osservazioni intorno ai restauri interni ed esterni della basilica di San Marco*, Venice, 1877, and 24:405–11.

25 *The North-West Porch of St. Mark's*, 1877, Ruskin Foundation, Ruskin Library, Lancaster. Ruskin completed the watercolour on 10 May 1877, shortly before his departure for England. His copy of part of it, made for C.E. Norton in 1879 and now at the Fogg Art Museum, Harvard University, is reproduced in *The Stones of Venice* II.

26 A.P. Zorzi, 'Ruskin in Venice', *Cornhill Magazine*, August/September 1906, pp 371–3.

27 Reproduced in *The Works of John Ruskin* 29, Letter 79. Whistler sued for libel, won the case and was awarded a farthing's damages.

28 A.P. Zorzi, *Sulla demolizione della Chiesa di S. Moisè*, Venice, 1877. Ruskin disliked the church of S. Moisè (see p.218). In view of this and his precarious mental health, he would have been unwilling to take an active part from England in Zorzi's campaign against its proposed demolition. In the event, the church was not destroyed.

29 Zorzi, 'Ruskin in Venice', p.376.

30 Published 1 November 1879, N. Kelvin (ed.), *The Collected Letters of William Morris*, vol.I, Princeton, 1984, p.529.

31 See p.225. *The West Front of St Mark's* (1877–82) by John Bunney was commissioned by Ruskin for the Guild of St George. The painting hangs in the Ruskin Gallery, Guild of St George Collection, Museums Sheffield.

32 The eight-page pamphlet was given to visitors to the Old Water Colour Society's winter exhibition and the Fine Art Society, New Bond Street. In 1880 it was reprinted in vol.19 of the *Art Journal*.

33 Principally that of Angelo Alessandri, J.W. Bunney, Raffaele Carloforti and T.M. Rooke.

34 See Hewison, *Ruskin on Venice*, p.383.

35 Pietro Saccardo (1830–1903), Venetian architect who became *proto* (architect) of St Mark's and of the Scuola Grande di S. Rocco. He replaced G.B. Meduna in 1883 and oversaw the revised plans for conservation work on the west front of the Basilica.

36 Dr Robertson (1846–1933) wrote: 'To those who knew Mr. Ruskin only through certain of his writings, the idea is not unnatural that he was dogmatic and brusque; but in reality he was gentle and unassuming and sympathetic' (*Good Words*, London, 1900).

37 Zorzi, 'Ruskin in Venice', pp 377–8.

38 Angelo Alessandri (1854–1931) studied at the Accademia delle Belle Arti in Venice, where he later became professor. He undertook many commissions for Ruskin and the Guild of St George, principally on the works of Carpaccio and Tintoretto.

39 Joan Evans and J.H. Whitehouse (eds), *The Diaries of John Ruskin*, 3 vols, Oxford, 1956–9, vol.III, p.1150.

40 Giovanni Bordiga (1854–1933), geometrician and art critic. Originally Professor of Geometry at the University of Padua, he became President of the Accademia in Venice (1916); first President of the Venice Biennale (1920–26); President of the Fondazione Querini Stampalia (1926–29); and President of the Ateneo Veneto (1929–33). In 1926 he founded the Istituto Universitario di Architettura di Venezia (IUAV).

41 Zorzi, 'Ruskin in Venice', pp 379–80.

42 Translation of the plaque reads as follows:

> John Ruskin
> Lived in this house, 1877
>
> High priest of art
> In our stones and in our St Mark's
> In almost in every monument of Italy
> He sought at one and the same time
> The craftsman's soul and the soul of the people
>
> Every marble, every bronze, every canvas
> Each of these things proclaimed to him
> That beauty is religion
> If the virtue of man inspire it
> And the people's reverence accept it
>
> The council of Venice, in gratitude
> 26 January 1900

(Ruskin died on 19 January 1900.)

GLOSSARY

abacus A narrow rectangular block forming the
   uppermost element of a capital and supporting an
   architrave

abbaino A dormer window

acanthus Herbaceous plant with prickly leaves; in Greek
   architecture, a conventional representation of its leaf
   used as a decorative motif on the Corinthian capital

alto rilievo High relief. Relief sculpture, carved deeply
   enough to suggest that the main parts of the design
   are almost detached from their support

annulet A fillet or ring encircling a column

apse A semicircular or polygonal vaulted space, usually
   placed at the eastern end of a church

arcade A series of arches carried on piers or columns

architrave The main beam resting on the abacus of a
   column; the horizontal parts surrounding a door or
   window; the lowest part of an entablature

archivolt The moulded architrave round an arch

arco a tutto sesto A rounded arch

arco a tutto sesto acuto An ogival arch

Arsenale The ship-building yard and armaments depot
   of the Venetian Republic

barrel vault A semi-circular arch-shaped roof

basso rilievo Low relief. Relief sculpture in which the
   figures project less than half their true depth from
   the background

boss An ornamental knot; a projecting ornament
   covering the intersection of ribs in a vault or ceiling

breccia Rock, naturally formed from mixed fragments of
   different kinds of stone

buttress A support built against the interior or exterior
   wall of a building

ca' (casa) Venetian term for a palace or house

cable A convex moulding resembling a rope or cable

calle A Venetian street or alley

campanile Bell tower, sometimes detached from the
   church or building to which it belongs

campiello A small square

campo A Venetian town square

capital The carved head of a column, pier, pilaster or
   pillar

casque Helmet or ornamental head

chequering A pattern of alternating squares or lozenges
   of contrasting colour or texture

clerestory The upper walls of the nave of a church, with a
   series of windows

colonnade A row of columns creating a sheltered area

cornice The third and uppermost part of the
   entablature; the projecting moulding at the
   top of a building

corte Courtyard

cortile An internal courtyard

crenellation Battlements, usually decorative; the spaces or
   indentations in an embattled parapet

crocket An ornament resembling an outward curving
   leaf, used on spires and pinnacles in Gothic
   architecture

cupola A small dome, ornamenting a roof or crowning
   another dome

cusp The point made where two curves meet, especially
   in Gothic tracery; the projecting points formed on
   the ribs or mullions of a traceried window. Also used
   by Ruskin for the pointed meeting-place at the top
   of an ogee-arched window

dentils Small square or oblong blocks, arranged like teeth and used as decoration for cornices and mouldings

diaper work A patterned wall decoration composed of adjoining identical units, such as diamond or squared shapes

Doge The chief officer or duke of the Venetian Republic, elected for life

dog-tooth An architectural carved moulding of raised four-pointed stars placed diagonally

dome A curved or spherical vault (may also be semi-circular with an oval section) found mainly in religious buildings

dripstone A projecting moulding, keeping rain from the parts below it

entablature The uppermost and horizontal part of a classical order (including the architrave, frieze and cornice), supported by columns or pillars

escutcheon A shield with a coat of arms; any shield-shaped ornament

extrados The exterior curve or surface of an arch or vault

eurythmia Harmony of proportion

façade The face of a building; its main elevation and principal front towards a street or open space

finial Ornament crowning an architectural feature; the uppermost part of a pinnacle

fluting Closely spaced parallel grooves used to ornament columns and pilasters

foliation Ornamental leaf carving, often found in Gothic architecture, especially in the decorated style

fondaco Store or warehouse; also a trading centre for foreign merchants in Venice

fondamenta A canal-side street in Venice

formella A decorative panel, usually oblong, of marble, stone, bronze or wood, carved or sculpted with figures or scenes and used on doors, walls and cornices

fregio a scacchi Frieze with Byzantine dentil decoration

frieze A horizontal band, with cornice above and architrave below

ghiera (it.) Archivolt

Greek cross A cross with vertical and horizontal shafts of equal length

iconostasis The screen separating the chancel from the nave in a Byzantine church

incrustation Decoration of precious material applied in low relief, e.g. the facing of sheets of marble onto a brick building

intaglio Incised or engraved ornamental carving

interstice Intervening space, chink or crevice

intonaco Plasterwork

intrados The inner curve or surface of an arch or vault

jasper Opaque variety of quartz, usually red, yellow or brown

keystone The central wedge-shaped stone at the summit of an arch, locking the whole together (and see *voussoirs*)

Latin cross A cross with its lower shaft longer than the other three

lintel The horizontal piece of timber or stone over a door or aperture, bearing the weight of the wall above it

loggia A gallery or balcony, open on one or more sides, with a roof supported by pilasters or columns

lunette Semi-circular space above a door or window, decorated with sculpture, fresco or mosaic

machicolations Openings that project out from the tops of walls, just below the battlements

meander In heraldry, an ornamental pattern of winding, undulating or interlocking lines

monolithic column Column made from a single block of stone

mosaic A design made by cementing small pieces (*tesserae*) of hard, coloured substances, e.g. marble, glass, ceramic or semi-precious stones, to a surface

nave The main body or central aisle of a church

oculus Oval or circular opening or window in a wall or dome

ogee arch Gothic arch shaped in a double curve, with the lower concave curves becoming convex towards the apex

opus Alexandrinum 'Alexandrian work'. Patterned surface decoration, made of slabs of coloured marble, often disc-shaped, with encircling bands forming a figure-of-eight motif

palazzo Palace; any dignified or important building

parapet Low wall bordering the edge of a balcony or roof. See *crenellation*

patera A flat stone medallion, plaque or ornament, often circular in shape and carved in low relief

pediment A gable or gable-like ornament over a portico, door or window, triangular or segmental in shape

pendentive The triangle formed by the intersection of a dome with two adjacent arches springing from supporting columns

piano nobile The main living floor of an Italian palace, usually on the first-floor level *piazza* An open space or square surrounded by buildings. In Venice, used only of Piazza San Marco

pier A solid support or pillar, of rectangular or square section, supporting an arch, the span of a bridge, etc.

pilaster A rectangular column or shallow pier engaged in a wall, and projecting only slightly from it. Its function is generally decorative rather than structural

pinnacle A small decorative feature crowning a spire or buttress in Gothic architecture

polychrome The decoration of architectural elements and sculpture, in a variety of colours

ponte A bridge

porphyry A hard rock anciently quarried in Egypt, composed of crystals of white or red felspar in red matrix

portico Porch or roofed arcade supported by columns, usually attached to the front or sides of a building

quadriga A chariot drawn by four horses abreast, often crowning a triumphal arch or monument

quatrefoil A four-lobed leaf or flower design, used in Gothic window tracery

rhomb Lozenge or diamond-shaped object

rib vault A vault divided by convex ribs or mouldings into compartments or cells

rio Venetian name for a waterway or canal, excepting the Grand Canal, the Cannaregio Canal and the Giudecca Canal

ripristino Rendering to the original

riva A bank or quayside street in Venice, generally wider than a *fondamenta*

scroll See *volute*

scuola Venetian guild or lay fraternity, dedicated to charitable works

serpentine A soft rock used as decorative material. Usually dark green, and mottled or spotted like the skin of a snake

shaft The part of a column between the base and capital; one of a group of clustered columns

soffit The underside of an arch, architrave or balcony

spandrel The triangular area of stone or brickwork formed by the outer curve of an arch; the horizontal drawn from the level of it apex and the vertical of its springing; the triangular space between two arches in an arcade

stemma Coat of arms; shield

stilted arch A round arch that rises vertically before it springs

string-course A decorative horizontal band on the exterior wall of a building

tesselated Covered in *tesserae*

tessera A small, usually cubic, piece of marble, glass or ceramic, used as the base unit in making a mosaic

tie beam The horizontal beam connecting the lower ends of rafters

tracery Stone open-work with a decorative pattern, used to fill windows and balconies, or as a relief ornament on solid walls

traghetto A gondola-ferry in Venice

vignette A design or illustration that fades into the surrounding space without a definite border

volute A spiral or scroll-shaped architectural ornament

voussoirs The wedge-shaped stones forming the curved part of an arch (and see *keystone*)

Zattere Rafts; the name still given to the south-east shore of Dorsoduro in Venice, where rafts were moored

BIBLIOGRAPHY AND
RECOMMENDED READING

Ammerman, Albert, *Venice before San Marco: Recent Studies on the Origins of the City*, Colgate, 2001

Arslan, Edoardo, *Gothic Architecture in Venice*, trans. Anne Engel, London, 1972

Bassi, Elena and Egle Renata Trincanato, *Il Palazzo Ducale nella storia e nell'arte di Venezia*, Milan, 1960

Birch, Dinah, *Ruskin's Myths*, Oxford, 1988

Bomford, David and Gabriele Finaldi, *Venice through Canaletto's Eyes*, London, 1998

Boucher, Bruce, 'Baroque architecture in Venice', *Apollo*, no.105, 1979, pp 388–95

Bradley, J.L. (ed.), *Ruskin's Letters from Venice: 1851–1852*, New Haven, 1955

Bradley, J.L. and I. Ousby (eds), *The Correspondence of John Ruskin and Charles Eliot Norton*, Cambridge, 1987

Brown, Patricia Fortini, *Venice and Antiquity: The Venetian Sense of the Past*, New Haven and London, 1988

Bunney, Sarah, 'John Bunney's "Big Picture" of St Mark's, and the Ruskin–Bunney relationship', *Ruskin Review and Bulletin*, vol.4, no.1, 2007, pp 18–47

Bunney, Sarah, 'J.W. Bunney's "Big Picture": an update', *Ruskin Review and Bulletin*, vol. 4 no.3, 2008, pp 13–15

Cicogna, Emmanuele, *Delle iscrizioni veneziane raccolte ed illustrate*, 6 vols, Venice, 1824–53

Clarke, Ashley and Philip Rylands, *Restoring Venice: The Church of the Madonna dell'Orto*, London, 1997

Clegg, Jeanne, *John Ruskin's Correspondence with Angelo Alessandri*, Manchester, 1978

Clegg, Jeanne, *Ruskin and Venice*, London, 1981

Concina, Ennio, *A History of Venetian Architecture*, Cambridge, 1988

Costantini, Paolo and Italo Zannier, *I dagherrotipi della collezione Ruskin*, Venice, 1986

Dearden, James S., 'The Ruskin Circle in Italy in 1872', *Connoisseur*, no.179, April 1972, pp 240–45

Dearden, James S., *John Ruskin: A Life in Pictures*, Sheffield, 1999

Deichmann, F.W., 'I pilastri acritani', *Atti della Pontifica Accademia Romana di Archeologia*, vol.50, 1980, pp 75–89

Demus, Otto and Ferdinando Forlati, *The Church of San Marco in Venice* (Dumbarton Oaks Studies VI), Washington DC, 1960

Demus, Otto with Lorenzo Lazzarini, Mario Piana and Guido Tigler, *Le sculture esterne di San Marco*, Milan, 1995

Dickinson, Rachel (ed.), *John Ruskin's Correspondence with Joan Severn: Sense and Nonsense Letters*, Oxford, 2008

Evans, Joan and J.H. Whitehouse (eds), *The Diaries of John Ruskin*, 3 vols, Oxford, 1956–9

Gianighian, Giorgio and Paola Pavanini, *Dietro i palazzi: Tre secoli di architettura minore a Venezia 1492–1803*, Venice, 1984

Goy, Richard, *The House of Gold: Building a Palace in Medieval Venice*, Cambridge, 1992

Grandesso, Espedita, *I Portali Medievale di Venezia*, Venice, 1988

Griffiths, Ralph and John Law (eds), *Rawdon Brown and the Anglo-Venetian Relationship*, Stroud, 2005

Hanley, Keith and Emma Sdegno (eds), *Ruskin, Venice and Nineteenth-Century Cultural Travel*, Venice, 2010

Harrison, Martin, 'Solomon's Temple and excavations in Byzantium', *New Scientist*, 10 February 1983, pp 388–9

Harrison, Martin, *A Temple for Byzantium*, London, 1989

Hewison, Robert, *The Argument of the Eye*, London, 1976

Hewison, Robert, *Ruskin on Venice*, New Haven and London, 2009

Hewison, Robert (ed.), *Ruskin's Artists*, Aldershot, 2000

Hewison, Robert, Ian Warrell and Stephen Wildman, *Ruskin, Turner and the Pre-Raphaelites*, exh. cat., Tate Britain, London, 2000

Hills, Paul, *Venetian Colour: Marble, Mosaic, Painting and Glass, 1250–1550*, New Haven and London, 1999

Hilton, Tim, *John Ruskin: The Early Years*, New Haven and London, 1985

Hilton, Tim, *John Ruskin: The Later Years 1859–1900*, New Haven and London, 2000

Howard, Deborah, *Venice and the East*, New Haven and London, 2000

Howard, Deborah, *The Architectural History of Venice*, 2nd edn, New Haven and London, 2002

Hunt, John Dixon, *The Wider Sea: A Life of John Ruskin*, London, 1992

Jacobson, Ken and Jenny, *Carrying off the Palaces: John Ruskin's Lost Daguerreotypes*, London, 2014

Keates, Jonathan, *The Siege of Venice*, London, 2005

Kite, Stephen, *Building Ruskin's Italy*, Aldershot, 2012

Landow, George, *The Aesthetic and Critical Theories of John Ruskin*, Princeton, 1971

Lauritzen, Peter and Alexander Zielcke, *Palaces of Venice*, London, 1978

Lazzarini, Lorenzo and Marisa Laurenzi Tabasso, *Il Restauro della Pietra*, Cedam, 1986

Lorenzetti, Giulio, *Venice and Its Lagoon*, trans. J. Guthrie, Rome, 1961

Lutyens, Mary, *Effie in Venice: Unpublished Letters of Mrs John Ruskin, Written from Venice between 1849 and 1852*, London, 1965

Mango, C., *Byzantine Architecture*, New York, 1976

Manno, Antonio, *Palazzo Ducale: Guida al Museo dell'Opera*, Venice, 1996

Manno, Antonio, *Il Poema del Tempo*, Venice, 1999

Maretto, Paolo, *La casa veneziana nella storia della città*, Venice, 1986

Morris, Jan, *The Venetian Empire: A Sea Voyage*, London, 1980

Newall, Christopher (ed.) with Christopher Baker, Ian Jeffrey and Conal Shields, *John Ruskin: Artist and Observer*, exh. cat., Ottawa and London, 2014

Norwich, John Julius, *A History of Venice*, New York, 1982

O'Gorman, Francis (ed.), *John Ruskin's Praeterita*, Oxford, 2012

Paoletti, Pietro, *L'architettura e la scultura del Rinascimento in Venezia*, Venice, 1893

Pemble, John, *Venice Rediscovered*, Oxford, 1995

Penny, Nicholas, *Ruskin's Drawings in the Ashmolean Museum*, Oxford, 1988

Penny, Nicholas, *The Materials of Sculpture*, New Haven and London, 1993

Perry, Marilyn, 'St Mark's trophies: legend, superstition and archaeology in Renaissance Venice', *Journal of the Warburg and Courtauld Institutes*, no.40, 1977

Pertot, Gianfranco, *Venezia 'Restaurata': centosettanta anni di interventi di restauro sugli edifici Veneziani*, Milan, 1988

Pertot, Gianfranco, *Venice: Extraordinary Maintenance*, trans. C. Donougher, London, 2004

Piamonte, Giannina, *Venezia vista dall'acqua*, Venice, 1968

Polacco, Renato, *Sculture romane e avori tardo-antichi e medievali del Museo archeologico di Venezia*, Rome, 1988

Quill, Sarah, 'The splendour of miscellaneous spoil: Ruskin's "Pillars of Acre" in Venice', unpublished typescript of a lecture to the Ruskin Society, London, 2005

Rizzi, Alberto, *Scultura esterna a Venezia*, Venice, 1987

Romanelli, Giandomenico, *Venezia Ottocento: Materiali per una storia architetettonica e urbanistica della città nel secolo XIX*, Rome, 1977

Romanelli, Giandomenico, *Venezia nell'Ottocento: Immagini e mito*, ed. G. Pavanello and G. Romanelli, Venice, 1983

Rosand, David, *Myths of Venice: The Figuration of a State*, UNC Press, 2005

Ruskin, John, *The Stones of Venice*, 3 vols, London, 1851–53

Ruskin, John, *The Works of John Ruskin*, ed. E.T. Cook and A. Wedderburn, Library Edition, 39 vols, London, 1903–12

Saccardo, G., 'I pilastri acritani', *Archivio Veneto*, no.24, 1887, pp 285–309

Sagredo, A., *Degli edifici consacrati al culto divino in Venezia o distrutti o mutati d'uso nella prima metà del sec.XIX*, Venice, 1855

Scarfi, Bianca Maria, *Il Leone di Venezia: studi e ricerche sulla statua di bronzo della Piazzetta*, Venice, 1990

Selvatico, Pietro, *Sulla architettura e sulla scultura in Venezia dal Medio Evo sino ai nostri giorni*, Venice, 1847

Selvatico, Pietro and Vincenzo Lazari, *Guida di Venezia e delle isole circonvicine*, Venice, 1852

Shapiro, H.I., *Ruskin in Italy: Letters to His Parents 1845*, Oxford, 1972

Strupp, Joachim, 'The colour of money: use, cost and aesthetic appreciation of marble in Venice, ca. 1500', *Venezia Cinquecento*, no.5, 1993, pp 7–32

Tassini, Giuseppe, *Alcuni palazzi ed antichi edifici di Venezia storicamente illustrati*, Venice, 1879

Tassini, Giuseppe, *Edifici di Venezia distrutti vôlti ad uso diverso*, Venice, reprinted 1969

Trincanato, Egle Renata, *Venezia Minore*, Milan, 1948

Tucker, Paul (ed.), *John Ruskin: Resumé of Italian Art and Architecture (1845)*, Pisa, 2003

Unrau, John, *Ruskin and St. Mark's*, London, 1984

Vickers, Michael, 'A "new" capital from St Polyeuktos (Saraçhane) in Venice', *Oxford Journal of Archaeology*, vol.8, no.2, 1989

Vickers, Michael, 'Wandering Stones: Venice, Constantinople and Athens', in K.-L. Selig and E. Sear (eds), *The Verbal and the Visual: Essays in Honour of William S. Heckscher*, New York, 1990

Vickers, Michael, 'The use of the royal cubit in country house design', in L. Schmidt, C. Keller, R. Jaeger, P. Burman (eds), *Looking Forwards: The Country House in Contemporary Research and Conservation*, Cottbus, 2001

Vio, Ettore, 'Le transformazioni architettoniche della facciata sud e la "Porta da Mar"', in *Da Cappella della Madonna a Cappella Zen, Arte, Storia restauri della Basilica di San Marco a Venezia*, Venice, 2012

Vio, Ettore (ed.), *Il manto di pietra della basilica di San Marco a Venezia*, Venice, 2012

Vucetich, Antonio, *Elenco degli edifici monumentali*, Venice, 1905

Wheeler, Michael, *Ruskin's God*, Cambridge, 2006

Wheeler, Michael (ed.), *Ruskin and Environment: The Storm-Cloud of the Nineteenth Century*, Manchester, 1995

Wildman, Stephen, *'A noble invention': Ruskin's Daguerreotypes of Venice and Verona*, exh. cat., Ruskin Library, Lancaster University, 2013

Wildman, Stephen, *Ruskin and the Daguerreotype*, exh. cat., Ruskin Library, Lancaster University, 2006

Wildman, Stephen, *John Ruskin: Photographer and Draughtsman*, exh. cat., Watts Gallery, Compton, 2014

Wilmer, Clive (ed.), *John Ruskin: Unto This Last and Other Writings*, Harmondsworth, 1985

Wilmer, Clive (ed.), *William Morris: News from Nowhere and Other Writings*, Harmondsworth, 1993

Wolters, Wolfgang, *La scultura veneziana gotica 1300–1460*, 2 vols, Venice, 1976

Wolters, Wolfgang with Umberto Franzoi and Terisio Pignatti, *Il Palazzo Ducale di Venezia*, Treviso, 1990

Zanotto, Francesco, *Venezia e le sue lagune*, Venice, 1847

Zanotto, Francesco, *Il Palazzo Ducale di Venezia*, Venice, 1853–61

Zorzi, Alvise Piero, *Osservazioni intorno ai ristauri interni ed esterni della Basilica di San Marco*, Venice, 1877

Zorzi, Alvise Piero, 'Ruskin and Venice', *Cornhill Magazine*, August/September 1906

Zorzi, Alvise, *Venezia scomparsa*, 2 vols, 2nd edn, Milan, 1984

LIST OF SITES BY *SESTIERE*

Venice is divided into six *sestieri* (districts). Sites included
in the book are listed below in order of the buildings'
postal address numbers within each *sestiere*.

SAN MARCO SESTIERE (VENICE 30124)

Piazza S. Marco	Basilica of S. Marco (St Mark's) and the campanile of S. Marco
S. Marco 1	The Porta della Carta, main entrance to the Ducal Palace
S. Marco 1–2	Palazzo Ducale (The Ducal Palace)
Piazzetta di S. Marco	The Pilastri Acritani ('Pillars of Acre') in the Piazzetta
Piazzetta di S Marco	Columns of the Lion of St Mark and St Theodore
Rio di Palazzo	Ponte della Paglia
Rio di Palazzo	Ponte dei Sospiri (Bridge of Sighs)
S. Marco 3–41 (Piazzetta)	Libreria Vecchia Sansoviniana (now Biblioteca Marciana) in the Piazzetta
S. Marco 42–70	Procuratie Nuove on the east side of Piazza S. Marco
S. Marco 72–78	Ala Napoleonica (on the site of the former church of S. Geminiano) on the south side of Piazza S. Marco
S. Marco 79–143	Procuratie Vecchie on the west side of Piazza S. Marco
S. Marco 1364	Palazzo Giustinian, Calle del Ridotto
Campo S. Moisè	Church of S. Moisè in Campo S. Moisè
Campo S. Maria del Giglio	Church of S. Maria Zobenigo (del Giglio) in Campo S. Maria del Giglio
S. Marco 2307 and 2318	Palazzo Contarini Fasan on the Grand Canal and in Campiello Contarini
S. Marco 2321	Palazzo Ferro Fini on the Grand Canal
S. Marco 2467	Palazzo Pisani Gritti on the Grand Canal and Campo del Traghetto, and known to the Ruskins as 'Casa Wetzlar'
S. Marco 2542–2546	Palazzo Moroni in Calle del Piovan o Gritti and on the rio della Fenice
S. Marco 2557	Façade of Palazzo Moroni on Fondamenta della Fenice
S. Marco 2840	Palazzo Barbaro on the Grand Canal and the rio dell'Orso
S. Marco 2847	Palazzo Cavalli on the Grand Canal and the rio dell'Orso
Campo S. Stefano	Church of S. Stefano
S. Marco 3327	Palazzo Contarini delle Figure on the Grand Canal and Calle Mocenigo Ca' Vecchia
S. Marco 3780, 3958	Palazzo Pesaro degli Orfei, now called Palazzo Fortuny, in Campo S. Beneto (Benedetto)
S. Marco 3877	Palazzo Corner Spinelli on the Grand Canal
S. Marco 3978	Palazzo Corner Contarini dei Cavalli on the Grand Canal and the rio di S. Luca
S. Marco 4038–9	Ca' Magno in Campiello S. Luca
S. Marco 4041	Palazzo Grimani on the Grand Canal and the rio S. Luca
S. Marco 4136	Palazzo Farsetti, on the Grand Canal and the Riva del Carbon
S. Marco 4137	Palazzo Loredan on the Grand Canal and the Riva del Carbon
S. Marco 4168	Palazzetto Dandolo on the Grand Canal and the Riva del Carbon
S. Marco 4299	Scala del Bòvolo, Palazzo Contarini (formerly Minelli), Calle della Vida

S. Marco 5282	Palazzo Moro (Campo S. Bartolomeo)
S. Marco 5346	Fondaco dei Tedeschi on the Grand Canal and Calle del Fondaco

CASTELLO SESTIERE (VENICE 30122)

Castello 69	Madonna and Child with angels, on the wall of the old Baptistery, Campo S. Pietro di Castello
Castello 1132	Gothic house at Fondamenta S. Anna
Castello 2390	Porta dell'Arsenale, in Campo dell'Arsenale and on the rio dell'Arsenale
Castello 2926	Palazzo Contarini della Porta di Ferro in Salizzada S. Giustina and on the rio S. Francesco
Castello 3608	Palazzo Gritti Badoer in Campo SS Giovanni in Bragora (Campo Bandiera e Moro)
Castello 4003	Palazzo Grandiben on the rio di S. Martino and Calle Erizzo
Castello 4196	Palazzo Dandolo Nani-Mocenigo (now Hotel Danieli) on the Riva degli Schiavoni
Castello 4328	Palazzo Trevisan Cappello on the rio di Palazzo and Calle della Malvasia
Castello 4907–8	Palazzo Zorzi Bon on the rio di S. Severo and Calle dell'Arco detta Bon
Castello 4930	Palazzo Zorzi on the rio di S. Severo and Salizzada Zorzi
Castello 4979/a and 4999	Palazzo Priuli on the Rio dell'Osmarin and Campo S. Severo
Castello 5245–7	Palazzo Vitturi in Campo S. Maria Formosa
Castello 5662–72	House in Salizzada S. Lio (Calle delle Vele)
Castello 5744–5	Gothic house, and Arco del Paradiso at Ponte del Paradiso and Calle del Paradiso, near Campo S. Maria Formosa
Castello 6041	Palazzo Bragadin Carabba on the rio del Malibran and Campo S. Marina
Campo S. Maria Formosa	Church of S. Maria Formosa
Campo SS Giovanni e Paolo	Basilica of SS Giovanni e Paolo
Campo SS Giovanni e Paolo	Equestrian monument to Bartolomeo Colleoni
Campo SS Giovanni e Paolo	Scuola Grande di S. Marco
Barbaria delle Tole	Church of the Ospedaletto (S. Maria dei Derelitti)

CANNAREGIO SESTIERE (VENICE 30121)

Campo S. Giobbe	Church of S. Giobbe in Campo S. Giobbe
Cannaregio 2040	Palazzo Vendramin Calergi on the Grand Canal and in Campiello Vendramin
Cannaregio 2291–2	Palazzo Giovanelli on the rio di Noale and the rio di S. Fosca
Campo della Madonna dell'Orto	Church of the Madonna dell'Orto (S. Maria dell'Orto) in Campo della Madonna dell'Orto
Cannaregio 3555	Gothic portal of Corte Nuova on the rio della Sensa and on Fondamenta dell'Abbazia
Cannaregio 3933	Ca' d'Oro (Palazzo Contarini) on the Grand Canal and Calle Ca' d'Oro
Cannaregio 4198–9	Palazzo Sagredo on the Grand Canal and in Campo S. Sofia
Cannaregio 4557–8	'Calle del Pistor' - Windows of a house in Salizzada del Pistor
Cannaregio 5549–50	Salizzada S. Canzian ('Calle del Bagatin'), terracotta parapet of Palazzo Contarini
Cannaregio 5631–2	'Palace at Apostoli': Ca' da Mosto on the Grand Canal and at Campiello del Leon Bianco
Cannaregio 5643	Palazzo Falier on the rio SS Apostoli and at Sotoportego Falier
Cannaregio 5701–11	Corte del Remer and Ca' Lion Morosini
Cannaregio 5856/a–58	Palazzo Polo in Corte Seconda del Milion
Campiello dei Miracoli	Church of S. Maria dei Miracoli

SAN POLO SESTIERE (VENICE 30125)

S. Polo 357–8	The former Palazzo Querini, in Campo delle Beccarie, Mercato di Rialto
S. Polo 2184–5	Palazzo Bernardo on the rio di S. Polo and Calle Ca' Bernardo
S. Polo 2766	Palazzo Pisani Moretta on the Grand Canal and Calle Pisani e Barbarigo
S. Polo 2802	Ca' Bosso at Ponte di S. Tomà and on the rio di S. Tomà
Campo dei Frari	Portal of the Cappella Corner of the Frari church
Campo dei Frari	Church of S. Maria Gloriosa dei Frari
Campo S. Rocco	Scuola Grande di S. Rocco

SANTA CROCE SESTIERE (VENICE 30135)

S. Croce 134	Palazzo Marcello on the rio del Gaffaro and Fondamenta Minotto
S. Croce 693	Church of S. Simeone Piccolo on the Grand Canal and Fondamenta S. Simeone Piccolo
S. Croce 1670	Archivolt and doorhead at Salizzada del Fondaco dei Turchi
S. Croce 1730	Fondaco dei Turchi on the Grand Canal and Salizzada del Fondaco dei Turchi
Campo S. Stae	Church of S. Eustachio (S. Stae) on the Grand Canal and Campo S. Stae
S. Croce 1979	Palazzo Priuli Bon on the Grand Canal at S. Stae
S. Croce 2060	Palazzo Agnusdio at Ponte del Forner and on the rio della Pergola
S. Croce 2076	Ca' Pesaro on the Grand Canal and Fondamenta Pesaro
S. Croce 2123	Palazzo Viaro Zane in Campo S. Maria Mater Domini
S. Croce 2172–75	Casa degli Zane in Campo S. Maria Mater Domini
S. Croce 2214	Palazzo Corner della Regina on the Grand Canal and Calle della Regina

DORSODURO SESTIERE (VENICE 30123)

Campo della Salute	Church of S. Maria della Salute on the Grand Canal
Campo S. Gregorio	Church of S. Gregorio
Dorsoduro 352–3	Ca' Dario on the Grand Canal and Ramo Barbaro
Dorsoduro 780	La Calcina (Hotel) on the Zattere ai Gesuati
Dorsoduro 874	Palazzo Manzoni, formerly Contarini dal Zaffo, now Contarini Polignac, on the Grand Canal
Dorsoduro 1050	Entrance to the Scuola di S. Maria della Carità, Campo della Carità
Campazzo S. Sebastian	Campanile of S. Sebastiano in Campazzo S. Sebastian
Dorsoduro 2376	Palazzo Arian Cicogna on the rio dei Carmini and Fondamenta Briati
Campo dei Carmini	Church of the Carmini (S. Maria del Carmelo) in Calle della Scuola and Campo dei Carmini
Dorsoduro 2615	Palazzo Guoro o Moro ('House of Othello') in Campo dei Carmini and on the rio di S. Margherita
Dorsoduro 2931–5	Palazzetto Foscolo Corner in Campo S. Margherita
Dorsoduro 3228	The Palazzi Giustiniani on the Grand Canal and Calle Giustinian
Dorsoduro 3246	Ca' Foscari on the Grand Canal and Calle larga Foscari
Dorsoduro 3368	'Rio Foscari House' on the rio di Ca' Foscari and Corte de l'Aseo

GIUDECCA, ISLAND (VENICE 30133)

Campo del Santissimo Redentore	Church of the Redentore, Campo del Santissimo Redentore

SAN MICHELE IN ISOLA, ISLAND

S. Michele in Isola	Church of S. Michele and the Cappella Emiliana

MURANO, ISLAND (VENICE 30141)

Campo S. Donato	Basilica of SS Maria e Donato
Fondamenta dei Vetrai	Lion at Ponte de Mezo on the rio dei Vetrai

TORCELLO, ISLAND (VENICE 30142)

Island of Torcello	Basilica of S. Maria Assunta
Island of Torcello	Church of S. Fosca

S. GIORGIO MAGGIORE, ISLAND (VENICE 30100)

Island of S. Giorgio Maggiore	Church of S. Giorgio Maggiore

S. GIORGIO IN ALGA, ISLAND

Island of S. Giorgio in Alga	Former church of S. Giorgio in Alga

INDEX

Figures in italics refer to illustrations